D0043951

90-661

796.6   Alley, Jean
ALL   Colorado cycling guide.

DEMCO

Other books by Jean and Hartley Alley

A Gentleman From Indiana Looks at Marblehead
Southern Indiana
A Gentleman From Indiana Looks at Newport

Colorado Cycling Guide

Jean and Hartley Alley

PRUETT PUBLISHING COMPANY
BOULDER, COLORADO

©1990 by Jean and Hartley Alley

All rights reserved. No part of this book may be reproduced without written permission from the publisher, with the exception of short passages for review purposes.

First Edition
1 2 3 4 5 6 7 8 9

Library of Congress Cataloging-in-Publication Data

Alley, Jean, 1920–
     Colorado cycling guide / Jean and Hartley Alley.
        p.   cm.
     Includes bibliographical references.
     ISBN 0-87108-768-5
     1. Bicycle touring—Colorado—Guide-books.   2. Colorado—Description and travel—1981– —Guide-books.   I. Alley, Hartley, 1919–   .   II. Title.
     GV1045.5.C6A43   1990
     796.6′4′09788—dc20   89-39910
                                                                                         CIP

Cover photograph by Robert Pollock.
Cover inset photographs and all interior photographs by Hartley Alley.
Cover and book design by Jody Chapel.

Contents

Acknowledgments

▲

Our thanks to all the people throughout the state of Colorado who helped us with this project, especially:
Boulder: Nancy Dutko
       Ron Kiefel
Colorado Springs: Craig Blewitt
             Steve Hall
Denver: Bill Litchfield
       Harvey McPhail
Durango: Ed Zink
Fort Collins: Gene Benedict
        Lee Cooper
        Rita Davis
Louisville: Scott Adlfinger
Pueblo: Richard Schaffer
Steamboat Springs: Bruce Alston
Vail: Cheryl Lindstrom
     Eric Johnson
And the many tourist information centers and chamber of commerce offices that furnished us with valuable information.

—Jean and Hartley Alley

Preface

▲

Jean and I have been serious cyclists since 1963. We've flown to Europe with our bicycles more than a dozen times on separate tours of England, Ireland, Scotland, Holland, Belgium, France, Germany, and Austria. In addition we've cycled in China, Mexico, and Guatemala, not to mention most areas of the U.S.

In 1965 we founded the Hilly Hundred Weekend, an annual bicycle touring event in southern Indiana that today attracts thousands of riders. After moving to Colorado I was Director of Bicycle Touring (1970–80) for the Boulder Group of the Colorado Mountain Club. We've led numerous tours in Colorado, two of them for the International Bicycle Touring Society.

We were so taken by cycling that we gave up freelancing as a photographer-writer team and went into the business of designing and manufacturing bicycle touring equipment. For fourteen years our firm, The Touring Cyclist Shop, ran ads in the leading bicycling magazines and sent out Touring Cyclist Brand panniers and handlebar bags to mail-order customers here and abroad.

Since retiring in 1984 we've been free to devote more time to cycling. As a kid I dreamed of someday taking a long solo bike trip. This led me to come up with the idea of cycling to my high school reunion. In April '87 I started out from Boulder and after 50 days (mostly headwind!) I arrived in Lynn, Massachusetts, in time for the reunion of the class of '37. 2200 miles of solo pedaling and just as much an adventure as I had dreamed it would be.

It's from this lifetime of bicycle riding that we approached the writing of this book.

—Hartley Alley
Boulder, Colorado

Please note:

This guide is not a substitute for your own experience and common sense. Use it to enjoy the sport of bicycle touring, but be aware that you must rely upon your own judgement as to your ability to deal with the dangers that are inherent in this risk sport. Road and traffic conditions are subject to change and may differ from the conditions that existed at the time this book was written.

Bicycle Touring in Colorado

▲

To enjoy bicycle touring in Colorado you need to be aware of some of the unique situations and problems that might arise. To discuss these I'll draw not only on our Colorado cycling experiences—we've lived in Boulder since 1970—but also on our tours abroad and in other parts of the United States.

Colorado Weather

Because of altitude and mountainous terrain the weather in Colorado can become severe rather suddenly. So severe that cycling becomes difficult and dangerous, if not simply impossible. If you're planning a tour in the mountains with a fixed schedule (i.e. motel reservations, etc.) it's best to go with June, July, and August. May and September are risky months. When an innocent September rain is falling in Denver the same storm can be producing a foot of snow up in the mountains.

Day trips or loosely scheduled multi-day tours have enough flexibility to allow you to work around most changes in the weather. Some of the most delightful cycling days that I can remember were in the spring and fall. On the other hand, Boulder club rides in April and September have on occasion been snowed out. So stay loose.

Heat and Sun

Most summer days in Colorado are warm and sunny, with hardly a cloud in the sky. While cycling along with day after day of blue skies and warm sunshine is a nice prospect, there is a down side: thought must be given to the possibility of dehydration and sunburn.

Dehydration

On a typical summer day in Colorado you'll find that you can be really working hard—going up a hill, for instance—and that you won't be sweating. This is an illusion. You'll be sweating profusely but it will disappear into the atmosphere because of the low humidity and the movement of air. You will be losing water at a great rate.

You can't count on your sense of thirst; it lags behind your real need for water. Fully hydrate yourself before and after the ride. When on the bike, drink every 15 minutes, at least a pint an hour—whether thirsty or not.

Have two cycling water bottles installed on your bike and learn to drink while under way. If you have to stop and get off the bike to drink you'll never get enough water. Carry enough water, or find it along the roadside, to wet down your head and your shirt.

Aridity and wind will take away the sweat from your skin so that you won't get any cooling effect. Take a tip from the Arabs and wear clothing that will cover your body and keep the moisture next to your skin.

Sunburn

Because of the high altitude you'll find that Colorado's sun is more intense than you'd expect. It has been estimated that you get 5 times more ultraviolet rays at 10,000 feet than at sea level.

Use a sunscreen. Wear a shirt that's light colored, lightweight, and has long sleeves that you can roll down or up. In his book *Bike Touring*, Ray Bridge points out that if you ride with a bare back you can get a bad burn before you know it. While under way the air cools you, so you don't feel the burn until you stop—and then it's too late.

Because of the sun's intensity, skin cancer is quite common in Colorado. People who are into tanning are gradually realizing that it leads in later life to that leathery look and that it's really just another macho trip.

Midday Heat

If you find that the midday heat is too much for you, head for the nearest oasis. Park and lock your bike and go shopping for food, take a swim in the city pool, call ahead for reservations, find some shade and clean and check your bike, write letters, write up your journal of the trip, or even take a nap. But stay away from beer or other alcohol—it has a dehydrating effect. Save the beer for the end of the day, when it will really taste good and will be a fitting reward for a day of hard pedaling.

Rain

Cycling in the rain can even be enjoyable if you have the right rain gear (more later) and if traffic and road conditions are favorable. However, you should keep in mind that your visibility and the vision of drivers is lowered. On my 2200-mile trek I had a few worrisome rain days. Anticipating that this would happen, I was ready. I wore a bright yellow rain suit and turned on my Belt Beacon—a strobe-like flashing light that was aimed at the overtaking traffic. Most drivers gave me a wide berth and I hardly got splashed.

When in touristy areas, such as most of the mountain region of Colorado, you should think twice about riding in the rain. A major danger is the RV driver. Often these vehicles are rented and unfamiliar to the driver, who might not have a feel for the width of the RV. More than one cyclist has been side-swiped in that situation—by an RV in the rain on a narrow mountain road.

Railroad tracks are always a hazard for the cyclist, but in the rain they can be deadly. The shiny steel surface becomes super slippery when wet. If wet tracks cross the road at an angle, the best bet is to get off the bike and walk across.

The worst set of tracks that I have seen are on Col. 133 just north of Paonia. The tracks cross the road three times at an extreme angle. Friends report that six of their group went down on these tracks on a rainy day—in spite of being experienced cyclists.

Cold

A common sight on Colorado's mountain passes in the middle of summer: a bare-limbed cyclist shivering because he's been caught in a sudden cold rain. The chances are that he is from a flatland state and that he "just can't believe how cold it got up here." He's a good candidate for hypothermia.

Hypothermia is the scientific term for, in plain words, getting chilled to the bone. In hypothermia the temperature of the body core drops dangerously low, affecting the function of all the bodily systems, especially the circulatory and mental processes. Physical coordination and judgement suffer. If the body continues to lose heat, hypothermia can result in death.

Here's a typical scenario: Sudden rain or wet snow hits cyclist who is clad only in shorts and jersey. The air temperature is as high as 50

Shivering cyclists at the top of Trail Ridge Road—three miles high (see Tour 7). Rain mixed with snow and a temperature of 36 degrees—typical weather on a July afternoon at 12,183 feet. A good place for leg warmers and other foul weather gear.

degrees but the fact that he is going downhill at 20 mph brings the wind-chill factor down to 30 degrees. His wet clothing, rather than warming him, is taking even more heat from his body. (On the flat on a dry day the same situation could develop with sweaty clothes in a 20-mph headwind.)

Clothing for Cold and Rain

Anytime that you are going to cycle in the mountains it's a good idea to carry leg and arm warmers—sleeve-like articles, made of wool or nylon. These are available in many Colorado bike shops and in most of the mail order stores that advertise in the bicycling magazines. Weighing hardly anything, they fit in a jersey pocket. You put them on at the top of the pass and you're all set for the chilly downhill run. They're also handy for casual everyday rides. On a cold summer morn you start out wearing arm and leg warmers and when the sun warms the day you peel them off.

On high, serious climbs, such as on the San Juan Mountains Circle (Tour 25) where rain or snow is more likely, you should have a rain suit in your handlebar bag. As most cyclists these days know, the best material for a rain suit is Gore-tex, or one of its equivalents. It's expensive, but well worth the investment. Because this stuff allows your sweat to pass through minute pores, you can wear it whether it's raining or not. On a chilly morning you wear it as a windbreaker and if it starts to rain or snow you don't need to stop and put on your rain suit. You've got it on already.

You'll need a pair of regular cold-weather gloves. Your hands are out front in the cold, really vulnerable. Coming down Mt. Evans (in July) we ran into a cold, spitting snow. I had good heavy gloves on, but even then I had to stop to warm my hands. Because of the potholes and hairpin turns I was braking constantly and my hands got cold and stiff.

Taking into account that your head and neck are the biggest losers of heat, carry a scarf and a wool hat. These weigh hardly anything. The hat you put on over or under your helmet. I carry a silk balaclava. It weighs about an ounce, covers my head, neck, and most of my face. You can find it at ski shops. Here's an old racer's trick: carry a newspaper and at the top of the pass stuff it in your shirt. It's light-weight, low budget, and you can use it on your rear carrier as a mudguard.

A final word: don't count on the sag wagon to carry your rain and cold gear. It could be miles away, and usually is when you need it. And if you do get caught in a hypothermic situation, don't be proud, stubborn, and stupid. Stick out your thumb, catch a ride, and get your cold body down to a warm motel and a hot bath.

Wind

As any bike rider can tell you, if it's windy the chances are the wind will be against you. A head wind is much worse than a hill. You know that a hill has a top and that you'll eventually reach it. But there seems to be no end to a head wind. Some cyclists have said that it's called a head wind because it starts to work on your head.

Trying to keep up to your usual speed against the wind is a waste of energy. The sensible approach is to conserve energy by going at an easy pace and by taking a low profile on the bike. On my long solo trip, with a day-after-day head wind, I worked out a plan: "Don't fight it, go slow. Take a rest every five miles and reward yourself with a handful of M&Ms. Be happy with a low mileage for the day."

In a head wind an oncoming truck will greatly increase the force of the wind. The first gust will want to tear your helmet off. Keep your helmet chin strap tight and get a good grip on the handlebars when you see a truck coming. In the rain this effect can be devastating. The bow wave will throw sheets of water in your face and blind you. In this circumstance, it's obviously best to take a day off and wait for a dry day.

It's safe to generalize about the wind in the mountains to this extent: in the early morning the air heats up and moves up-slope; in the late afternoon the air cools and goes down-slope. This of course means that you should do your mountain riding in the early hours. You'll have a tail wind on the way up and a head wind on the down side to help slow you to a safe speed.

Because of the effect of the mountains, Colorado winds seem to be coming from all directions. The only constants that we have found:

in the a.m. there is a strong southwest wind from Pueblo to Denver; in good weather the flat part of Boulder county has a southeast wind. The U.S. Weather Bureau and the U.S. Geological Survey publish maps and charts of prevailing wind patterns. However, I have learned not to count on these things. As I said in the beginning, the chances are the wind won't go the way you want to go.

If you want to experience a bike rider's heaven, try this some year when you have nothing to do. Take a "Tail Wind Tour." You start somewhere in the middle of the U.S. And you must always cycle with the wind, regardless of where it takes you. The tour isn't over until you hit an ocean. It could take years!

Four of us left Boulder one weekend for a short tail wind tour. Having only four days to spare, we took a sag wagon along just in case we ran out of time way out in eastern Nebraska. But there was no need for the sag. Riding about 80 miles a day, the wind took us, on succeeding days, east, north, west, and south. We wound up right where we started: back home in Boulder.

One last wind story. The wind really blows sometimes in Boulder. In the winter and spring it has blown over 100 miles an hour. These big winds are always from the west. So one day with a 60-mph wind I headed east on my bike. The wind was so strong that you could barely stand up. I flew along with this tremendous wind howling behind me. Whether uphill or down I was spinning out a 100-inch gear. I, a nonracer in so-so shape, covered the 25 miles to Brighton in just over 50 minutes! Did I cycle back against the wind? Are you kidding? Jean came and got me in the pickup.

Lightning

If you're going to be cycling in the mountains you need to be aware of the danger of lightning. Lightning tends to strike (i.e. go to ground) at the highest point that it can find. The most dangerous time of day seems to be around noon. With these generalities in mind, here are a few suggestions.

1. Get an early start on any day that you will be climbing a peak or high pass. Plan on finishing those sectors well before noon. In par-

ticular, think of this before cycling up Mt. Evans or over Trail Ridge—see Tours 11 and 7.

2.   A good general rule of thumb: avoid being near a high point. In other words, don't seek shelter under a lone tree. Instead look for a forest of trees that are close together and mostly the same height.

3.   If caught in an open space, the danger is that you yourself will be the high point. In this case, weather bureau experts recommend that you get down on all fours—in the low ground of a ditch if there is one nearby.

4.   In any case, get away from your bicycle, which because of its conductivity could attract a strike.

Cycling Techniques

Climbing

As far as I'm concerned, the very essence of bicycling is hill-climbing. A hill is a challenge that must be met. A really dyed-in-the-wool cyclist accepts the challenge eagerly. He accepts the fact that he might hurt on the way up the hill. He looks forward to reaching the top and to that wonderful feeling of easy pedaling when he finally gets there.

So the first thing in hill-climbing is putting yourself in the right mood. Take on a positive mind-set and look forward to enjoying the challenge of getting up the hill. In addition, you certainly need to know something about climbing techniques.

Pacing   Learn to pace yourself, so that you don't run out of energy and become discouraged before you get to the top. There are climbs in Colorado that go up and up for as much as 20 miles.

Ron Kiefel tells me that cyclo-tourists often make the mistake of "attacking" at the start of a climb. He says, "take it easy at the start of a long climb and wait until you're warm and your pulse is up before you start to really crank it. But save some for the final slopes.''

Ron should know about climbing. He's a pro racer, perennial winner of the hill-climb prologue of the Coors Classic, Olympic medalist, and as a member of the surprisingly successful Seven-11 team has raced the European circuit, including the Tour de France.

Take a rest   If the climb gets too long or too steep, get off and walk, or stop for a breather. One way or another you'll make it to the top under your own power. Stop and take a moment to enjoy the fact that you've made it this far.

Position   When climbing don't get down in the drops—the lowest part of the handlebars. This low position will constrict your diaphragm and thorax and thus restrict the deep breathing that you'll be doing because of the hill. Instead, place your hands on the tops of the bars and sit up. After all, when you're climbing your speed is reduced and you will get no streamline advantage from being in the drops. (Watch the racers, they don't climb in the drops.) In addition, see that your elbows are slightly bent out. This will keep your chest open.

In fact, anytime that you are cycling, whether climbing or on the flat, make sure that your elbows are bent. Because if your arms are straight you will needlessly tense and tire your shoulder and back muscles. Try it. You'll see that bending your arms is one of the secrets of keeping relaxed and efficient while pedaling.

Different strokes   Simply put, you can climb while sitting on the saddle or you can climb by standing on the pedals. While seated you can "spin" in a low gear or "grind" in a medium gear. Pedaling while standing, often called in this country "honking" or "jamming," is usually done in a higher gear. You should practice and refine all three of these climbing techniques. You'll find that each of these methods uses a different set of muscles. When you switch from, say, grinding to honking you'll be resting one set of muscles while another set is doing the work. (Catch the TV coverage of the next Tour de France and notice the climbing technique. You'll see that they alternate between sitting and standing.)

Grinding   Grinding it out is the most common way of climbing. Hands are placed on the middle of the bars, on either side of the stem. Seated, you turn a medium-size gear at a moderate rate, say 40 to 60 pedal cadence, and you slide your butt back quite far on the saddle.

Sliding back on the saddle is very important. It allows you to use your arm and back muscles; it makes it possible for you to apply power sooner at the top of your pedal stroke. And sliding back in effect is the same as raising your saddle, giving you more mechanical advantage in the job of pushing the pedals.

Spinning   This is the rather delicate art of turning the pedals at a fast rate—60 to 100 rpm or more—in a low gear. In this instance don't bother to slide your butt back; instead concentrate on keeping your pedaling action smooth and round, avoiding bouncing your butt up and down.

Honking   Honking, climbing in a standing position, is done in a bigger gear, turning the pedals at a comparatively slow rate—35 to 65 rpm. This is a skill that many cyclists neglect. It takes some practice for most of us, but it certainly is worth mastering, if only because it gives you a change of muscle use. In addition, if the grade is really steep and you've run out of low gears, honking is the only way you have left, unless you get off and walk.

When gears are not low enough, walking up a hill is an honorable solution. This is the steepest grade on the Hardscrabble Circle (Tour 22).

When honking it is most important that you use the muscle power of your arms and upper body. Place your hands on the brake lever hoods and pull up in opposition to the downthrust of your leg. The right arm pulls up when the right leg pushes down, and, of course, the left arm opposes the left leg. This arm action will cause the bike to rock from side to side, the top tube even hitting the insides of your thighs. However, the bike will track in a straight line. Swaying the bike is proper form and the way it should be, but don't let your body sway. Body sway is counterproductive in that the heavier mass of your body is not following the straight line of the direction of travel.

On the down stroke your leg should be quite straight, because at this point you are using the weight of your body to push the pedal down.

The word   I consider honking and jamming to be inappropriate names because they somehow imply that climbing while standing is an awkward, pile-driving, strength-is-all movement. To get a better feel for the grace, elegance, and ease that the great riders show in this style of climbing maybe we should adopt the term that's used in Europe: "dancing." The British speak of dancing on the pedals; in France it's *danseuse*, in Spain, *bailar*—the same word, of course. If you think "dancing" rather than "honking," perhaps you'll be more relaxed and efficient.

Downhill   You'd think that there's not much to say about going downhill on a bicycle. Anybody can do it—just get on the bike and without turning a pedal you zoom downward like a skier on a slope. But there are several points that concern safety, especially when you are flying down a mountain road in the Colorado Rockies.

Back when I was coaching a local racing team I often drove a follow car behind the pack at races. On long downhill stretches in the mountains I regularly clocked them at 55 mph. That's really moving! I'd guess it's like going 110 mph in a VW bug. As a cyclo-tourist I get scared if I go over 40 on a bike—I certainly don't recommend that you try for any downhill speed records.

Spinning in a low gear. Off to an early start, climbing out of Ouray, heading toward Durango on U.S. 550 (see Tour 25).

Triathletes honking and grinding up the "Wall" on the Morgul Bismarck course (see Tour 8). Note how the arms and upper body add climbing strength.

Here are a few pointers on downhill cycling:

1.   The faster you go the more you should move away from the side of the road. Leave yourself a margin for error. If you should flat or break a spoke or somehow run off the side of the road at a fast descending speed there's a good chance that you'll smash into rocks or trees and suffer serious injuries. At speed, take a position in the middle of the right-hand lane.

2.   High-speed shimmy or wobble. Some bikes will at 15 mph or more develop a violent oscillation in which the whole frame is involved in a side-to-side shimmy. Even the most expensive bikes will sometimes have this problem. There are many theories as to the cause, but it's hard to pinpoint. Some experts blame frame geometry, claiming it can be caused by the seat tube and fork being parallel to each other. Others think that having an imbalance of weight between the front and rear is the culprit. In any case, it's a serious and potentially life-threatening situation. The handlebars will shake violently and all of your arm strength will not be enough to stop it. Steering is affected, the bike will go straight ahead but it does not want to make any turns. I and other grown men have whimpered with fear when a shimmy takes over the bike on a fast downhill run.

3.   Okay. How do you stop the shimmy? You simply clamp the top tube with your knees. This immediately dampens out the vibration, and the problem is solved. I understand that some racers routinely clamp the top tube with knees anytime that they are on a descent. If you want to test your bike and your ability to handle shimmy, do this: While coasting down a gentle grade, take both hands off the handlebars and slap the top tube smartly. This will usually induce shimmy. Put your hands back on the bars and you'll probably find that the shimmy persists. Then clamp the top tube with both knees and voilà! the shimmy is gone. Practice this a few times and you'll have peace of mind on the downhill runs.

4.   Braking on a fast downhill run is quite different from braking on the flat. Sudden strong braking could cause you to go over the

handlebars. To counteract this, when you apply the brakes throw your butt to the rear and take a low profile.

5. To avoid heating up the brakes, rims, and tires use the brakes intermittently rather than continuously. Heat build-up can be a serious problem if you use sew-up (racing) tires. Until the early '70s there were no high quality clincher tires. Before that all serious cyclists used sew-ups. On a 1969 tour of Nova Scotia we all used sew-ups, which was fine until we hit the hilly Cabot Trail Highway.

We braked so much on the winding steep downs that the rims heated up and melted the rim glue. The front sew-up now started to creep around on the rim, cocking the valve stem at a perilous angle. The only solution was to stop, remove the wheel, reverse it, and put it back on the bike. When you braked on the next long down, like magic, the tire slipped back to its proper position on the rim.

6. You can save your brakes on a long down by sitting up straight and sticking your knees out. I use these "air brakes" to keep from getting too close to the cyclist in front of me.

7. Brake *before* the curve. If you brake *in* the curve you could skid sideways. Watch for loose gravel on curves. If you brake or try to turn in gravel you'll crash and wind up with a case of "road rash"— the racers' name for skin abrasions.

8. Avoid pedal scrape by keeping your inside pedal high on curves. Or, better still, coast with both pedals at the same height. In that way you're ready for either right or left turns.

9. Keep yourself physically and mentally relaxed on the bike. Keep your arms bent and use a soft touch on the handlebars.

10. After you feel comfortable going downhill at speed, practice coming to a complete stop in the middle of a steep down, remembering to throw your butt back. This will not only prepare you for panic stops but will teach you to respect the tremendous force that's involved in downhill cycling.

Getting Into Shape

It's quite obvious that you should be in your best possible physical shape before you tackle any multi-day cycle tour. This is especially so if you are going to be riding in the mountains of Colorado.

You have two ways to go: you can train ahead of time, or you can start your tour out of shape and gradually pick up fitness as you go along. To put it another way: If you don't get in shape ahead of time you'll have sore muscles and be gasping for breath on every climb throughout most of your two-week vacation. And on the last day you'll finally round into shape and wish you had another week of vacation. Or you can spend, say, three months of gradual training and arrive ready to tackle the toughest mountain climbs, enjoying every mile. Getting in shape ahead of time *is* important, unless you want to feel like quitting or staying in bed after a tough first day of attacking the Colorado Rockies.

If you'll be starting your tour in just so-so shape, your best bet is to stay away from the long climbs for the first week. For an easy break-in we suggest that you take Tour 3, Cheyenne Circle. (See page 51.)

Here's a good general rule for your training: It should result in your being ready to ride 50 miles a day, day after day, with relative ease. And you should feel comfortable riding two hours straight without stopping and getting off the bike.

If you will be carrying all your gear (i.e. no sag wagon), you should take some local test rides with your bike loaded down with the 30 pounds or so of the things you'll be taking on tour. You'll notice that a loaded bike handles very differently, and, of course, that you'll be using lower gears on the climbs. You'll have to relearn honking (climbing while standing on the pedals) with a loaded bike, but you'll soon get over the awkwardness.

Ideally your training should start no later than six weeks before your tour, with a minimum of three days a week of at least an hour on the bike. On weekends pile up some miles on long club rides. (If there's no cycling club in your town, start one. Faced with this situation when we moved to Boulder, we started a club and it's still going strong after 18 years.)

James McCullagh, the publisher of *Bicycling* magazine, has written an excellent book on how to work yourself into shape for bicycle touring. Titled *The Complete Bicycle Fitness Book*, it contains elaborate day-by-day and week-by-week training schedules and easy-to-read discussions of the physiological aspects of cycling.

If you can't be cycling ahead of time, you can at least prepare your cardiovascular system by jogging, swimming, tennis. This won't save you from sore cycling muscles, but it will cut down on your gasping as you climb in the thin air, two miles above sea level.

Staying Alive on the Road

1. Colorado has some of the most demanding cycling in the world: long, steep climbs and very fast downs. You risk your life if you don't start out with good equipment in the best of condition. Brakes and tires, especially, are most important.

If you flat or break a cable on a down you could in no time be out of control and in danger of running off the road at the next curve. Inspect your tires and brakes before descents. Be ready in your mind to lay the bike down and take a fall if while under way you should have a blowout or break a brake cable. After all, losing skin on the pavement is certainly preferable to crashing head first into a tree.

2. On a narrow road that has high-speed car traffic, don't ride in a tight bunch. Spread out so that you're each about 50 yards apart. This allows the cars to safely weave around each rider. And it eliminates the possibility that the cyclists, their attention diverted by the cars, will run into each other—possibly the biggest danger. We developed this approach after some scary stretches of cycling on high-speed roads in Germany.

3. Colorado state law for bicyclists is similar to that of other states, with the following 1988 additions: On a two-lane road with no shoulder you must move to a single file when overtaking cars reach a distance 300 feet to your rear. You must move to a single file if the sight distance front or rear is less than 300 feet.

In essence, this means that to be safe and/or legal your best bet is to ride single file anytime you're on a two-lane road that has traffic, or where the road winds and thus cuts down on the visibility. Otherwise, two abreast is okay. The only time that more than two abreast is legal is when you're on a shoulder, and if all the bicyclists are completely on the shoulder.

Bicycling is allowed on the shoulder of Interstates in Colorado, except in cities and where an alternative adjacent road is available, as indicated by signs.

4. Don't let traffic pile up behind you on a narrow, winding road where the cars can't safely pass. Get off the road and let them pass. When a slow-moving RV or truck approaches you from the rear, there is a good chance that he has been collecting a long line of cars behind him. Pull over and let the whole line get by. Then get back on and enjoy a spell of traffic-free cycling.

5. On the other hand, don't encourage motorists to pass when to do so would endanger you—for instance, where the road is too narrow for two cars and a bicycle to safely pass each other at the same time. If you stay far over to the right at the edge of the road, the drivers will be tempted to squeeze by you whether it is safe for them to do it or not.

So move out and, as we say, "take a lane."

6. Taking a lane. On a narrow two-lane road, anytime you see a vehicle coming from the front immediately check in your mirror to see if there is traffic coming up behind you. If there is overtaking traffic you should move out smartly to the middle of the lane, continuing to watch in both directions. 99 times out of 100 the rear car will slow down and wait for a safe opening before he passes you. If he doesn't, you still have time and room to move to the edge of the road.

This manuever of taking a lane is endorsed by most of the authors listed in the Bibliography. John Forester is a bicycle safety authority who has for years advocated taking a lane. Richard Ballantine in his book *Richard's New Bicycle Book* sums it up nicely when he says: "If somebody objects to your 'obstructing', ignore them. You are not obliged to risk your life for their convenience." Ballantine has had extensive experience with cycling in New York City traffic. His book is well worth reading, if just for his discussion of cycling in traffic.

17

Taking a lane requires that you keep ever alert and that you use a rearview mirror. It takes courage at first, but practice it and use it and it will help save you from side-swipes and close calls.

Group Riding

The solo cyclist is in a rather simple situation. Simple, in that he only has to deal with these two basic variables: motor vehicles and roadway hazards. But just as soon as two or more cyclists get together for a ride, the situation gets complicated. Now there's the danger that the cyclists will run into each other. And there is the possibility that some will stray from the group and get lost.

Chaos results if you don't have rules for cycling safety—rules for a standard procedure for passing, stopping, swerving around road hazards, etc. In our Boulder touring club we call it the "Rules of the Road." Before each club ride the leader for the day gathers the first-time riders around and recites and explains the rules. I strongly suggest that all cycling groups adopt these procedures, whether twosomes, family groups, club rides, or mass rallies.

The rules of the road
1.   When overtaking a slower rider, pass on the left, yelling out "passing" or "on your left" or giving an audible signal with a bell or horn.

The author measuring a paved shoulder on Col. 12 near La Veta (see Tour 33). As much as possible the tours in this book are routed on roads with paved shoulders, usually at least 2 feet wide.

2. If an unusual situation forces you to overtake on the right, yell out "passing on the right" and proceed to pass, with caution.

3. To avoid bike-to-bike collisions, hand signals must be given at turns. The lead biker gives the hand signal and calls out "right turn" (or "left turn") and the riders following are to repeat the sign and the vocal backup, thus passing the word along.

4. To avoid confusion, the hand signal for a right turn is made by pointing to the right with the right arm. Not the left arm. The traditional sign for a right turn was designed with the motorist in mind. Our right turn signal was designed for the cyclist, and can mean only one thing: right turn.

5. When stopping, the leader of a large group holds his hand high and yells "stopping." Those behind will make the sign and do a vocal backup. If only two riders are present, the stop signal is made with the arm down, palm to the rear.

6. When you see glass in the road, or another hazard that could cause a flat or a fall, the warning signal is made by pointing at the object and pumping your arm up and down, and yelling "glass."

7. When a car approaches from behind, the last rider will yell out "car behind." The signal will be passed forward so that all members of the group will be warned, and move to a single file if that is necessary. When moving to a single file the rider on the left will move forward to make the single file. Do not move back—too hazardous.

8. To avoid losing anybody it is understood that nobody will get ahead of the leader, nor will anybody get behind the sweep-up rider. (The sweep-up is chosen for his cycling experience, roadside repair expertise, and for having a sympathetic attitude toward beginning riders. He stops to give aid when needed.)

9. At changes of direction, the leader will stop at the intersection and wait until the sweep-up comes along with the last rider before

going on in the new direction. This gives the leader a chance to count noses and to see that all is okay.

10.   Whenever the group stops, all riders will move off the pavement to a safe position well away from motor traffic.

Equipment

The marketplace is flooded with new equipment for bicycle touring. The bicycling magazines and the mail order houses tempt us with four-color ads. I feel no need to add to that torrent of ink. But I would like to discuss a few pieces of equipment that I personally find necessary and desirable for touring in Colorado.

What Kind of Bike?

The best kind of bicycle for riding on paved roads is a regular touring bicycle with drop handlebars, toe clips, the usual relatively skinny tires, and 10 or 15 gears that go low enough to take you up the steepest and longest grade that you want to climb. I generalize intentionally about the gears, because the proper low gear for you will be determined by your strength, fitness, skill, and the weight of you and the load that you'll carry on the bike. (For what it's worth, my favorite bicycle is a 21 speed with a low of 25 inches and a high of 108.) If you're going to cycle in the Colorado Rockies, just make sure that you have a low enough gear.

A mountain bike with its upright bars and fat tires is ideal for riding on off-road trails, but not ideal for riding on pavement. Richard Ballantine in his *Richard's New Bicycle Book* sums it up by saying that "a mountain bike can be compared with a Jeep—it's made for traveling on rugged terrain." On the 1988 Ride the Rockies Tour less than 10% of the 2000 riders had mountain bicycles. The mountain bike's extra weight and tire drag just didn't make sense for 7 long days of climbing passes, when all the route was paved.

Useful Gadgets

1.   I love my bicycle computer. You've already got one or you've seen

them in the catalogs. For solo riding or training they can't be beat. Besides showing the mileage covered, a computer can help teach you to spin, show your top speed on downs, and in general keep you informed and entertained.

2.   I think that the Flickstand is the most useful and original device that has come on the touring scene in my 25 years of cycling. The Flickstand does what a kickstand is supposed to do: it keeps a loaded bike from falling over when you park it. You flip this gadget over your front tire and lean the bike against a wall, tree, or anything. The bike can't fall over because the handlebars can't turn—even when your panniers and handlebar bag are loaded with 40 pounds of stuff. The Rhode Gear Co. makes it. (I own no stock.)

3.   When we cycle in a new area, on roads that are strange to us, I usually carry a compass. I always have it with me anytime that we go to Europe, whether for a bike or motor trip. It's so easy to get turned around in a strange place, especially when the sky is overcast.
    I use the Huntsman compass. You can carry it in your pocket or, better yet, pin it to your handlebar bag, so you can read it without stopping. We used it on long walks in the winding streets of Vienna and Budapest, never got lost, and always found our way back to the hotel.

Rearview Mirrors

    I'm convinced that the rearview mirror is cycling's most important safety device. It has saved me and other cyclists from countless life-threatening situations.
    If you read the important books on bicycle touring (see the Bibliography) you'll see that the majority of these authors use and recommend the rearview mirror. Among others, Eugene Sloane, Fred Delong, Richard Ballantine, Raymond Bridge, Karen and Gary Hawkins, and John Rakowski are all advocates of the rearview mirror.
    You wouldn't for a moment think of driving a car without a rearview mirror. A mirror gives you instantaneous access to vital information: it tells you what's behind you and what's about to overtake you.

The most common bike-auto collision occurs when an overtaking car side-swipes a bicyclist. With a mirror you can see overtaking vehicles and swerve out of the way, if that is necessary. The mirror helps you to anticipate all sorts of dangerous situations.

There are three types of rearview mirrors, differing mainly in their method and place of attachment. They mount on eyeglasses, helmet, or handlebars. I much prefer the eyeglass type, mainly because it's always mounted in the same place, thus requiring no readjustment. I find that the helmet type requires almost constant readjustment, and the handlebar type vibrates on bumps in the road and delivers a blurred image.

The rearview mirror will warn you of big trucks and RVs that are about to overtake you. It will help you in making turns, changing lanes, or taking a lane. On city bikepaths you won't be surprised by the pseudo-racer who zooms past without an audible signal.

On club rides the leader can look back in his rearview mirror and check on the other riders. It also comes in handy when a twosome is out for a spin. A mirror-equipped strong rider is not so apt to motor away from a weak rider in the rear.

A safety note. Don't make the mistake of making a turn with just a glance in the mirror. Remember that turning your head and looking back is a preliminary signal to the cars and bikes behind that you want to make a turn, or change lanes. Look over the left shoulder for a left turn and, of course, over the right for a right turn. To sum up, check in your mirror, turn your head and look over your shoulder, and if all is clear give a hand signal and then make the turn.

In a lighter vein. On club rides our bunch usually keeps their eyeglass mirrors on when we stop at a restaurant for lunch. Comes in handy for checking out bikies of the opposite sex. And we once cheered the Dodgers to a World Series win—with our backs to the screen.

Emergency Communication

There are many communication problems that can pop up on a bicycle tour. On a club ride the sweep-up rider on the rear often needs to be in touch with the leader—and sometimes there's as much as a mile from the front to the back of the group. If one of your riders has a bad fall you'll need to call for an ambulance. On a back road there might not be any passing motorist to lend a hand. Radio communication could be the answer. A hand-held radio that weighs just over a pound could do the job.

There are two ways that you can go if you'd like to be able to talk on the radio while you're pedaling along on your bike. There's Citizen Band (CB) and Amateur Radio (nicknamed "ham radio").

Radio Shack sells CB walkie-talkies from $20 to $140. Excellent for communication from the front to the rear of a club ride. Power varies from 1/4 watt to 5 watts. Effective range varies from 1/4 mile to 2 miles, depending on the power and the terrain.

Amateur radio is perhaps a better way to go. A ham walkie-talkie costs more, about $300, but it has a working range of up to 120 miles. Power is the same: 1/4 to 5 watts.

To operate amateur radio gear you must pass a test for a license from the Federal Communications Commission. The FCC test is given by ham clubs, in friendly surroundings. To prepare for the test you can attend free classes provided by a ham club or you can study tapes.

The hand-held amateur radio's wide range of coverage is provided by a series of repeaters located on high points all across the country. (There are over 100 ham repeaters in Colorado alone.) The signal from your small hand-held radio is sent to the repeater and then instantaneously rebroadcast at a greater power, thus accounting for the greater range than has CB.

Jean and I are both amateur radio operators and make much use of our ham gear on bike rides. On weekdays we sometimes go on separate breakfast rides; she'll be cycling with her group and I'll be 40 miles away, with mine. Over that distance we'll easily make bike-to-bike radio contact, and check that all is okay and chat a bit. These tiny radios provide peace of mind.

On my solo bicycle trip from Colorado to Massachusetts I used my ham walkie-talkie as I pedaled along, to get information about road and weather conditions, the location of motels and restaurants, and just for companionship. In those wide-open spaces it provided me with someone to chat with as I covered the miles—and to perhaps meet for lunch in the next town down the road. And, most important, to bring help if I needed it.

Sure enough, disaster did strike: one windy day a side-wind gust knocked me down. I wound up on the pavement somewhat bloodied. On hearing about this over his radio, a friendly ham drove out on the lonely eastern plains of Colorado, bandaged me up, fed me, and led me to the local motel, where he arranged a special low rate.

Some of the repeaters owned by ham clubs have a phone patch, which means that by activating the patch you can make a telephone call on your hand-held radio—to your home or any other local phone. You can dial 911 in an emergency. It's almost like having a cellular phone on your bike. Let's say you're riding alone on a back road. You've had three flats, and you've run out of spare tubes, tire glue, and daylight. And it starts to rain. You just phone home from your bike and your family driver comes and gets you. I think that you as a bike rider will find that getting into ham radio is very worthwhile. For more information about becoming an amateur radio operator contact your local ham club or write to: Amateur Radio Relay League, 22 Main St., Newington, CT 06111. (203) 666-1541.

Roadside Repairs, Tools, and Spares

As any experienced cyclo-tourist knows, mechanical problems are apt to develop on any bike ride, local or long distance. The most common are flat tires, derailleurs or brakes in need of adjustment, loose nuts and bolts, broken cables, and broken or loose spokes. Anytime you get on your bike you should have with you the tools and spare parts that you'll need to take care of these problems. If you don't know how to make these roadside repairs, at least carry the tools and parts so that anybody can help you—even a passing motorist.

The Basics

1. For flats: a frame pump, 2 spare inner tubes, a patch kit (in case you puncture both of your spare tubes), 2 tire irons.

2. For tightening nuts and bolts: a 4″ crescent wrench and/or the appropriate allen wrenches.

3. For adjusting or replacing cables: 1 rear brake cable, 1 rear derailleur cable (they will fit front or rear), 1 small screwdriver, 1 pair 4″ pliers (for pulling on cable).

4. For replacing or tightening spokes: spoke wrench, freewheel remover, 6 spare spokes (must fit your wheels exactly).

5. Additional tools that might come in handy: a 6″ crescent wrench, for removing the pedals when you put the bike on a plane or bus; an 8-9-10 combination wrench for nuts and bolts.

Beginning cyclists have more flat tires than do experienced riders, mainly because beginners are apt to ride in the gutter where all the junk is. And they don't scan the roadway for glass and potholes. Veteran riders avoid flats by riding where the right tire of the cars sweeps the road clean. They scan the roadway, and "glove" their tires. In other words, they reach down with a gloved hand and wipe the tires clean when they have just run through a patch of glass or junk that they can't avoid.

Weeks before your group leaves on a tour, have a professional bike mechanic demonstrate how to deal with roadside repairs. Make it a hands-on session where everybody brings his or her bike and actually changes a tire, installs a cable, etc.

Start a long multi-day tour with new tires. They're cheap. You don't want a blowout when you're flying down a canyon at 40 mph. Check tire pressure daily. At speed a soft tire could blow because of heat build-up.

At the end of the day wipe your bike clean and inspect it. A good way to check for loose parts is to lift the bike a couple of inches off the floor and drop it. Anything loose will rattle.

When it rains, don't take a muddy bike into a motel room. Ask at the desk for "some rags so that I can clean my bike before I take it into the room." A master PR stroke that will endear you and other bikies to the management.

Besides doing your own roadside repairs you should set up your own bike repair area at home and learn to take care of the more complicated work on your bike. Buy tools at your local bike shop and ask the owner to come to your group meeting and show you how to use them. Most shop owners will teach you the tricks of the trade if you buy all your tools and parts from them.

There are many excellent books on bike repair. I like and list these books in the Bibliography:

For roadside repairs: *Sloane's Handy Pocket Guide to Bicycle Repair*.
For maintenance and inspection: *The Bicycle Touring Book* by Tim
    and Glenda Wilhelm.
For routine home repairs: *Richard's New Bicycle Book*.

You should learn to do all but the most complicated repairs on your own bike. It makes you a better rider because you understand how the bike works, and you'll feel confident that nothing will break at the wrong time. But if it does, you'll be able to fix it!

Helpful Hints

Tender Butts

Nothing takes the fun out of cycling faster than a pain in the butt. When your fanny hurts you just don't want to ride any farther. Staying off the bike for a few days always helps. But if you're on a scheduled tour you have to keep pedaling day after day.

Let's look at the condition. The problem starts with the skin in the crotch being rubbed raw as a result of friction between you and the shorts you're wearing. The dampness of your sweat contributes to the problem. Fanny problems are less apt to occur if you are wearing cycling shorts—lined with either chamois or a man-made terry cloth. But sometimes even the most experienced cyclists will be plagued by this problem.

The first stage is a simple rawness of the skin. The second stage is where the skin is broken and the bacteria in the sweat enters the skin and causes an infection. Painful pimples and even boils develop in the infected area.

The first rule here is cleanliness. Wash the area thoroughly with soap and water after every ride—do this daily whether or not you have access to a shower. Then apply peroxide or alcohol. My dermatologist tells me that peroxide is better because the skin is less apt to become irritated from repeated application.

Here's a prevention trick that's been around the cyclo-tourist world for years. At the drugstore you buy some Dr. Scholl's moleskin or the new Foamskin. This is a soft, thick material that is sticky on one side. Then cut the moleskin into squares about 3 inches across. At the slightest discomfort you duck in somewhere and wash and dry the tender area. Then, bending forward to approximate your position on the bike, you apply the moleskin so that it covers the area. You'll find that this padding gives instant relief. Wash carefully every night and apply peroxide. Use new moleskin daily until the tenderness is gone. I've ridden hundreds of miles, day after day, with moleskin protecting me from agony. It works.

Getting An Early Start

If you want to get all of the good out of your bike tour, you've got to be an early riser. Get up before dawn and be on the road as soon as the sun gets up. If you start riding at dawn you'll get in 3 or 4 hours of cycling on quiet highways—the motor tourists and RVs usually don't get moving before 9:30. You'll eat in uncrowded restaurants: breakfast at 6 and lunch at 11. You'll arrive at your destination early (maybe 2 P.M.) and have your pick of motels or campgrounds. Then during the heat of the midafternoon you can shower and take a nap and a swim, and be all ready to go out on the town in the evening, eating dinner at 5:30 in an uncrowded restaurant. You'll have plenty of time to shop before the stores close. This could be an important advantage: in the early morning you're apt to have an upslope tail wind helping you climb the long grades in the mountains. With this approach to scheduling you'll be using the daytime hours wisely and you'll be on the road during the best cycling hours.

Packing Lists

I have a simple approach to making a list of the things that I take on tour. First I list all of the conditions that I might meet, such as: hot, cold, rain, on-bike time, off-bike time, repairs, emergencies, hunger, thirst, etc. These subject heads remind me of all the items that I need to put on my packing list. I make it a very long list, including all kinds of things that I may or may not need. I want this

27

long list so that I can give careful consideration to each little item. Then I pare the list to the bone by doing a lot of crossing out. In this way I go lightweight but I don't forget anything important.

If you need help, these three books have excellent packing lists with discussions of each item on the list:

Bike Touring by Raymond Bridge.

The Bicycle Touring Manual by Rob Van der Plas.

The Complete Book of Bicycling by Eugene A. Sloane.

Carrying too much weight and stuck with gears not low enough, this cyclist was struggling up U.S. 550 toward Ouray (see Tour 25). Relief came the next day when he joined a Heart Cycle group and put all his heavy packs in the sag wagon.

How to Use This Book

▲

The tours in this book vary in length from one day to seven days. Of course you can tour for longer periods of time by tying several tours together. Our connecting routes (Tours 5, 8, 17, 24, 28, and 31) will help you to plan your own tours of varying lengths.

If you are enjoying bicycling in a certain area, you may want to spend several days there and ride a series of the one-day tours that we have included, returning to the same location each night.

The mileages of most of the tours are figured to make logical cycling days, depending somewhat on where you can find a place to stop for the night. But it's certainly possible for you to ride more or less miles in your cycling day.

Accommodations

We've tried to give you some basic information about the location of campgrounds and motels, and we've listed telephone numbers for those accommodations where it would be wise to call ahead for a reservation. These are in places where there are not many motels, or where all lodging is likely to be taken after 5 or 6 P.M. during the height of the tourist season.

Actual Climbing

You will note that at the beginning of each day's ride we list an actual climbing figure. A word of explanation is in order.

Every bike rider wants to know the amount of climbing that he faces in a day's ride. It represents the work to be done. In calculating the "Actual Climbing" we roughly measured all of the large and small upgrades and got a total for the day. We did not subtract for the downgrades.

Oftentimes you'll be misled by a look at the altitude difference between two towns. Cycling from Idaho Springs down to Golden is an example. Golden is 2000' lower, so it must be all downhill. Not so. In that stretch there are two upgrades of 600' and 400'. So there is 1000' of "Actual Climbing" between Idaho Springs and Golden.

Helpful Maps

At the beginning of each tour we have listed maps that will be helpful to you. The *Colorado Road Atlas* (see Appendix A) is the best bet for getting a good detailed picture of Colorado roads and the layout of major towns.

For even more detail, refer to the National Forest Maps also listed at the beginning of each tour. (See Appendix A for information about ordering these maps.)

Colorado State Highway Bicycle Maps

Anyone planning to tour in Colorado should certainly send for the *Bicycling Colorado* maps compiled by the Colorado Department of Highways. These include an overall map of the state showing the shoulder width on all state and national highways in Colorado, with suitability for cycling indicated by color. Also included in the package is a more detailed set of strip maps showing the Interstate Corridor Bicycle Routes through the state.

These strip maps, titled *Across the Rockies, Over the Plains, Front Range Route*, and *South Platte Route* show you where you can ride on I-25, I-70, or I-76, and what roads to take when you are not allowed on them. The maps show you how to cycle through Denver and other cities on the routes—invaluable knowledge for a touring cyclist. (See Appendix A for information about how to send for a set of these maps).

Bicycling the Interstate Highway Corridors

Because of the motor vehicle noise and the proximity to high speed traffic, some cyclists may feel that it is somewhat unpleasant to cycle on the shoulder of an Interstate highway.

But in Colorado, as in many other western states, it is sometimes necessary and even desirable to ride on the Interstates. In some remote areas it may be your only choice. Cycling on the Interstates is legal in Colorado, except when going through cities, and where no-cycling signs are posted.

We have ridden many miles on Colorado Interstate highways and find them safe, if not always ideal. You usually have a smooth 10'-wide shoulder, free of debris and potholes, giving you a good separation from traffic.

It's the on- and off-ramps that you have to pass while on the Interstates that can be dangerous. Eugene A. Sloane in his fourth revised edition of *The Complete Book of Bicycling*, published by Simon and Schuster, has some good suggestions about riding the Interstates safely.

As you arrive at an off-ramp, where traffic on your left may exit and cross in front of you, you must stop. Do not depend on a rear-view mirror to check how far away or how fast traffic is coming up from behind you. Traffic is always going faster than you think it is.

As you approach the exit ramp stop and look back. Only when you are positive that traffic coming in the right lane is not going to exit should you proceed across the ramp.

On-ramps are a little safer. When crossing an on-ramp, what you do is stop at the point where the on-ramp merges with the highway. When traffic coming down the on-ramp is clear (i.e. when you see no cars on the ramp) simply take a straight cut to the right, across the ramp, and turn left down the ramp's shoulder. You can then safely merge with the highway shoulder at the base of the ramp.

Transportation for Your Bicycle and You

By Airline

Airlines will carry your bicycle as part of your luggage. Cost and boxing requirements vary with the different carriers. To avoid surprises, contact your airline ahead of time.

There are plenty of flights into Denver, and from there you can make air connections to other cities in the state. Consult with your travel agent about the flights that are currently available.

Airport Vans and Buses

From the Denver airport van-shuttle service is available to these cities:

Boulder (303) 499-1559
Fort Collins (303) 398-2284
Cheyenne, WY (303) 398-2284
Colorado Springs (719) 634-3518
Pueblo (719) 634-3518

All these shuttle services tell us that they are able to transport boxed bicycles.

Tickets for these shuttles are available at the airport, but they all say that advance notification or reservation is a good idea. We have found that if you check in early they can more easily load a couple of boxed bicycles in the luggage compartment before putting in other luggage.

There is also public bus service—RTD (Regional Transportation District)—from the airport to Boulder, which almost always has room for bicycles whether boxed or not.

Long Distance Bus Lines

Greyhound/Trailways offer connections between major cities in Colorado. They will carry your bicycle, but the official word is that it must be in a box. But it's really up to the bus driver, and a smiling approach may get your bike on without a box. For information about Greyhound/Trailways Bus schedules call (303) 292-6111.

By Train

Amtrak trains cross Colorado with stops in Denver, Winter Park, Granby, Glenwood Springs, Grand Junction, La Junta, and Trinidad. The biggest problem in going by train is that during the summer months the trains are crowded, and you would probably have to make your reservations months ahead. You can find out about schedules and reservations by calling Amtrak (800) 872-7245.

At present the Amtrak office tells us that you need to box your bike and check it through. However, an Indiana-based tour company, Endless Summer Tours (800) 345-3389 or (219) 874-6996, handles numerous cycle vacations using Amtrak. They have been able to arrange to carry on bicycles in bicycle bags. They can make Amtrak reservations for you whether you are on one of their tours or not. They will also rent or sell you a bicycle bag (or advise you as to the kind to use). You may want to call Endless Summer Tours for Amtrak advice. Or write to them at 1101 Franklin St., Michigan City, IN 46360.

By Auto

Of course you can drive to the starting point of any one of these tours. Many of the motels in Colorado will allow you to leave your car in their parking lot for a week or so, but would expect you to book a room there for your first and last nights.

Cycling From Denver's Stapleton Airport

If you want to start riding from the airport, it's certainly possible. We and other cycling friends have done it often.

See Tour 1 for a cycling route to Boulder. You could as easily continue to Fort Collins. If you choose to go south, the Interstate Corridor Bicycle Route will take you to Colorado Springs and beyond. The State Highway Department Bicycle Strip Maps have detailed directions for following the Interstate. The I-25 corridor takes you north or south through the state within sight of the eastern slope of the Rocky Mountains.

To cycle in Denver you should have the *Bicycling Denver* route map, prepared by the Denver Bicycle Touring Club, to help you find recommended routes for getting through the city, and thus joining up with the Interstate Corridor Bicycle Routes that are shown on the above mentioned Colorado Highway Department strip maps. See Appendix A for addresses. Or call the Hot Line of the Bicycle Program of the Colorado Department of Highways (303) 757-9281 for more information.

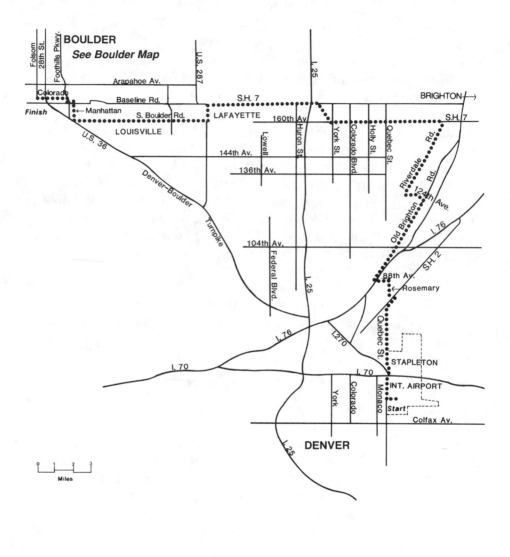

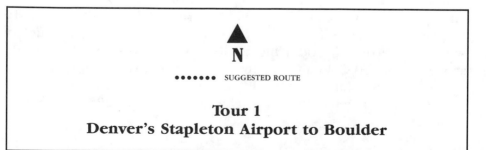

N

•••••• SUGGESTED ROUTE

Tour 1
Denver's Stapleton Airport to Boulder

Denver's Stapleton Airport to Boulder

Connecting route

Distance	44 mi from Stapleton (5280′) to Boulder (5363′)
Actual Climbing	600′
Helpful Maps	*Colorado Road Atlas*, pages D14, T10, T3. (See Appendix A.)
Terrain	Flat most of the way, with some climbs through rolling country after the route heads west toward Boulder.
Roads and Traffic	For the first 5 mi out of Stapleton Airport you will be riding in city traffic. After that the roads will have a low traffic count, or very adequate shoulders.
Special Notes	We live in Boulder, and have cycled from Stapleton to Boulder on various occasions after returning from bicycle tours in Europe. We usually spend the night of arrival at a motel near the airport, and cycle home the following morning. Best not to try it late in the day.

0.0   **Leave** Stapleton Airport on exit road going **west** to Quebec St.

0.5   **Right** (N) on Quebec St. (Col. 35).

Follow arrow pointing to Smith Rd. and Col. 35, avoiding underpass, but don't turn on Smith Rd.

1.5   **Cross** Smith Rd.

Follow Col. 35 **north** and get in lane for I-70 **West** at top of overpass.

1.6   **Pass under** I-70.

1.9   **Pass over** I-270, staying on Quebec St.

Keep to the right through S curve and **continue north** on Quebec St.

2.8   **Pass** Air Cargo Facility at traffic light. 2′ to 4′ shoulder.

5.7   **Right** (NE) at stop sign onto Col. 2 and **cross** old R.R. tracks carefully. They are slanted across road. Cross them at 90-degree angle.

6.0   **Left** (W) at first possible left turn onto East 80th Ave. and **cross** more R.R. tracks.

6.1   **Immediate right** (N) on Rosemary St.

7.1   **Left** (W) at T on E. 88th Ave.

7.7   **Pass over** I-76.

7.8   **Immediate right** (N) on frontage road along **west** side of I-76.

8.8   **Cross** E. 96th Ave.

Continue (N) on now-called Old Brighton Rd. to town of Henderson.

10.0   **Cross** E. 104th Ave.

12.6   **Pass** Henderson Post Office on right.

12.9   **Left** (W) on 124 Ave. (Follow Regional Park sign).

13.9   **Right** (N) at T on Riverdale Rd.

14.1   **Bear right** and stay on Riverdale Rd.

17.9   View of South Platte River on right side of road.

18.8   **Left** (W) on E. 160th Ave. (Col. 7). 8′ shoulder. Start of short climb and rolling countryside.

24.8   Road curves right—**follow** Col. 7.

26.2   Denver North campground. Entrance to the left on Washington St.

26.3   **Pass over** I-25 and **continue west** toward the mountains.

27.9   Spectacular view. Your first good, unimpeded view of the Rocky Mountains. On a clear day you can see 14,256′ Longs Peak to the northwest. The Continental Divide reaches its easternmost point along this ridge of mountains.

30.2   **Cross** Boulder County line.

32.6   **Left** (S) at traffic light on Public Road (U.S. 287) and through small town of Lafayette. Restaurants and stores.

33.5   **Right** (W) on South Boulder Rd. Wide 4-lane road now all the way to Boulder, with the exception of 0.5 mi of narrow road on this stretch.

35.0   **Cross** Col. 42 at traffic light and continue on South Boulder Rd. through edge of Louisville, famous for its spaghetti restaurants, which are south on Main St. A good bike shop, The Louisville Cyclery, is on your left just before crossing R.R. tracks.

37.6   **Pass** traffic light at McCaslin Blvd. **Continue west** on South Boulder Rd. 6′ shoulder. As you approach Boulder you will be riding through agricultural land, part of the greenbelt the city and county of Boulder have bought to preserve the open space around the city. You will be looking west toward the famous Flatirons rock formations. Boulder's spectacular mountain backdrop has been preserved, and saved from developers, as part of the greenbelt acquisition program.

41.0   **Right** (N) on Manhattan Dr. signed Bike Route. Note motel on northwest corner.

42.0   **Left** (W) on Baseline Rd. for 2 blocks.

42.1   **Right** (N) on Col. 157 (Foothills Parkway). 8′ shoulder.

42.8   **Left** (W) **dangerous turn** on Colorado Ave. Follow signs directing you toward C.U. stadium. 4-lane road.

43.5   **Cross** 30th St.

44.1   **Cross** busy 28th St. (U.S. 36) at traffic light and **continue west** for 2 blocks.

44.3   **Finish** in Boulder at the northeast edge of the University of Colorado, at the corner of Colorado Ave. and Folsom St. This is also the starting point for other tours out of Boulder. For more information about Boulder see page 41.

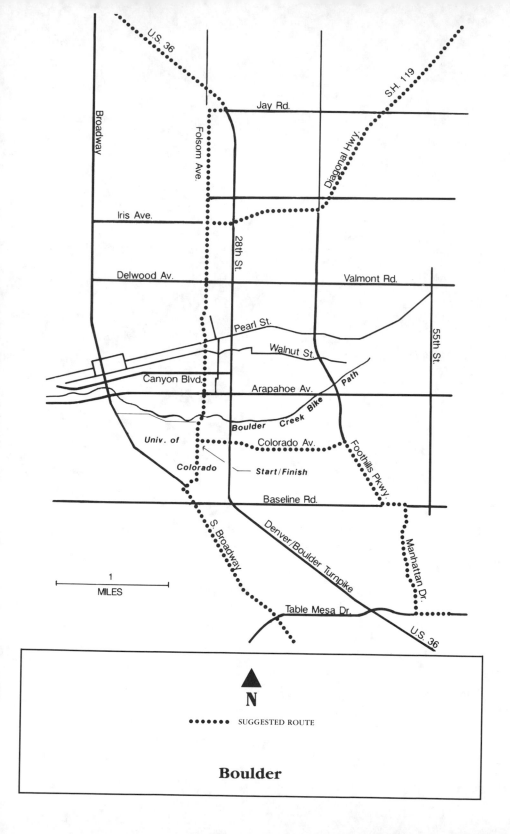

U.S. 36

Broadway

Folsom Ave.

Jay Rd.

Diagonal Hwy.

S.H. 119

Iris Ave.

28th St.

Delwood Av.

Valmont Rd.

55th St.

Pearl St.

Walnut St.

Canyon Blvd.

Arapahoe Av.

Path

Boulder Creek Bike

Univ. of

Colorado Av.

Foothills Pkwy.

Colorado

Start/Finish

Baseline Rd.

S. Broadway

Denver/Boulder Turnpike

Manhattan Dr.

1
MILES

Table Mesa Dr.

U.S. 36

N

•••••••• SUGGESTED ROUTE

Boulder

Boulder

Population 80,002, elevation 5363'

▲

Boulder is a bicycle town. Many world-class cyclists live here, or come here to train. It was the original location of the Red Zinger Bicycle Race—later called the Coors International Bicycle Classic. There are many other amateur and professional races here during the summer months. There are also weekend rides with the Boulder Bicycling Group of the Colorado Mountain Club, the Boulder Velo Club, and others. (See Appendix B.) For the schedules of rides inquire at one of the local bike shops.

In 1858 the first settlers in search of gold came to the Boulder valley. They established the town at the edge of the Rocky Mountains at the base of the distinctive Flatiron rock formations. It became a supply town for the gold and silver camps farther up in the mountains. The University of Colorado was established here in 1876 and helped the town to survive when the gold and silver veins ran out. Boulder didn't become a ghost town as many others did.

The Mapleton Hill Historic District on the west side of town was laid out in 1888 and the maple trees planted there transformed the area from a windswept, native-grass covered hill to a delightfully shaded neighborhood. A tour through this area will give you a view of a great variety of turn-of-the-century architecture.

The Pearl St. Mall is a fascinating place to stroll (but don't ride your bikes there because cycling is forbidden on the Mall proper). Musicians, jugglers, and entertainers of various kinds will hold your interest if you want to stop and watch, and there are numerous shops to explore. It's been rated one of the most successful downtown malls in the country.

Bike Routes

The city of Boulder has an excellent bike map with many bikepaths, routes, and recommended streets indicated. It's available from the

41

city, and if you plan to spend time in Boulder, it's worth sending for. (See Appendix A.) *Bike Rides of the Colorado Front Range* by Vici DeHaan, published by Pruett Publishing of Boulder, will also furnish you with a selection of other short rides starting in Boulder.

Accommodations

Boulder has plenty of motels, restaurants, stores, and, as you would expect, many bike shops. To find a good motel, easy to reach by bicycle, **follow** the Folsom St. bike lane **north** from the northeast edge of the University of Colorado campus at the corner of Folsom and Colorado Ave. **Continue downhill**, crossing Boulder Creek, for 3 blocks to Walnut St. **Right** (E) on Walnut for 1 block. **Right** (S) on 26th St. for 1 block. You will see the Best Western Golden Buff Motel Lodge on the left. (303) 442-7450. Call ahead.

To find a campground near Boulder, you will have to ride 1.5 mi up Boulder Canyon from the western edge of town to the Boulder Mountain Lodge Campground. The road up this canyon is a busy, dangerous highway, and you should not attempt to ride all the way up Boulder Canyon. (There are better canyons to climb. See Tour 2 and 7A.) However, if you need to find a campground, this 1.5 mi stretch of highway has 1' to 2' shoulders and can be negotiated with caution. To get to the Boulder Mountain Lodge Campground, **follow** the Boulder Creek Bikepath, which you can pick up at the bridge over the creek on Folsom (just south of Taft Dr.) or at any point along the creek. Follow the bikepath through the city to its western edge. There a bridge will take you across the creek to Eben Fine Park. **Go through** the parking lot to Arapahoe Ave. directly to the **south**. **Right** (W) on Arapahoe and merge with Canyon Blvd. at stop sign at the mouth of Boulder Canyon. **West** on Canyon Blvd. (Col. 119) for 1.5 mi. **Right** (N) on Four Mile Canyon Rd. and you will see Boulder Mountain Lodge Campground straight ahead.
(303) 444-0882. It is a small campground, so it would be a good idea to call ahead before making the trip up the canyon.

For more Boulder-and-vicinity route information, see Tours 1, 2, 3A, 3D, 4, 5, and 8.

Boulder

The Boulder Bicycling Group of the Colorado Mountain Club riding out of Boulder on the Boulder/Long-mont Diagonal Highway—the famous Flatiron rock formations are in the background.

A lunch stop in the small town of Niwot makes this club ride a very social occasion.

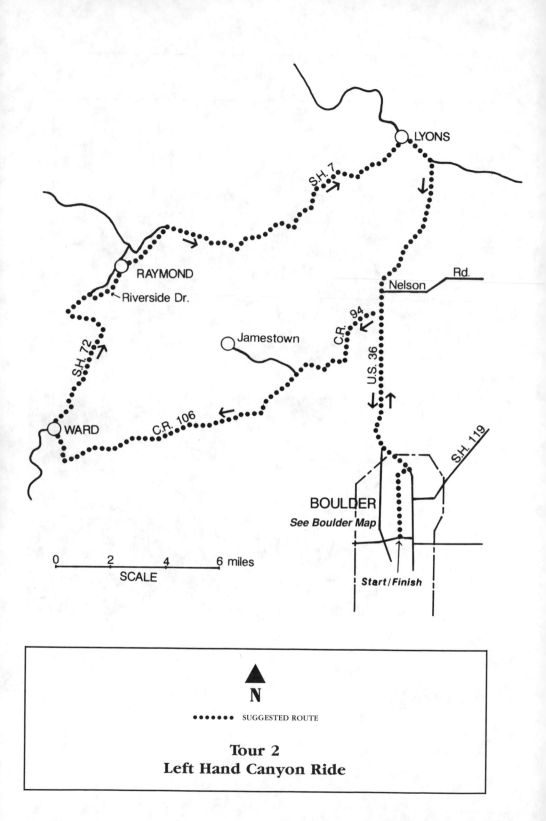

LYONS

S.H. 7

RAYMOND

Riverside Dr.

Nelson   Rd.

C.R. 94

Jamestown

S.H. 72

U.S. 36

C.R. 106

WARD

S.H. 119

BOULDER
See Boulder Map

Start / Finish

0   2   4   6 miles
SCALE

N

●●●●●●● SUGGESTED ROUTE

**Tour 2
Left Hand Canyon Ride**

2

Left Hand Canyon Ride

Distance   65 mi round trip from Boulder (5363′)

Actual Climbing   4800′

Helpful Maps   *Colorado Road Atlas*, pages T3, D14. National Forest Map: Roosevelt. Boulder County Cycling Guide. (See Appendix A.)

Terrain   Gentle climbing at first, then just before Ward a very steep 1.8 mi climb. Once you have joined the Peak-to-Peak Highway after passing through Ward, it's mostly downhill to Lyons.

Roads and Traffic   Good shoulders and smooth pavement on U.S. 36 and on the Peak-to-Peak Highway. Left Hand Canyon Dr. has a low traffic count. There is some rough pavement in spots, but since you are going up you can pick your way. The back road going down through Raymond is also rough, but has a low traffic count.

Special Notes   From the Boulder elevation of 5363′ you climb up through a very scenic canyon to the old mining town of Ward, elevation 9253′. Then you can follow the Peak-to-Peak Highway on a route through the mountains and finally make an exciting descent to Lyons and a return along the foothills to Boulder. Connie Carpenter-Phinney trained on this route before the

1984 Olympics, where she won a gold medal in the women's cycling road race.

0.0   **Start** tour in Boulder at the **northeast** edge of the University of Colorado campus, corner of Colorado Blvd. and Folsom St.

Ride north on Folsom St. using bike lane.

2.0   **Cross** Iris Ave.

3.0   **Right** (E) on Jay Rd. for 1 block.

3.1   **Left** (N) on 28th (U.S. 36 West). 5' shoulder.

9.3   **Left** (W) on Left Hand Canyon Dr. (County Rd. 94).

11.7   **Curve right** just after Buckingham Park, staying on County Rd. 94. Note Bikeway Information sign after turn. Use caution—lots of blind curves. But not much traffic on this road except at commuting time. Picnic spots at various places along the creek on the way up.

14.5   **Left** (SW) over bridge, staying on Left Hand Canyon Dr. (now County Rd. 106). The canyon gets a little steeper here. Be alert for loose gravel on turns, which could cause a spill. You're still following Left Hand Canyon Creek.

24.3   There are 2 unpaved roads going off to the left, but **follow** paved road which bends to the **right**.

Continue on steep climb (1.8 mi) through Ward.

25.5   Ward, population 129, elevation 9253', is an old gold mining town dating from 1860. There is a small general store in town, one restaurant overlooking the town, and one restaurant after you have turned onto the Peak-to-Peak Highway.

25.9 Leaving Ward you will come to a sharp hairpin turn to the right and a 0.2 mi very steep climb to the Peak-to-Peak Highway. You may have to walk this bit!!!

26.1 **Right** (N) on Peak-to-Peak Highway (Col. 72).

26.4 The Millsite Inn is 0.3 mi down the road, on the Peak-to-Peak Highway. To reach the other Ward restaurant you must turn **left** (S) upon reaching the Peak-to-Peak Highway and go **south** less than 0.5 mi to the first road to the left. The Old Depot Cafe is about 0.5 mi down this road, overlooking the town.

26.4 **Continue** (N) from Millsite Inn on Peak-to-Peak Highway. This is a beautiful downhill—smooth pavement with 3′ shoulder. Check brakes and tires before you start down, and be alert for gusts of wind from side canyons as you descend.

The Peak-to-Peak Highway between Ward and Raymond is a perfect cycling road. Low traffic and a wide, smooth shoulder.

34.0 **Important! Right** (E) at sign pointing to Raymond, on Riverside Dr. This road takes you through the summer cabin town of Raymond. A gentle descent following South St. Vrain Creek on narrow, rather rough but quiet road. Small store at intersection in 1.6 mi.

Continue along creek to join main highway (now Col. 7).

37.8 **Right** (E) on Col. 7 and continue down. Good road but with less shoulder as you descend. You will pass through the Narrows with high rock formations on both sides of the road. As you reach the flat, the road cuts through the Dakota Hogback, a famous geological formation which runs north/south along the foothills.

49.3 **Right** (E) as you enter Lyons onto U.S. 36 toward Boulder.

Lyons Population 1137, elevation 5374'.

Restaurants, grocery store, small motel, and an interesting historical museum in the old Redstone Schoolhouse on High St.

51.3 **Right** (S) still on U.S. 36 over R.R. tracks heading toward Boulder. Narrow shoulder for 4 mi on this road. Ride single file. Then 5' shoulder to Jay Rd. at the edge of Boulder.

63.3 **Right** (W) on Jay Rd. to Folsom (signed 26th St. at this point).

63.4 **Left** (S) on Folsom St. and join bike lane.

65.4   **Finish** tour in Boulder at **northeast** edge of the University of Colorado campus, at the corner of Colorado Blvd. and Folsom St.

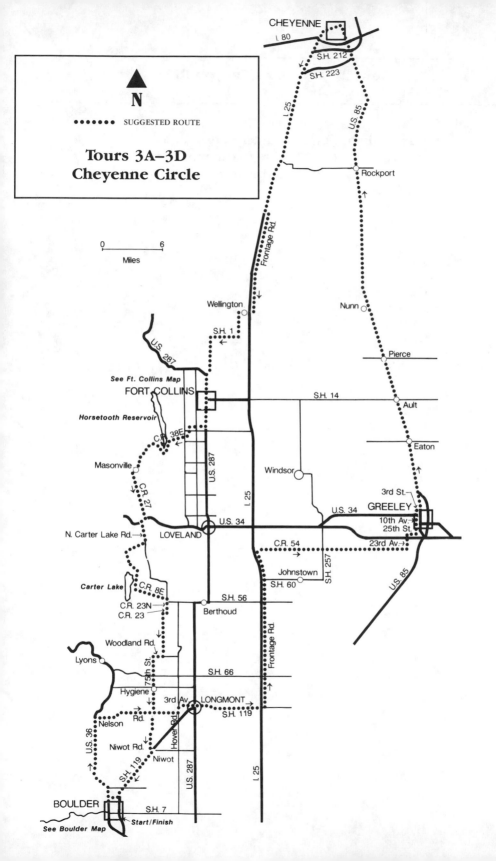

CHEYENNE

I. 80

S.H. 212

S.H. 223

I. 25

U.S. 85

Rockport

Nunn

Frontage Rd.

Pierce

Wellington

S.H. 1

S.H. 14

Ault

See Ft. Collins Map

FORT COLLINS

Eaton

Horsetooth Reservoir

C.R. 38E

U.S. 287

Masonville

Windsor

3rd St.

GREELEY

C.R. 27

I. 25

10th Av.
25th St.

N. Carter Lake Rd.

U.S. 34

LOVELAND

U.S. 34

23rd Av.

C.R. 54

Carter Lake

C.R. 8E

Johnstown

S.H. 257

U.S. 85

C.R. 23N
C.R. 23

S.H. 56

Berthoud

S.H. 60

Woodland Rd.

Frontage Rd.

Lyons

75th St.

S.H. 66

Hygiene

3rd Av

LONGMONT

Nelson Rd.

Niwot Rd.

S.H. 119

U.S. 36

Hover Rd.

S.H. 119

Niwot

U.S. 287

I. 25

BOULDER

S.H. 7

See Boulder Map

Start/Finish

N

•••••• SUGGESTED ROUTE

Tours 3A–3D
Cheyenne Circle

0   6
Miles

Cheyenne Circle

Distance	219 mi
Suggested Time	4 days
Total Climbing	3900′

This is a 4-day loop from Boulder to Greeley, north to Cheyenne, Wyoming, then south to Fort Collins and back to Boulder. It's a tour of medium difficulty along the foothills on the east side of the Rockies, with great views of the mountains and a stretch of wide-open cowboy country as you near Cheyenne.

Terrain Rolling roads for the first three days. Then some steep climbs between Fort Collins and Boulder.

Roads and Traffic Good shoulders on the busy roads including a stretch of I-25, and low-traffic, country roads the rest of the time.

Special Notes In 1973 shortly after we moved to Colorado we led a tour covering this territory for 30 members of the International Bicycle Touring Society (IBTS). It was so popular that we did it again two years later. It's an ideal break-in tour for flatlanders. In the second year, our tour was followed by a week in the mountains, led by another IBTS member, which included the climb over Trail Ridge Road to elevations of more than 12,000', and some other high passes. The Cheyenne Circle was a good preparation for the second week of climbing in higher altitudes.

Since that time the Cheyenne Circle has also been a favorite tour for the Boulder Bicycling Group of the Colorado Mountain Club.

For the IBTS this was planned as a motel-oriented tour. There are no conveniently located campgrounds on the route, so we suggest that you take this tour only if you plan to stay in motels. The overnight stops are made in cities that are interesting and worth exploring after you check into your motel.

3A

Boulder to Greeley

Distance	61 mi from Boulder (5363′) to Greeley (4663′)
Actual Climbing	600′
Helpful Maps	*Colorado Road Atlas*, pages T3, D14, T19, D11, T16. (See Appendix A.)
Terrain	Mostly flat with some roller-coaster hills.
Roads and Traffic	Good shoulders where traffic demands it. Otherwise quiet, low-traffic roads.

0.0   **Start** tour in Boulder at the **northeast** edge of the University of Colorado campus, at the corner of Colorado Blvd. and Folsom St.

2.0   **Ride north** on Folsom St. using bike lane.

Cross Iris Ave.

3.0   **Right** (E) on Jay Rd. for 1 block.

3.1   **Left** (N) on 28th (U.S. 36 West), riding along the foothills that run along the eastern edge of the Rocky Mountains. 5′ shoulder.

Continue (N) on U.S. 36 to Nelson Rd.

10.4   **Right** (E) on Nelson Rd., a wonderful downhill run usually with the wind behind you.

17.4   **Left** (N) at traffic light onto Hover Rd. Good 4-lane highway which also has a bikepath on the east side.

18.4   **Right** (E) on 3rd Ave. and into Longmont. Motels, restaurants, and bike shops. Note fine old turn-of-the-century mansions as you near downtown.

20.0   **Cross** Main St. and go 1 more block **east** to Kimbark St., where you will see a sign directing you to "Museum." It's well worth a side trip to turn left following the sign to visit the Longmont Museum, on the west side of the street in the first block. Historical displays interpreting the history of Longmont and the St. Vrain Valley from the time of the Indians to the present day are fascinating and informative.

　　　　Continue (E) out of town on 3rd Ave., which becomes Col. 119, a 4-lane highway with 5' shoulder.

26.8   **Pass under** I-25 to frontage road on **east** side. Motels and restaurants at intersection.

26.9   **Left** (N) on frontage road. Very little traffic and generally good roadbed on this roller-coaster road with some long but not steep hills.

41.2   **Pass** Johnson's Corners, a big truck-stop restaurant and motel. A logical stop for lunch because you won't find any more restaurants until you reach Greeley. We've eaten here many times. For years it has been a favorite bikies' stopping point.

　　　　Continue north for 1 mi on frontage road to first right-hand turn. No road sign here but later sign shows it to be Weld County Rd. 54.

42.4   **Right** (E) on Road 54 for another roller-coaster ride through one of the richest farming counties in the U.S.

56.8   **Left** (N) at 4-way stop on 23rd Ave.

57.8   **Pass under** U.S. 34 and continue **north** to 25th St.

58.2   **Right** (E) on 25th St.

59.3   **Left** (N) on 10th Ave., which is marked bike route. This will take you past the University of Northern Colorado.

60.8   **Finish** tour in Greeley at corner of 10th Ave. and 10th St.

Greeley   Population 53,066, elevation 4663′.

This is a pleasant college town with wide streets. It's easy to get around by bicycle. First settled in 1870, Greeley was named for the publisher of the New York *Tribune*, Horace Greeley, whose advice at

On the first day of the Cheyenne Circle tour, at mile 26.9 while following the I-25 corridor, cyclists can ride on the low-traffic frontage road, nicely removed from the heavy traffic on the Interstate.

that time was "Go west, young man!" Motels, restaurants, groceries, and bike shops. The Holiday Inn (303) 356-3000 at the corner of 8th Ave. (U.S. 85 Business) and 6th St. is easy to reach by bicycle.

3B

Greeley to Cheyenne

Distance 53 mi from Greeley (4663') to Cheyenne (6062')

Actual Climbing 1500'

Helpful Maps *Colorado Road Atlas*, pages T16, D11. (See Appendix A.)

Terrain An all-day gradual climb.

Roads and Traffic You will have an adequate shoulder riding out of Greeley. Then for 18 mi the shoulder will vary from none to narrow. After that an 8' shoulder all the way to Cheyenne. Traffic is usually quite light after you get away from Greeley until you approach Cheyenne.

Special Notes Start early on this day. It's likely to be hot and windy. You will ride through several small towns with grocery stores and/or restaurants just north of Greeley, but then you will be in wide-open cowboy country with no water or food stops. So be prepared with plenty of water and picnic supplies.

0.0 **Leave** Greeley from the corner of 10th Ave. and 10th St.

Continue **north** on 10th Ave. to 3rd St. **Right** (E) on 3rd St. for 2 blocks to 8th Ave. **Left** (N) on 8th Ave.

(U.S. 85 Business) and out of town toward Cheyenne, Wyoming.

7.3 Eaton. 2 restaurants, supermarket.

11.3 Ault. Restaurant, grocery.

15.3 Pierce. Cafe, grocery.

20.3 Nunn. Last possible grocery.

Continue north on U.S. 85 to Cheyenne. Now you get that 8' shoulder the rest of the way.

34.0 Rockport with a small roadside snack bar and gas station, which may or may not be open. But there are shade trees and a good spot for a picnic stop. This highway passes through the Pawnee National Grasslands. Buffalo once roamed these windswept plains, hunted by the Indians for food and skins. Today, the buffalo and Indians are replaced by range cattle and the occasional cowboy rounding them up. And often a herd of antelope grazing peacefully not too far from roadside.

41.1 **Cross** Wyoming state line.

As you enter Cheyenne you'll be passing through the ugliest part of town. But continue on, it gets better. Actually Cheyenne is a very attractive town.

49.5 **Pass under** I-80.

49.8 **Continue** (N) over the bridge across the extensive Union Pacific R.R. tracks.

50.7 **Cross** Lincoln Way (16th St.) (U.S. 30) at end of bridge.

50.8   **Left** (W) onto one-way 17th St.

Cheyenne

Population 51,458, elevation 6062'.

Cheyenne was first settled in 1867 when the Union Pacific Railroad crossed the high plains en route to the West Coast. It was named for the Indian tribe that roamed the grasslands of the area. When you cross Capital Ave. while you are riding through town, be sure to stop long enough to look north and south, from one end of the street to the other. On one end you will see the historic Union Pacific Depot and on the other the gold-domed Capitol Building. To explore more of Cheyenne pick up a *Magic City Tour Map* from the Chamber of Commerce at 301 W. 16th St. Motels, restaurants, groceries, bike shops.

Note: Don't plan your visit during the annual Frontier Days—the last full week in July. There will be no room for you in any motel and the whole town will be overcrowded.

Continue (W) through town on 17th St. to Thomes Ave.

51.3   **Left** (S) on Thomes Ave. for 1 block.

51.4   **Right** (W) on Lincoln Way (16th St.) You'll pass several motels along here.

52.5   Just a little farther on you'll see our favorite motel in Cheyenne, The Hitching Post Inn. (307) 638-3301. Calling ahead for a reservation would be a good idea.

3C

▲

Cheyenne to Fort Collins

Distance 44 mi from Cheyenne (6062') to Fort Collins (4984')

Actual Climbing 300'

Helpful Maps *Colorado Road Atlas*, pages D10, T13. National Forest Map: Roosevelt. (See Appendix A.)

Terrain Relatively flat riding.

Roads and Traffic To leave Cheyenne you will have to negotiate the entrance to I-25 and ride on the shoulder for 20 miles. (See page 30 for safe Interstate riding suggestions.) Then you will have a no-traffic, frontage road and finally a beautiful, quiet country road as you approach Fort Collins.

Special Notes Start this day with water bottles filled. You'll be riding through unpopulated grasslands for more than half of the trip.

0.0 **Start** by cycling **west** on Lincoln Way (Business U.S. 30) from the Hitching Post Inn to I-25 **south—** toward Denver.

1.6 **Enter** I-25 with care and head **south**. It's okay to ride on shoulder of the Interstate, but be very alert at these Cheyenne interchanges. Use your rearview mirror, and follow the safe Interstate riding suggestions.

10.6   **Cross** Colorado state line.

13.6   Point of Interest: geological formation.

Continue south on I-25 to off-ramp at Buckeye Rd. Exit #288.

21.6   **Take** Exit #288 (no bicycles on Interstate beyond this point).

Pass under I-25 to frontage road on **east** side and **continue south**.

31.6   **Right** (W) on Wellington Rd. (Col. 1), **passing over** I-25 at Exit #278.

32.1   Small town of Wellington. Population 1215, elevation 5201′. Cafe, grocery store. This is the only possible lunch stop. The park in the center of town is a good picnic spot.

Continue on Col. 1 through town and out onto 10 mi of a perfect cycling road—smooth pavement with an 8′ shoulder.

You are out of ranching country and back to farmland. Midway on this stretch you will see the antenna towers of WWV, the transmitting station for the National Bureau of Standards.

42.3   **Left** (S) at T and onto U.S. 287.

42.8   As you enter Fort Collins you'll pass a stretch of motels (low to medium price) and restaurants along this 2 mi stretch of U.S. 287 to downtown. More motels, restaurants, and bike shops farther along.

44.3   **Left** (E) at Mountain Ave. for 1 block to Remington St. Note restored Old Town to your left.

44.4   **Finish** in downtown Fort Collins at corner of Mountain Ave. and Remington St.

For an easy-to-reach motel, **continue south** on Remington St. for 1 mi to Elizabeth St. **Right** (W) on Elizabeth for 1 block to College Ave., where you will find the Best Western University Motor Inn. (303) 484-1984.

For more information about Fort Collins see page 81.

3D

▲

Fort Collins to Boulder via Carter Lake

Distance	61 mi from Fort Collins (4984′) to Boulder (5363′)
Actual Climbing	1500′
Helpful Maps	*Colorado Road Atlas*, pages T13, D10, D14, T3. National Forest Map: Roosevelt. Fort Collins Bike Map. (See Appendix A.)
Terrain	An exciting into-the-foothills ride with three climbs at Horsetooth Reservoir, a ride through a valley between two hogback ridges, and a 1.4 mi very steep climb up to Carter Lake.
Roads and Traffic	Avoid weekends for this ride because of possible heavy boat and RV traffic around Horsetooth Reservoir. Otherwise traffic should be no problem and roads are good.

0.0 **Start** tour in downtown Fort Collins at the corner of Mountain Ave. and Remington St.

South on Remington St. for 2 mi.

2.0 **Left** (E) on Spring Park Dr. for 1 block.

Right (S) on Mathews St. When Mathews St. jogs to the **left**, **follow** it to Drake Rd. for 0.5 mi.

Right (W) on Drake for 1 block.

Left (S) on Harvard St. for 0.3 mi.

Left (S) on Remington St. for 0.2 mi.

Right (W) on Swallow Rd. and **cross** College Ave.

Continue west on Swallow (signed Bikeway) for 1.6 mi to Dunbar Ave.

4.7 **Important left** (S) at stop sign on Dunbar Ave.

5.4 **Right** (W) at T on Horsetooth Rd. 2′ shoulder.

5.7 **Left** (S) on Taft Hill Rd.

6.2 **Right** (W) on County Rd. 38E. You will see a big gas station at this corner. 3′ shoulder.

7.3 **Road swings left**. Beginning of first climb.

7.6 **Sharp right** and road narrows and gets steeper.

8.0 Top of climb.

Bear left (don't go over the dam) and, continuing on 38E, ride alongside and around the end of the reservoir.

10.1 Start of second climb.

10.9 Top of climb.

11.7 Bottom.

12.0 Start of third climb.

13.0 Top of climb, and then a nice long down.

16.2 **Important left** (S) on County Rd. 27. Masonville Trading Post just after turn on the left. A good snack and regrouping stop.

Continue south on County Rd. 27 through pleasant rolling country in a valley between two hogback ridges.

21.5   **Right** (W) at T on U.S. 34. 3′ shoulder. Riverview Campground on left and motel and restaurant on right.

22.3   **Left** (S) onto N. Carter Lake Rd. after crossing bridge (County Rd. 29).

22.8   **Pass** Carter Valley RV Campground.

24.4   **Right** (W) staying on pavement onto County Rd. 18E, following Carter Lake sign.

26.5   **Left** (S) on County Rd. 31S, following Carter Lake sign.

26.6   **Start** the steepest climb of the day. 1.4 mi to the top, **crossing** two **dangerous** cattle guards (consisting of railroad rails approximately 6″ apart). So when you come to the cattle guard you should be sure to have enough momentum to cross without

Crossing the first of two dangerous cattle guards on the steepest climb of the day up to Carter Lake. It's important to maintain sufficient momentum to cross without danger of your front wheel turning and falling between the rails.

danger of your front wheel turning and catching—or you should walk it.

28.0   Top. Restaurant/bar and a general store.

28.6   Carter Lake Landing. Restaurant.

Continue along edge of lake.

31.5   **Left** at Y at stop sign and **continue east** on County Rd. 8E.

35.0   **Right** (S) at T on County Rd. 23N (Col. 56).

35.6   **Right** (S) at first road to right (County Rd. 23). It becomes 83rd St. at Boulder County line—signed Bike Route.

41.2   **Right** (W) at T on Woodland Rd.

42.2   **Left** (S) on 75th St.

44.2   **Cross** Ute Highway (Col. 66).

After leaving Fort Collins the route climbs into the foothills, skirting Horsetooth Reservoir.

45.2   **Pass** small town of Hygiene. Cafe and grocery.

49.9   **Cross** Nelson Rd. and **continue south** on N. 75th St.

51.6   **Left** (E) at T on Niwot Rd. (County Rd. 34).

Right (SW) at traffic light on Col. 119 (Diagonal Highway). 4 lanes with 10′ shoulder.

59.4   **Stay** on Col. 119 following Diagonal Highway signs.

59.7   **Merge** into Iris Ave., heading **west**.

60.4   **Straight** ahead crossing 28th St. (U.S. 36) and leaving Col. 119. Stay on Iris Ave.

60.6   **Left** (S) on Folsom St. and join bike lane.

62.6   **Finish** tour in Boulder at **northeast** edge of University of Colorado campus, at the corner of Colorado Blvd. and Folsom St.

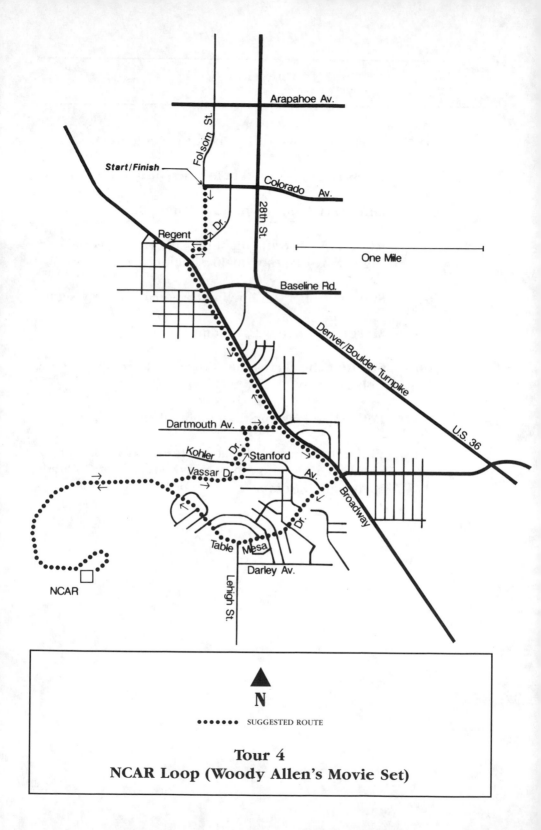

Arapahoe Av.

Folsom St.

Start/Finish

Colorado Av.

28th St.

Regent Dr.

One Mile

Baseline Rd.

Denver/Boulder Turnpike

U.S. 36

Dartmouth Av.

Kohler Dr.

Stanford

Vassar Dr.

Av.

Broadway

Dr.

Table Mesa

Darley Av.

Lehigh St.

NCAR

N

•••••• SUGGESTED ROUTE

**Tour 4
NCAR Loop (Woody Allen's Movie Set)**

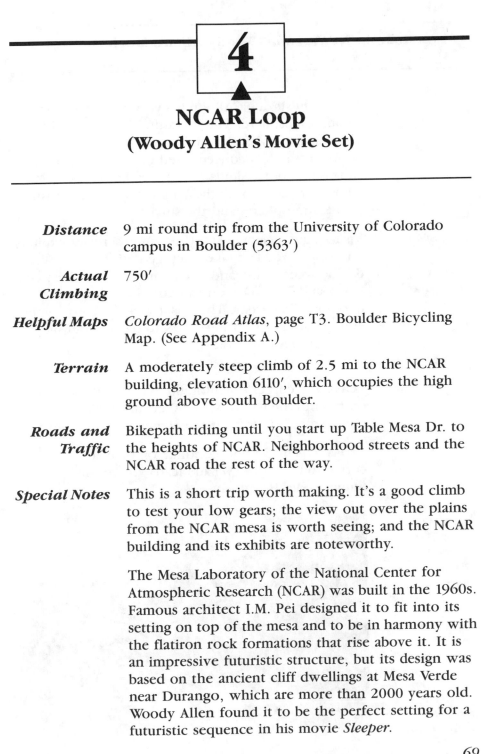

4

NCAR Loop
(Woody Allen's Movie Set)

Distance 9 mi round trip from the University of Colorado campus in Boulder (5363′)

Actual Climbing 750′

Helpful Maps *Colorado Road Atlas*, page T3. Boulder Bicycling Map. (See Appendix A.)

Terrain A moderately steep climb of 2.5 mi to the NCAR building, elevation 6110′, which occupies the high ground above south Boulder.

Roads and Traffic Bikepath riding until you start up Table Mesa Dr. to the heights of NCAR. Neighborhood streets and the NCAR road the rest of the way.

Special Notes This is a short trip worth making. It's a good climb to test your low gears; the view out over the plains from the NCAR mesa is worth seeing; and the NCAR building and its exhibits are noteworthy.

The Mesa Laboratory of the National Center for Atmospheric Research (NCAR) was built in the 1960s. Famous architect I.M. Pei designed it to fit into its setting on top of the mesa and to be in harmony with the flatiron rock formations that rise above it. It is an impressive futuristic structure, but its design was based on the ancient cliff dwellings at Mesa Verde near Durango, which are more than 2000 years old. Woody Allen found it to be the perfect setting for a futuristic sequence in his movie *Sleeper*.

69

Tour 4   NCAR Loop (Woody Allen's Movie Set)

The scientists at NCAR study everything that pertains to our atmosphere. The literature that is available to visitors at the Mesa Laboratory states that currently, NCAR research is concentrated in four main areas: storms and other similar-sized weather phenomena, climate (weather over the long term), the chemistry of the atmosphere, and the sun.

Visitors are welcome at NCAR, and there are exhibits on display. You can take a self-guided tour any weekday between 8 A.M. and 5 P.M., or weekends between 9 A.M. and 3 P.M. Or you can go on a guided tour at noon on Wednesday. There is a small cafeteria where you can eat lunch. Bring a lock to secure your bicycle to the outdoor bike rack.

0.0   **Leave** the corner of Colorado Ave. and Folsom St. on the **northeast** corner of the University of Colorado campus, following the bikepath going **south**.

Cross Regent Dr. and continue on bikepath that curves to the **right** (W) and leads you to the bikepath tunnel under Broadway.

The Mesa Laboratory of the National Center for Atmospheric Research (NCAR) blends into the famous Flatiron rock formations west of Boulder. The design was inspired by the ancient cliff dwellings at Mesa Verde near Durango.

0.8   **West** through tunnel.

Immediately left (S) on bikepath.

Continue south along **west** side of Broadway.

1.0   **Cross** Baseline Rd. Be alert for turning traffic at all the bikepath crossings that are coming up.

1.3   **Cross** 27th Way, **pass** U.S. Department of Commerce Boulder Laboratories (Bureau of Standards), and **continue** on bikepath.

1.8   **Cross** Dartmouth Ave. at traffic light and **continue south** on marked bike route on Harvard Ln.

Staying on Harvard Ln., swing **right** to the **west** of the Exxon station to reach Table Mesa Dr. Ignore bikepath sign that sends you straight ahead over small bridge on east side of the gas station.

2.3   **Right** (W) on Table Mesa Dr. 4-lane road.

2.5   **Pass** Gillaspie Dr. at pedestrian traffic light and start on moderate climb that gets steeper as you progress.

3.5   **Enter** NCAR grounds and begin steeper climb. Watch for deer grazing on either side of the road on the NCAR grounds. You will be cycling toward the impressive and unique Flatirons rock formations.

4.8   **Right** at the top of the climb following arrow on sign "Visitor drop-off and bicycle parking."

4.9   **Stop** at front of the NCAR Mesa Laboratory building and lock your bike at the bike racks. You can enjoy a leisurely visit to the exhibit areas of the building, have lunch in the cafeteria, and view the eastern plains with Boulder immediately below and Denver in the distance.

Retrace down steep, winding NCAR road. Use caution—the road gets steeper and steeper as you descend.

Note: The return route is different. It takes you through an interesting neighborhood and allows you to avoid the busy left turn at Broadway and Table Mesa Dr.

Be alert for **left** turn as soon as you leave the NCAR grounds. Don't sweep past it as you fly downhill.

6.1 **Immediate left** (NE) at edge of the NCAR grounds on Vassar Dr.

6.6 **Left** (N) on Drake St. for 2 blocks.

6.7 **Left** (W) on Stanford Ave. for short, steep downhill for 1 block.

6.8 **Almost immediately right** (N) on Kohler Dr.

7.0 **Right** (E) at T on Dartmouth Ave.

7.2 **Left** (N) at traffic light onto bikepath running along the **west** side of Broadway.

Pass U.S. Department of Commerce Boulder Laboratories.

8.0 **Cross** Baseline Rd.

8.2 **Right** (E) through bikepath tunnel under Broadway to University of Colorado campus.

Follow bikepath across Regent Dr. going **north**.

9.0   **Finish** tour at **northeast** edge of the University of Colorado campus, at the corner of Colorado Blvd. and Folsom St.

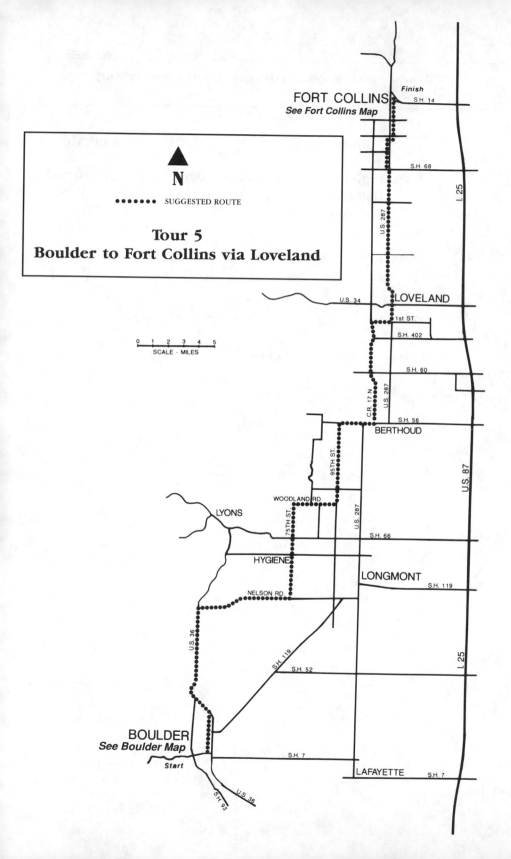

N

•••••• SUGGESTED ROUTE

Tour 5
Boulder to Fort Collins via Loveland

0 1 2 3 4 5
SCALE - MILES

FORT COLLINS
See Fort Collins Map
Finish
S.H. 14

S.H. 68

I. 25

U.S. 287

LOVELAND
U.S. 34
1st ST.
S.H. 402

S.H. 60

C.R. 17 N
U.S. 287
S.H. 56
BERTHOUD

95TH ST.

WOODLAND RD.

U.S. 287

LYONS

75TH ST.

U.S. 87

S.H. 66

HYGIENE

LONGMONT
S.H. 119

NELSON RD.

U.S. 36

S.H. 119

S.H. 52

I. 25

BOULDER
See Boulder Map
Start

S.H. 7

S.H. 93
U.S. 36

LAFAYETTE
S.H. 7

5

Boulder to Fort Collins via Loveland

Connecting route

Distance	54 mi from Boulder (5363′) to Fort Collins (4984′)
Actual Climbing	600′
Helpful Maps	*Colorado Road Atlas*, pages T3, D14, D10, T20, T13. National Forest Map: Roosevelt. Fort Collins Bike Map. (See Appendix A.)
Terrain	An easy ride with no steep climbs.
Roads and Traffic	Where you encounter traffic there will usually be an adequate shoulder, and back roads will have very little traffic.

0.0   **Start** tour in Boulder at the **northeast** edge of the University of Colorado campus at the corner of Colorado Ave. and Folsom St., riding **north** on Folsom.

         Follow bike lane out of town.

2.0   **Cross** Iris Ave.

3.0   **Right** (E) on Jay Rd. for 1 block.

3.1   **Left** (N) on 28th St. (U.S. 36 West). 5′ shoulder.

         Continue north on U.S. 36, riding along the foothills that form the eastern edge of the Rocky Mountains.

10.4 **Right** (E) on Nelson Rd. (toward Longmont). Wonderful downhill run!

16.2 **Left** (N) on 75th St.

17.8 **Pass** small town of Hygiene. Small cafe and grocery.

18.8 **Cross** Col. 66 (Ute Highway).

20.9 **Right** (E) on Woodland Rd. (when pavement turns to the right).

Continue (E) past 83rd St. to T at 95th St.

24.9 **Left** (N) on 95th St.

26.0 **Jog left** at next T onto Yellowstone Rd. for 0.1 mi and **right** again back to 95th St., heading **north**.

29.7 **Right** (E) on Col. 56 (stay on pavement).

31.3 **Straight ahead** (E) at stop sign to join busy U.S. 287 for 0.5 mi.

Riding north out of Boulder on U.S. 36, the highway that follows the foothills along the eastern edge of the Rocky Mountains.

Note: Shoulder here okay for riding for this short distance, but U.S. 287 not recommended for cycling until north of Loveland. It's a busy, narrow road from Longmont to Campion.

31.8   **Left** (N) at traffic light on County Rd. 17N (Taft Rd.) through rolling wheatfields with mountains to the west. 2′ shoulder.

37.0   At edge of Loveland, **continue across** 14th St., staying on Taft Rd.

38.1   **Right** (E) on 1st St. at **south** side of Loveland.

39.2   **Cross** 1-way Cleveland Ave. and **continue east** for 1 more block.

39.3   **Left** (N) on 1-way Lincoln Ave. (U.S. 287) through Loveland.

Loveland

Population 30,244, elevation 4982′.

Restaurants, motels, groceries, bike shops.

After crossing U.S. 34, note Indian statue on left, by Loveland sculptor Fritz White. It's called *Winning the Iron Shirt* and is based on the little-known fact that Spanish Conquistadors left behind in the plains quite a number of "Iron Shirts"—breastplates and shirts of mail. According to the legend a Cheyenne brave wore one of these shirts of mail and was considered invincible because arrows could not penetrate it. But he was finally killed by a member of a weaker tribe—a Pawnee warrior. Since the Cheyenne were noted for their oppression of the Pawnee tribe, this was a classical case of the legendary underdog winning, and capturing the "Iron Shirt." Incidentally, there are at least 30 professional sculptors in Loveland, drawn there by the presence of two foundries in the town.

Continue north on U.S. 287 toward Fort Collins.

42.0 Beginning of 10′ shoulder.

48.6 **Left** (W) on Harmony Rd. at traffic light at **south** edge of Fort Collins for 1 block.

Right (N) on Mason St. signed bikeway.

Jog left on Horsetooth Rd.

Immediate right (N) onto McClelland Dr. for 1.5 mi.

Right (E) on Swallow Rd. and **cross** College Ave. (U.S. 287).

Note: Bikes not allowed on U.S. 287 (College Ave. for 3 mi between Horsetooth Rd. and Laurel St.). You will see the signs prohibiting bikes, but they don't tell you what alternate routes to take. If you plan to spend any time here you should send for the Bike Map from the City Transportation Division. (See Appendix A.) Or pick one up at any bike shop in town. It will help you find your way around if you want to explore the town on other streets than those designated in this tour.

50.3 **Continue east** 1 more block to Remington St.

Left (N) on Remington St. for 0.2 mi.

Right (E) at stop sign onto Harvard St. and follow around 0.3 mi to Drake Rd.

Right (E) at stop sign for 1 block on Drake Rd.

Left (N) on Mathews St., following an S curve that keeps you on Mathews for 0.5 mi to Spring Park Dr.

Left (W) for 1 block to Remington St.

51.6   **Right** (N) on Remington, signed bikeway, for 2 mi to downtown Fort Collins.

53.6   **Finish** tour in downtown Fort Collins at the corner of Remington St. and Mountain Ave.

Restored Old Town is at end of Remington St. straight ahead. It's an interesting area of renovated shops and offices. Worth a visit.

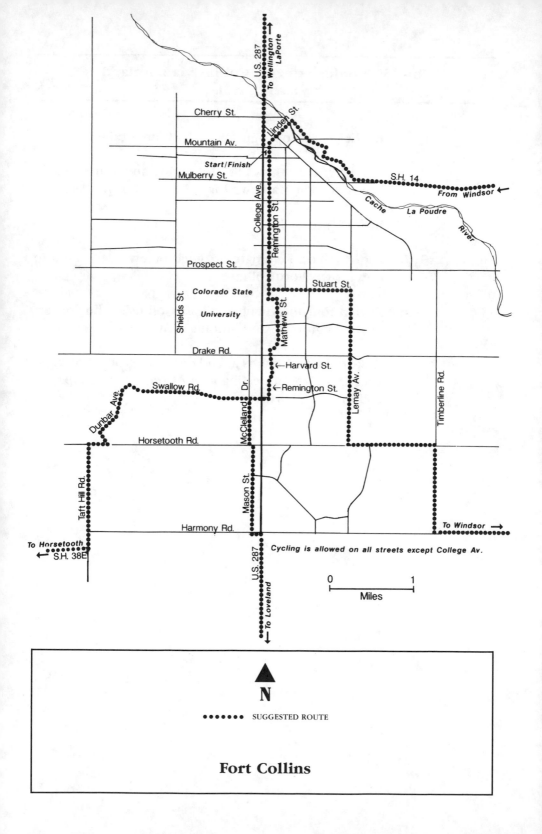

Fort Collins

Fort Collins

Population 87,700, elevation 4984'

▲

The history of Fort Collins began in 1836 when a party of French trappers proceeding northward along the Rocky Mountain foothills were caught in a heavy snowstorm. They buried their excess supplies, including gunpowder, intending to return for them later. The area, and later the nearby river, were called Cache la Poudre (French words for "hide" and "powder"). Because the river was more easily crossed at nearby LaPorte, it became an important station on the Overland Stage. In 1864 an army camp was established, moved to higher ground, and named Fort Collins.

Colorado State University was established here in 1870, six years before Colorado became a state.

Bike Routes

It's quite easy to get around Fort Collins by bicycle. The streets are wide, and bike routes are designated by sign throughout most of the town. A bicycle map of Fort Collins is available from bicycle shops, or you can send for one from the City Transportation Division. (See Appendix A.)

Fort Collins bicycle clubs also have rides scheduled for most weekends. Ask at one of the local bike shops for a schedule.

Accommodations

There are plenty of motels, restaurants, stores, and bicycle shops. The nearest campground is the KOA 10 mi north on U.S. 287 just beyond the town of LaPorte. For an easy-to-reach motel, ride **south** on Remington St. from the Old Town area for 1 mi to Elizabeth St. **Right** (W) on Elizabeth St. for 1 block to College Ave., where you will find the Best Western University Motor Inn. (303) 484-1984.

For more Fort Collins-and-vicinity route information see Tours 3C, 3D, 5, 6, and 12A.

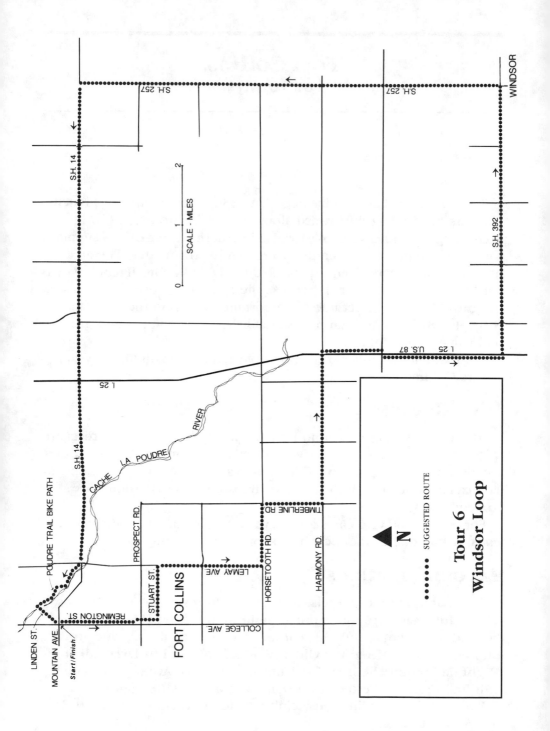

N

SUGGESTED ROUTE

**Tour 6
Windsor Loop**

SCALE - MILES

0   1   2

WINDSOR

S.H. 257

S.H. 257

S.H. 14

S.H. 392

I 25   U.S. 87

L 25

S.H. 14

CACHE LA POUDRE RIVER

POUDRE TRAIL BIKE PATH

PROSPECT RD.

TIMBERLINE RD.

HORSETOOTH RD.

HARMONY RD.

STUART ST.

LEMAY AVE.

COLLEGE AVE.

REMINGTON ST.

LINDEN ST.

MOUNTAIN AVE.

Start / Finish

FORT COLLINS

Windsor Loop

Distance	33 mi round trip from Fort Collins (4984′)
Actual Climbing	300′
Helpful Maps	*Colorado Road Atlas*, pages T13, D10. Fort Collins Bike Map. (See Appendix A.)
Terrain	Easy riding through pleasant countryside.
Roads and Traffic	Low-traffic country roads, and good shoulders on roads that are more heavily traveled. Total of only 2 mi in the whole trip with no shoulder where you would like one.

0.0 **Begin** this tour from Old Town area of Fort Collins at the corner of Mountain Ave. and Remington St.

Ride south on Remington St. for 2 mi.

2.0 **Left** (E) at stop sign on Stuart St.

2.9 **Right** (S) on LeMay Ave.

4.7 **Left** (E) at T at traffic light on Horsetooth Rd.

5.7 **Right** (S) on Timberline Rd.

6.7 **Left** (E) on Harmony Rd. Up to this point you have had 2′ to 8′ shoulders, but on this stretch of Harmony Rd. you will have a 1.3 mi section of 4-lane road with no shoulder.

9.1   **Pass over** I-25 to frontage road on **east** side of Interstate.

9.3   **Right** (s) on frontage road.

10.3   **Pass back over** I-25 to frontage road on **west** side of Interstate.

12.5   **Left** (E) at Windsor exit #262 on Col. 392, **crossing over** Interstate again. 6′ shoulder.

16.7   For a lunch stop note the Firehouse Restaurant in the shopping center on the south side of the road at the west edge of town.

17.1   **Continue east** on Col. 392 to junction of Col. 257 at traffic light. Straight ahead is the main street of town.

Windsor   Population 4277, elevation 4800′.

This is a typical eastern plains town, except for the large, ultra-modern Eastman Kodak plant here.

To return to Fort Collins, ride **north** on Col. 257 from the corner of Col. 257 and Col. 392, passing bird-watching ponds on the right. 8′ shoulder.

24.9   **Left** (W) on Col. 14 to edge of Fort Collins. 0.5 mi no shoulder, then 6′ shoulder the rest of the way.

28.7   **Pass over** I-25.

31.8   **Cross** LeMay Ave. just after city limits. Don't cross the bridge over the Cache la Poudre River just ahead.

31.9   **Join** signed Poudre Trail Bikepath on the **east** side of the river, heading **north**.

   Follow Poudre Trail along the river to Linden St.

32.0   **Left** (S) on Linden St. and **cross over** bridge to Old Town Fort Collins. You can walk your bike through the mall.

32.5   **Left** (E) to Remington St.

32.8   **Finish** tour at corner of Remington St. and Mountain Ave.

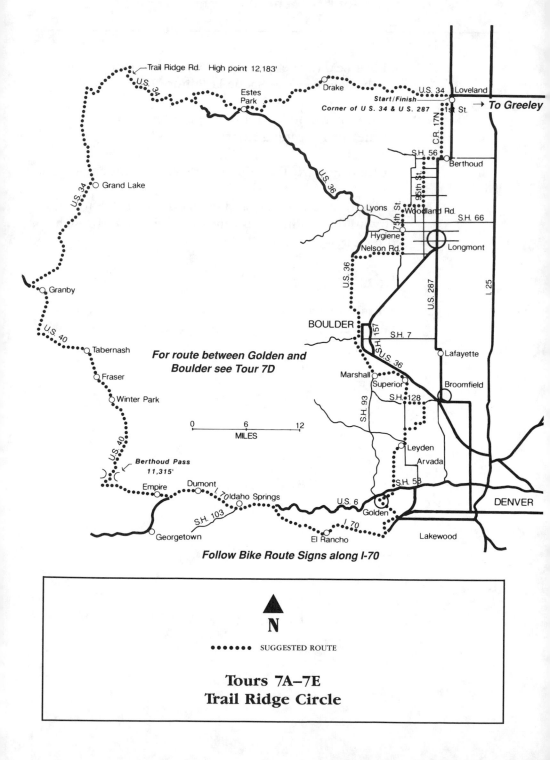

Trail Ridge Rd. High point 12,183'

U.S. 34

Estes Park

Drake

U.S. 34 Loveland

→ To Greeley

Start/Finish
Corner of U.S. 34 & U.S. 287

1st. St.

CR. 17N

S.H. 56

Berthoud

95th St.

U.S. 34 Grand Lake

U.S. 36

Lyons

175th St.

Woodland Rd.

S.H. 66

Hygiene

Nelson Rd.

Longmont

I. 25

Granby

U.S. 36

U.S. 287

U.S. 40

Tabernash

BOULDER

S.H. 157

S.H. 7

*For route between Golden and
Boulder see Tour 7D*

Fraser

U.S. 36

Lafayette

Winter Park

Marshall

Superior

Broomfield

0   6   12
MILES

S.H. 93

S.H. 128

Berthoud Pass
11,315'

Empire

Dumont

Idaho Springs

Leyden

Arvada

U.S. 40

S.H. 58

DENVER

U.S. 6

S.H. 103

Golden

Georgetown

I. 70

El Rancho

Lakewood

Follow Bike Route Signs along I-70

▲
N

●●●●●●● SUGGESTED ROUTE

**Tours 7A–7E
Trail Ridge Circle**

7

Trail Ridge Circle

Distance	248 mi
Suggested Time	5 days
Total Climbing	13,208'

Starting in Loveland (4982'), you will climb up through one of the most beautiful and best-for-cycling canyons in the area.

Then this tour takes you through Rocky Mountain National Park, and you climb to 12,183' on the world's highest continuous paved highway. There are 11 mi of road above timberline, and you will pass through areas of unique alpine tundra. You should be in good cycling condition to make this trip, and you should have adequately low gears on your bicycle. And because of the high altitude, you should be ready for freezing temperature, snow flurries, or cold rain.

You will return with a climb over 11,307' Berthoud Pass, and continue through Idaho Springs, Golden, Boulder, and back to Loveland.

Big Thompson Canyon—
Loveland to Estes Park

Distance 29 mi from Loveland (4982') to Estes Park (7522')

Actual Climbing 2700'

Helpful Maps *Colorado Road Atlas*, pages T20, D10, D9, T12. National Forest Map: Roosevelt. (See Appendix A.)

Terrain This is a beautiful canyon to climb or descend. The scenery is spectacular. Climbs are not exceptionally steep.

(Of course this also makes a delightful one-day trip from Loveland to Estes Park for lunch and return to Loveland.)

Roads and Traffic The road is recently rebuilt with good, wide shoulders most of the way. Traffic is sometimes heavy during the tourist season, but on this wide road you don't have to worry about it.

Special Notes This was the scene of the disastrous Big Thompson flood in 1975. Houses, cars, and people were swept away as a wave of water rushed through the canyon. You will see signs posted in Colorado canyons advising you to "climb to safety in case of a flash flood." 139 people died in the Big Thompson flood mainly because they tried to outrun it by car rather than climbing up on foot away from the river.

Loveland

Population 30,244, elevation 4982'.

Motels, restaurants, stores, bike shops. Yogi Bear's Jellystone Campground, (303) 667-1204, with good tent sites, is 3 mi east of town on U.S. 34. See Tour #5 for more Loveland information.

0.0   **Leave** from corner of U.S. 34 and U.S. 287 (Lincoln Ave. and Eisenhower Blvd.) in Loveland.

      Head west on U.S. 34 (W. Eisenhower Blvd.) out of town on 4-lane road.

6.7   **Pass** Riverview Campground.

8.9   **Pass** Dam Store and Big Thompson Power Plant.

9.1   **Enter** the Narrows, following Big Thompson River. Steep canyon walls leave room for just the road and the river.

11.0   Then out into the open, still following the river. There

Entering Big Thompson Canyon going west on U.S. 34. This is a beautiful canyon to ride—good pavement and wide shoulders most of the way.

89

are a few stretches of narrow shoulder, but 4'
shoulder persists most of the way.

16.0   **Pass** River Bend Store.

16.8   **Pass through** small town of Drake. Small store.

16.9   **Bear left** on U.S. 34 through a wider canyon, passing summer cottages and several motels.

27.8   Break out into the open with view of Estes Park
ahead.

28.2   KOA Campground, and beginning of strip of motels
and restaurants on edge of town.

29.4   **Finish** in Estes Park at junction of U.S. 34 and Wonderview Ave.

Estes Park   Population 2703, elevation 7522'.

The delightful climate makes Estes Park a popular

*Descending into
Estes Park, a
popular moun-
tain resort with
a delightful
summer climate,
at the end of the
Big Thompson
Canyon climb.*

tourist attraction. The town is picturesque, and usually crowded with tourists during the summer.

F.O. Stanley, the inventor of the Stanley Steamer automobile, came to Estes Park in 1903 to recover from tuberculosis. The mountain air was so beneficial that he settled here and built an opulent resort hotel. He used to meet his guests, when they reached the end of their railroad journey in Lyons at the bottom of the mountain, with a fleet of his steam-driven, locomotive-like Stanley Steamers, and carry them up to the hotel. The Stanley Hotel, featuring turn-of-the-century elegance, is still open today.

Motels, restaurants, stores, bike shops. National Park Commercial Campground, (303) 586-4563, is on U.S. 34 just before the Fall River entrance to Trail Ridge Road, and just inside the entrance is the Aspenglen National Forest Campground.

If continuing over Trail Ridge Road you should plan to make an early start on your next day's ride. See Tour 7B.

7B

Trail Ridge Road—
Estes Park to Grand Lake

Distance   50 mi from Estes Park (7522′) to Grand Lake (8369′)

Actual Climbing   5000′

Helpful Maps   *Colorado Road Atlas*, pages T12, D1, D9, D13.
National Forest Map: Roosevelt. (See Appendix A.)

Terrain   Trail Ridge Road, through Rocky Mountain National Park, is the world's highest continuous paved highway. (The road up Mt. Evans is higher, going to 14,260′, but it dead-ends at the summit.) The highest point on Trail Ridge Road is 12,183′ above sea level. The road runs for 42 mi from the Fall River Gate to the Grand Lake Gate. There are 11 mi of road above timberline. You will ride through unique alpine tundra. Snowbanks alongside the road are often still there at the end of summer. There is plenty of climbing, but grades are not exceptionally steep.

Roads and Traffic   The road is in good condition. Shoulders vary from none to 3′. Traffic may be heavy, especially after noon, but it tends to move slowly. Trail Ridge is usually open from Memorial Day until mid-October, but even in the middle of the summer it may be closed temporarily due to storms. So you should plan your trip carefully with an eye to weather forecasts.

Special Notes   It is essential that you make your start from Estes Park very early in the day. Thunder and lightning at this high altitude can be especially dangerous; and these storms are more likely to occur in the afternoon. Starting early in the morning you will also avoid most of the auto-tourists and have the road to yourself. Be advised that you might encounter rain, sleet, or even snow. Dress accordingly. Be sure to carry warm clothing for the long descent from the high point of 12,183′ to the 8369′ level of Grand Lake.

0.0   **Leave** Estes Park, elevation 7522′, on U.S. 34, turning **northwest** onto Wonderview Ave.

0.3   **Pass** Stanley Hotel on hillside to the right.

1.9   **Begin climb**. Road now called Fall River Rd.

4.9   **Pass** National Park Commercial Campground on right just before entrance gate.

5.1   Fall River Entrance Station to Rocky Mountain National Park. It will cost you $2.00 to enter the park as a bicyclist. Ask for a map at the gatehouse. Aspenglen National Forest Campground is just beyond entrance gate.

Long straight stretch of 2-lane, no-shoulder road leads you into the park.

7.7   Start of climb.

9.1   **Right** at intersection with U.S. 36, staying on U.S. 34. The long, most difficult climbing is just ahead.

13.6   Mummy Range overlook.

16.8   Another good overlook, from 2 mi above sea level, looking down at the roads you have just climbed.

17.4   **Pass** Rainbow Curve at elevation of 10,829.

17.6   Tree line. You will be riding through alpine tundra. Snowbanks remain alongside the road most of the summer. Winds are often strong and gusty.

High point at 12,183′ is unmarked because if it were marked there would be a traffic jam of snap-shooters. Mountains to the left mark the Continental Divide.

26.1   Visitors Center with store and restaurant at 11,796′.

26.3   Fall River Pass, and you are on the way down, through alpine tundra.

27.5   **Pass** tree line, and ride through pine forests.

30.4   **Cross** Milner Pass on the Continental Divide at 10,758′, and on the way down negotiate six hairpin curves.

36.7   **Pass** Colorado River Trailhead. 3′ shoulder begins on gentle downhill to Grand Lake Gate.

46.7   **Exit** at East Gate, Grand Lake Station.

49.5   **Left** (E) at intersection of Col. 278.

50.0   **Finish** in Grand Lake Village.

Grand Lake Village   Population 382, elevation 8369′.

A sparkling little town with the Old-West look of boardwalks on its main street. Motels, restaurants, stores, and near the east end of town a bike shop that offers to let you park your bike safely there

while you explore the town on foot. For campgrounds, retrace to U.S. 34 and turn **left** toward
Granby. You will pass two lakes and several campgrounds on your left on this next 10 mi stretch.

*Grand Lake
Village with its
boardwalk, small
shops, and
restaurants.*

7C

Grand Lake to Idaho Springs

Distance	72 mi from Grand Lake (8360') to Idaho Springs (7540')
Actual Climbing	3508'
Helpful Maps	*Colorado Road Atlas*, page D13. National Forest Maps: Arapaho, Roosevelt. (See Appendix A.)
Terrain	Relatively flat as far as Winter Park, with view of mountains ahead marking the Continental Divide. After Winter Park you will have a long climb up to Berthoud Pass at 11,315' on the Continental Divide.
Roads and Traffic	Good road with wide shoulders from Grand Lake to Winter Park. On the ascent to Berthoud Pass 3' shoulder, but on the down side 4.8 mi with no shoulder. Then frontage roads will take you along the I-70 corridor to Idaho Springs. Traffic usually not a problem.

0.0 **Leave** Grand Lake on Col. 278 going **west** to intersection of U.S. 34.

1.0 **Left** (S) on U.S. 34. 8' shoulder. Road follows shoreline of Shadow Mountain Lake and then Granby Reservoir. Nice cycling.

5.7 **Pass** road on left to Cutthroat Bay Campground.

7.1 **Pass** road on left to Stillwater Campground.

10.2 **Leave** lake shore and start downhill through open fields.

12.1 **Cross** Colorado River.

14.8 **Left** (E) to join U.S. 40. 10″ shoulder.

16.9 Granby. Population 963, elevation 7935′. Motel, restaurant, stores.

21.9 **Start climb** of 2.6 mi and then a down with a view of the valley, and in the distance, mountains marking the Continental Divide.

27.9 **Pass through** the small town of Tabernash and continue on through a wide, green valley.

Road crosses R.R. bridge and then runs alongside the Denver & Rio Grande railroad tracks. This is the track that leads to the West Portal of the Moffat Tunnel, which runs for 6.2 mi through the mountains under the Continental Divide on the way to Denver.

31.9 Small town of Frazer with Safeway supermarket.

34.7 Winter Park. Population 480, elevation 9110′. Motels, restaurants, stores, Idlewild National Forest Campground.

37.3 **Pass** Winter Park Resort Ski Area. Start of climb up to the pass. 3′ shoulder.

37.6 Moffat Tunnel Overlook.

48.6 Top of Berthoud Pass, the Continental Divide. Elevation 11,315′. Motel and restaurant at top.

No shoulder for 4.8 mi on the descent.

54.6 At Berthoud Falls sign, 3′ shoulder starts as you continue down.

60.5 Mountain Meadows Campground.

62.0 Small town of Empire. Population 423, elevation 8602′.

The climb over Berthoud Pass, elevation 11,315′, will seem easy after the previous day's ride over Trail Ridge Road with a high point of 12,183′.

Restaurants, and the Peck House, a Victorian hotel.

63.3   **Pass over** I-70 straight ahead.

63.4   **Enter** I-70 going **east** and ride on shoulder for 1.5 mi to next exit.

64.5   **Take** exit #233 to frontage road.

65.2   **Pass under** I-70 to **north** side and **continue east** on frontage road, straight ahead through the next intersection with the big gas sign.

66.8   **Right** (S) immediately after passing Dumont Fire Station on left, again crossing over I-70 to **south** side.

66.9   **Left** (E) on Stanley Rd. Continue parallel to I-70 along a rushing mountain stream, passing mines and tailings as you approach Idaho Springs.

70.8   **Cross** stream and **pass under** I-70.

71.0   **Right** (E) on Colorado Blvd. (Business Loop 70).

Just after entering town, turn **right** (S) on 13th St. for 1 block.

Left on Miner St., the main street of this Old-West mining town, where there are restaurants, saloons, and stores with the flavor of the gold-rush days.

72.0   **Finish** in Idaho Springs at corner of Miner St. and 13th Ave.

Idaho Springs Population 2077, elevation 7540'.

In 1859 the first major gold strike in the Colorado mountains was made near Idaho Springs at the junction of Chicago Creek and Clear Creek. There are still gold mines around Idaho Springs, and the historic Argo Gold Mill and Museum is open for tours.

To find motels and restaurants, **continue** (E) on Miner St. Safeway supermarket on right, and motel strip ahead after Miner St. merges with Colorado Blvd. The Indian Springs Resort, (303) 567-2191, is a favorite overnight stopping place for bikies. The resort hotel is 0.5 mi south of Miner St. on Soda Creek Rd. Hot mineral springs were discovered here in 1859. You can avail yourself of a hot mineral bath, or you can swim in their covered mineral water swimming pool.

7D

Idaho Springs to Boulder

Distance	57 mi from Idaho Springs (7540′) to Boulder (5363′)
Actual Climbing	1500′
Helpful Maps	_Colorado Road Atlas_, pages D14, T3. National Forest Map: Arapaho. (See Appendix A.)
Terrain	Though mostly downhill from Idaho Springs to Golden, you'll have two significant climbs to contend with—a 4-miler and a 2-miler. Then a roller-coaster back roads trip from Golden to Boulder.
Roads and Traffic	Following the I-70 corridor, you will have good frontage roads or will be riding on the shoulder of I-70. (See page 30 for safe Interstate riding suggestions). There will be some traffic to deal with as you approach Golden. From Golden to Boulder the roads are not busy, with the exception of 1.4 mi on Indiana St. where you could experience commuter traffic on a no-shoulder road in the late afternoon.

0.0 **Leave** Idaho Springs going **east** on Miner St. Merge with Colorado Blvd. (Business Loop 70).

0.8 **Bear right** over I-70 following Bike Route signs.

0.9 **Left** (E) **immediately** onto **south** side frontage road.

1.3   1 mi of gravel road along here. This road allows you to avoid going through the tunnel on I-70.

2.3   Back to pavement.

2.9   **Left** at Hidden Valley sign and **immediate right** to enter I-70 at exit #243 and ride on shoulder. Start of 4 mi climb.

6.7   **Leave** I-70 at exit #247.

6.8   **Left** (W), **crossing over** I-70 to frontage road on **north** side of Interstate (U.S. 40).

6.9   **Right** (E) on frontage road, and down.

9.7   **Cross** two bridges at bottom of descent and start 2 mi climb.

11.6   **Pass over** I-70 at top of climb to **south** side frontage road.

   Left toward El Rancho restaurant.

12.3   **Left** (NE) on Col. 74 for 0.5 mi.

12.8   **Enter** I-70 **east** at exit #252 and ride on shoulder.

   Pass Chief Hosa Campground at exit #253.

   Leave I-70 on steep ramp at exit #254.

14.7   **Left** at top and over I-70 to **north** side.

14.8   **Right** (E) on frontage road (U.S. 40) following Buffalo Bill's Grave sign. 4' shoulder.

Continue east passing Lookout Mountain Rd.

Pass road to Cabrini Shrine.

20.4   **Left** (NE) at traffic light, staying on U.S. 40 & East Business 70. Immediately on right you will pass Point of Geological Interest sign. No shoulder, but road is wide enough.

Pass Heritage Square on left.

Pass Zeta St. on left.

Pass East Tin Cup Village Campground on left.

22.2   **Pass** Rooney Rd. on right and be alert for arrow pointing to West U.S. 6—Golden sign.

22.6   **Left** (N) **before** traffic light following sign to U.S. 6 West.

Left (W) at stop sign on U.S. 6 for 1 block.

22.8   **Right** (N) **immediately** on Ulysses St. at traffic light. 3' shoulder.

23.7   **Left** (NW) at T at traffic light onto S. Golden Rd. 6' shoulder.

24.7   **Bear right** on Ford St. which becomes 1-way into Golden.

25.5   **Left** (W) at 14th St. (at end of 1-way) for 2 blocks.

25.7   **Right** (N) on Washington St.

25.9   **Pass under** Welcome Arch on Washington St.

See Tour 9 for more Golden information.

Continue north on Washington St.

26.0 **Right** (E) at traffic light on 10th St.

26.2 **Pass** Coors Brewery on right. (For info about touring the brewery and tasting the beer, see Tour 9.)

26.7 **Caution!** Slanted R.R. tracks. Cross at 90-degree angle.

27.6 **Left** at sign to Easley Rd. and up slight grade.

27.8 **Right** (N) on Easley Rd. at stop sign.

Pleasant, low-traffic, winding roads will take you through the next few miles.

31.2 **Right** (E) on 64th Ave. (County Rd. 172).

32.7 **Left** (N) on Quaker St.

Pass through tiny town of Leyden.

35.1 **Right** (E) at T on Leyden Rd.

36.2 **Left** (N) at stop sign on Indiana St. (Col. 72).

36.4 **Straight ahead**, leaving Col. 72 and going **north** on Indiana St. (County Rd. 17). (Follow Jefferson County Airport sign.)

Steep downhill on Indiana St. 1.4 mi of no-shoulder road where you could encounter commuter traffic.

37.8 **Right** (E) on 96th St. No shoulder, but less traffic on

these roads to the east than you would have on
Indiana St.

38.8   **Bear left** (N) at Y on Alkire St.

39.3   **Right** (E) on 100th Ave.

40.3   **Left** (N) on N. Simms St.

41.3   **Pass** 108th Ave.

43.1   **Left** (W) on Col. 128 (120th Ave.).

44.7   **Pass** Indiana St.

45.0   **Right** (N) on McCaslin Blvd. (signed Bike Route).
4' shoulder.

Steep downhill. This is part of the famous Morgul-
Bismarck Race Course. This grade is known as ''The
Wall.'' (See Tour 8.)

Short climb and then a descent.

48.5   **Left** (W) toward Marshall on Col. 170. Road runs
along **west** side of the Boulder-Denver Turnpike.

50.0   Magnificent views of the Front Range and the Flatirons rock formations ahead.

52.3   **Right** (E) leaving Col. 170 at T, for 50 yards to
Marshall Rd.

Left (N) **immediately** on Marshall Rd. signed Bike
Route and through tiny town of Marshall, where coal
miners of the area used to live.

53.3   **Straight ahead** (N) at Dead End sign.

53.6   **Join** concrete bikepath running along **east** side of Broadway.

54.4   **Left** (W) through tunnel under Broadway on downslope just past Brookfield Dr. You must dismount to enter the tunnel.

Immediate right (N) on bikepath on **west** side of Broadway and **continue north**, following Broadway.

54.9   **Cross** Table Mesa Dr. at traffic light, and follow marked Bike Route on Harvard Ln. Use caution and watch for turning cars at all the crossings as you follow the Bike Route **north** along Broadway.

55.3   **Cross** Dartmouth Ave. and continue on bikepath past the U.S. Department of Commerce Boulder Laboratories (The Bureau of Standards).

55.9   **Cross** Baseline Rd.

Down to tunnel running under Broadway.

56.1   **Right** (E) through tunnel, and you will be on the University of Colorado campus.

Continue north on campus bikepath.

56.5   **Finish** in Boulder at **northeast** edge of University of Colorado campus, at the corner of Colorado Blvd. and Folsom St.

See pages 41–42 for more Boulder information.

7E

Boulder to Loveland

Distance   40 mi from Boulder (5363′) to Loveland (4982′)

Actual Climbing   500′

Helpful Maps   *Colorado Road Atlas*, pages T3, D14, D10, T20. National Forest Map: Roosevelt. (See Appendix A.)

Terrain   An easy ride with no major climbs.

Roads and Traffic   Where you encounter traffic there will usually be an adequate shoulder, and back roads will have very little traffic.

0.0   **Leave** Boulder from **northeast** edge of the University of Colorado campus, riding **north** on Folsom St. Follow bike lane out of town.

2.0   **Cross** Iris Ave.

3.0   **Right** (E) on Jay Rd. for 1 block.

3.1   **Left** (N) on 28th St. (U.S. 36 West). 5′ shoulder.

Continue north on U.S. 36 along eastern edge of Rocky Mountain foothills.

10.4   **Right** (E) on Nelson Rd. toward Longmont.

16.2   **Left** (N) on 75th St.

17.8 **Pass** small town of Hygiene. Small cafe and grocery.

18.8 **Cross** Col. 66 (Ute Highway).

20.9 **Right** (E) on Woodland Rd.

Continue (E) past 83rd St. to T at 95th St.

24.9 **Left** (N) on 95th St.

26.0 **Jog left** at next T onto Yellowstone Rd. for 0.1 mi and **right** again back to 95th, heading **north**.

29.7 **Right** (E) on Col. 56.

31.3 **Straight ahead** (E) at stop sign to join busy U.S. 287 for 0.5 mi.

31.8 **Left** (N) at traffic light on County Rd. 17N (Taft Rd.) through rolling wheatfields with mountains to the west. 2' shoulder.

37.0 At edge of Loveland **continue across** 14th St. staying on Taft Rd.

38.1 **Right** (E) on 1st St. at south side of Loveland.

39.2 **Cross** 1-way Cleveland Ave. and **continue east** 1 more block.

39.3 **Left** (N) on 1-way Lincoln Ave. (U.S. 287).

40.3 **Finish** Tour in Loveland at corner of U.S. 287 and U.S. 34 (Eisenhower Blvd. and Lincoln Ave.).

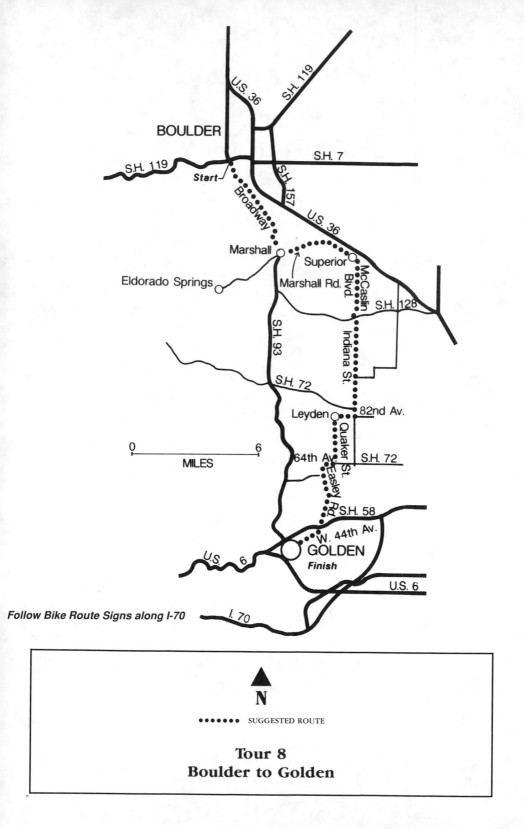

Follow Bike Route Signs along I-70

SUGGESTED ROUTE

Tour 8
Boulder to Golden

8

Boulder to Golden

Connecting route

Distance	26 mi from Boulder (5363′) to Golden (5675′)
Actual Climbing	800′
Helpful Maps	*Colorado Road Atlas*, pages T3, D14. (See Appendix A.)
Terrain	2 steep climbs on McCaslin Blvd. Lots of roller-coaster riding on other country roads.
Roads and Traffic	You will be riding out of Boulder on bikepaths. Then you will join part of the famous Morgul-Bismarck race course. Traffic should be no problem until you reach Indiana St., where you will join a very rolling up-and-down road (no shoulder for 4.4 mi) that will take you past the east gate of the Rocky Flats plant. There can be a lot of traffic on this road at commuting time—early in the morning, and after 3 P.M. So avoid riding here at those times.
	This road (Indiana St.) always has less traffic than the more direct route to Golden (Col. 93), which is narrow most of the way, always busy, and not recommended for cycling.
	Note: Col. 93 may be widened and improved after this book goes to press. For updated info call the Colorado State Public Information Dept. at (303) 757-9228.

0.0   **Leave** the corner of Colorado Ave. and Folsom St. at the **northeast** corner of the University of Colorado campus, following the bikepath going **south**.

Cross Regent Dr. and continue on bikepath that curves to the **right** (W) and leads you to the bikepath tunnel under Broadway.

0.8   **West** through tunnel.

Immediately left (S) on bikepath.

Continue south along **west** side of Broadway.

1.0   **Cross** Baseline Rd. Be alert for turning traffic at all the bikepath crossings that are coming up.

Pass U.S. Department of Commerce Boulder Laboratories (Bureau of Standards) to the west of the bikepath.

1.6   **Cross** Dartmouth Ave. at traffic light and **continue** on marked Bike Route on Harvard Ln.

2.0   **Cross** Table Mesa Drive at traffic light and **continue south** past shopping center on your right.

2.5   The bikepath will lead you through another tunnel under Broadway to Bike Route on the **east** side of Broadway.

Continue (S) following the marked bike routes through the small town of Marshall.

4.7   **Right** (SE) on Cherryvale Road.

Immediately left (E) on Col. 170. (Marshall Dr.).

You are now on part of the famous Morgul-Bismarck race course.

8.4 **Right** (S) on McCaslin Blvd. (signed Bike Route). 4' shoulder.

Pass small town of Superior on right.

8.7 Start of half-mile climb up "The Hump."

11.3 Start climb up "The Wall," which gets quite steep near the top.

These climbs were named by local bicycle racers. The Morgul-Bismarck course is world-famous for its tough climbs and its barren, treeless landscape—and was an important stage of the Coors International Bicycle Classic. The 1981 Coors over-all title was won by the U.S.'s Greg LeMond, who later upset all Europe by winning the 1986 Tour de France. Subsequent winners of the Coors: in 1986, Bernard Hinault, 5-time winner of the Tour de France; in 1987, Raul Alcala of Mexico; in 1988, Davis Phinney, Boulder's hometown cycling hero.

12.0 **Left** (E) at stop sign at the top, onto Col. 128.

12.2 **Immediate right** (S) on Indiana St. and steep downhill. No shoulder.

Continue on roller-coaster road along **east** side of Rocky Flats plant.

13.6 **Pass** gate to Rocky Flats.

16.4 At top of climb join Col. 72 and **continue south**.

16.8 **Right** (W) at 82nd Ave. (Leyden Rd.). No shoulder, but usually very light traffic on these back roads.

17.8 **Left** (S) on Quaker St.

20.2 **Right** (W) at T and stop sign on 64th Ave. (Jefferson County Rd. 172).

20.7 **Left** (S) on Easley Rd. Delightfully winding road at the base of a majestic mesa.

23.9 **Left** at "To 44th Ave." sign. Make tight turn around curve to 44th Ave.

24.1 **Right** (W) on W. 44th Ave.

25.2 **Caution**—bad R.R. track crossing. Cross at 90-degree angle.

Pass Coors Brewery—world's largest one-location brewery.

Enter Golden on 10th St.

This connecting route takes you over the famous Morgul-Bismarck race course, which you will reach at 5 mi south of Boulder. These Coors Classic racers are approaching the top of "The Wall," a steep climb to the finish line.

26.0   **Left** (S) on Washington St. at traffic light.

26.2   **Finish** under the Welcome Arch on Washington St.

See Tour 9 for more Golden information.

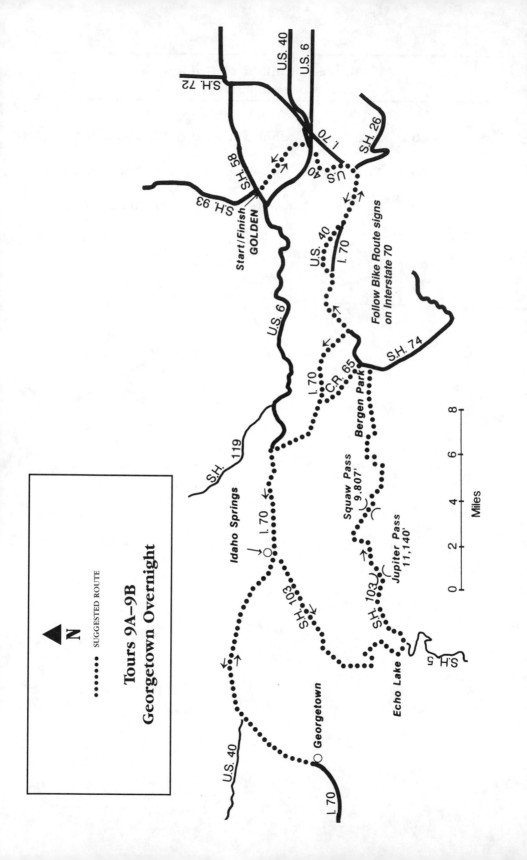

N

SUGGESTED ROUTE

**Tours 9A–9B
Georgetown Overnight**

Start/Finish GOLDEN

S.H. 72

U.S. 40

U.S. 6

I.70

S.H. 26

S.H. 58

S.H. 93

U.S. 40

U.S. 40

I.70

Follow Bike Route signs
on Interstate 70

S.H. 74

U.S. 6

I.70

C.R. 65

Bergen Park

S.H. 119

Squaw Pass
9,807'

Idaho Springs

I.70

Jupiter Pass
11,140'

S.H. 103

S.H. 103

Echo Lake

S.H. 5

U.S. 40

Georgetown

I.70

Miles

0   2   4   6   8

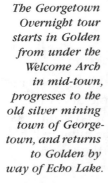

9

Georgetown Overnight

Distance	108 mi
Suggested Time	2 days
Total Climbing	7800′

This tour takes you through some beautiful eastern slope foothills territory between Golden and Georgetown. In the late 1800s Georgetown was the Silver Queen of the Rockies, producing more silver ore during its bonanza days than any other mining location in the country.

The Georgetown Overnight tour starts in Golden from under the Welcome Arch in mid-town, progresses to the old silver mining town of Georgetown, and returns to Golden by way of Echo Lake.

WEST ROUTT LIBRARY DISTRICT
HAYDEN PUBLIC LIBRARY

9A

Golden to Georgetown

Distance 41 mi from Golden (5675') to Georgetown (8519')

Actual Climbing 3600'

Helpful Maps *Colorado Road Atlas*, pages D14, D13. National Forest Map: Arapaho. (See Appendix A.)

Terrain The climb to Idaho Springs from Golden is steep at times. From Idaho Springs to Georgetown it is a gentle but steady upgrade alongside a rushing mountain stream.

(See Tour 10, Lookout Mountain Climb, for an alternative route out of Golden.)

Roads and Traffic You will have city traffic to deal with getting out of Golden. After that you are following the I-70 corridor, on quiet frontage roads most of the time. See page 30 for safe Interstate riding suggestions.

Golden Population 12,237, elevation 5675'.

The Colorado School of Mines is located in Golden. The Geology Museum at 16th and Maple St. in the geology building contains extensive displays of rocks, minerals, fossils, and an early Colorado mine exhibit. Golden is also famous as the home of the Coors Brewery. You can take a tour of the brewery and, if you are over 21, sample the product. Call 277-BEER for information about the brewery tour schedule.

There are restaurants, stores, a bike shop, 2 motels, and a B&B—The Dove Inn (303) 278-2209—in the downtown area. Other motels are toward Denver adjacent to I-70 and Colfax Ave. Closest campground is Tin Cup Village, (303) 279-6279, on our route out of town (see below). Chief Hosa Campground (303) 526-0364 is 12 mi farther along also on this route.

0.0   **Leave** Golden from under the Welcome Arch on Washington St. and head **south**.

Left (E) **immediately** on 12th St. for 1 block.

0.1   **Right** (S) on Jackson which becomes 1-way. Has parking and/or bike lane.

1.0   **Curve left** and then **right** to merge with S. Golden Rd. now 2-way.

2.0   **Right** (S) on Ulysses St.

2.9   **Left** (E) at traffic light on U.S. 6. **Cross** both lanes and turn **right** (S) **immediately**, following Red Rocks Park sign.

3.1   **Join** U.S. 40, heading **west**.

3.6   **Pass** Tin Cup Village Campground on right.

5.4   **Continue west** on U.S. 40 at traffic light following Mt. Vernon Canyon Rd. sign. Do not turn onto I-70.

Start of climb on U.S. 40 running parallel to I-70 at

first, then curving away. 4′ shoulder on smooth, quiet road.

9.6   **Pass** Lookout Mountain Rd. on right.

10.6 **Cross** Mt. Vernon Country Club Rd. at top of climb and go straight ahead on entrance ramp to join I-70.

12.0 **Pass** Chief Hosa Campground, (303) 526-0364, with good tent sites, at exit #253. Best to call ahead if you want to camp here.

13.0 **Take** exit #252 and leave I-70.

13.1 **Cross** bridge over I-70 to **south** side.

13.3 **Right** (W) following U.S. 40, El Rancho Restaurant on left.

14.0 **Right** (N) and pass over I-70 to **north** side of Interstate.

          Left (W) on frontage road and start long descent through pine forested canyon to bridge at bottom. Back up on a gentle climb.

19.0 Steep descent. Use caution on sharp curves near the bottom.

20.8 **Left** on U.S. 6 after crossing bridge at bottom.

          Immediately join I-70 at interchange #244. **Stop** and use caution at entrance where you must cross 2 traffic lanes to get to shoulder on right.

22.5 **Take** exit #243 onto frontage road.

22.8   **Follow** Bike Route sign and **pass under** I-70.

Right (W) on frontage road on **south** side of I-70.
(Riding on 1 mi of gravel on this stretch keeps you
out of tunnel on I-70.)

24.4   **Left** over bridge crossing I-70, following Bike Route
sign, into town of Idaho Springs.

Idaho Springs   Population 2077, elevation 7540′.

There are numerous motels and restaurants along this
entrance into town. Continuing straight west following Central Business District sign will bring you to
Miner St., the main street of this Old-West gold mining
town. On Miner St. you will find more restaurants,
saloons, and stores that retain the flavor of the gold-
rush days.

Continue through Idaho Springs on Miner St.

26.6   **Right** (N) on 13th Ave. for 1 block.

Left (W) on Colorado Blvd. (Business Loop 70).

27.4   **Left** on Stanley Rd. **passing under** I-70 and crossing bridge on marked Bike Way. Stanley Road runs
parallel to I-70 and along a rushing mountain stream.
Notice tailings and mines along the roadside.

31.2   **Right** (N) when you reach unpaved Dead End section
and cross bridge to **north** side of I-70.

Left (W) on frontage road, immediately passing
Dumont Fire Station.

Continue straight ahead past next area of restaurants
and Ski Rental sign for 2 mi.

33.2   **Left** (S) and **pass under** I-70.

Right (W) on frontage road on **south** side.

33.6   **Important left** on Alvarado Rd. Do **not** pass under I-70 again.

Immediately cross stream and **continue west** on Alvarado Rd. Rocky cliffs on each side of the valley become steeper and higher as you approach Georgetown.

40.7   **Finish** in Georgetown at Rose and 6th St.

Georgetown   Population 830, elevation 8519'.

Georgetown is a jewel of a town with many perfectly restored buildings. Its late 1800s prosperity was based on the rich deposits of silver that made it the greatest producer of silver in the country. It had a population of 5000 during that time. Then in 1893 silver lost its value, and in just months the town was almost deserted. Since Georgetown never was destroyed by a major fire, most of the fine buildings dating from its days of prosperity remained to be restored, including the impressive Hotel de Paris (now a museum), built and run by a Frenchman who came to Georgetown during the silver bonanza.

You will find motels, restaurants, and stores here. The Georgetown Motor Inn (303) 569-3201 is 1 block south of Alvarado Rd. before you reach the old restored town area. The closest campground is 6 mi away on U.S. 40. To reach it you would **backtrack** on Alvarado Rd. to **cross** I-70 at exit #232 and take U.S. 40 **west** to 1.5 mi beyond Empire for Mountain Meadow Campground, (303) 569-2424.

9B

Georgetown to Golden via Echo Lake

Distance 67 mi from Georgetown (8519′) to Golden (5675′)

Actual Climbing 4200′

Helpful Maps *Colorado Road Atlas*, pages D17, D18. National Forest Map: Arapaho. (See Appendix A.)

Terrain After retracing downhill to Idaho Springs, you will have a moderate climb to Echo Lake (10,650′), and more serious climbing over 11,140′ Juniper Pass before making the descent back to Golden.

Roads and Traffic The road to Echo Lake and over the pass is 2-lane without shoulder, but has a low traffic count.

0.0 **Leave** Georgetown going **east** out of town, and retrace the route on Alvarado Rd.

7.1 **Right** on frontage road and follow bike route signs directing you to the north and south frontage roads of I-70 and into Idaho Springs on Stanley Rd.

13.3 **Right** (E) on Colorado Blvd.

14.0 **Right** (S) at 13th St. (Col. 103), the Mt. Evans Rd.

Pass over I-70 and on the right pass the National Forest Information Center—a good place to buy maps.

Start gentle climb on good, smooth road, following Chicago Creek.

20.8   **Bear left** crossing bridge over Chicago Creek and beginning steeper grades and hairpin turns.

26.8   Road levels out at elevation of 10,650′. Echo Lake Lodge and Restaurant. Echo Lake National Forest Campground.

26.9   **Left** (E) to continue on Col. 103. No shoulder but very little traffic.

29.5   Jupiter Pass, elevation 11,140′.

30.6   Start down. Great views of mountain tops to the left, with pine forests to the right on this quiet road.

33.5   Squaw Pass, elevation 9807′.

36.9   **Continue** straight ahead at end of Col. 103 onto County Rd. 103 and continue down.

43.9   Jefferson County line.

46.1   **Important left** (N), as you enter the town of Bergen Park, onto County Rd. 65, (just **before** you reach T at busy Col. 74). After turning onto Rd. 65 you will immediately pass Bergen Park Community Church on your right. No shoulder on County Rd. 65, but much less traffic than you would encounter on Col. 74.

Continue (NW) on County Rd. 65 downhill on curvy road to cross Soda Creek at bottom, and climb up to I-70.

48.8   **Pass over** I-70.

48.9   **Right** (E) on frontage road (U.S. 40) on **north** side of Interstate.

Down to cross 2 bridges at bottom and start up.

52.6   **Pass over** I-70 to **south** side frontage road.

Left (E) on frontage road toward El Rancho Restaurant.

52.9   **Left** (N) at stop sign at junction of Col. 74.

53.1   **Enter** I-70 East on entrance ramp straight ahead and ride on shoulder.

54.1   **Pass** Chief Hosa Campground at exit #253.

55.1   **Take** steep uphill exit ramp at exit #254.

55.6   **Left** at top and **pass over** I-70 to **north** side.

55.7   **Right** (E) on frontage road (U.S. 40) following Buffalo Bill's Grave sign. 4' shoulder.

57.0   **Continue east** passing Lookout Mountain Rd.

59.7   **Pass** road to Cabrini Shrine.

61.2   **Left** (NE) at traffic light, staying on U.S. 40 & East Business 70. Ride downhill, passing Point of Geological Interest sign immediately on right. No shoulder, but road is wide enough.

62.3   **Pass** Heritage Square on left.

Pass Zeta St. on left.

Pass East Tin Cup Village Campground on left. (Closest campground to Golden.)

63.0   **Pass** Rooney Rd. on right and be alert for arrow pointing to West 6 in 0.4 mi.

63.4   **Left** (N) **before** traffic light following sign to U.S. 6 West.

Left (W) at stop sign on U.S. 6 for 1 block.

63.6   **Right** (N) **immediately** on Ulysses St. at traffic light.

64.5   **Left** (NW) at T at traffic light onto S. Golden Rd. 6' shoulder.

65.5   **Bear right** on Ford St., which becomes 1-way into Golden.

66.3   **Left** (W) at 14th St. at end of 1-way, for 2 blocks.

66.4   **Right** (N) on Washington St.

66.5   **Finish** tour under the Welcome Arch in Golden.

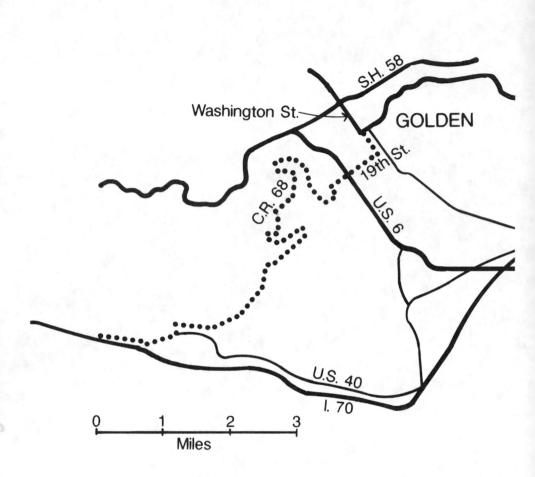

Washington St.

S.H. 58

GOLDEN

19th St.

C.R. 68

U.S. 6

U.S. 40

I. 70

0   1   2   3
Miles

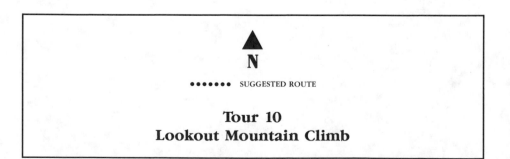

N

•••••••• SUGGESTED ROUTE

Tour 10
Lookout Mountain Climb

10

▲

Lookout Mountain Climb

Distance	18 mi round trip from Golden (5675′)
Actual Climbing	1700′
Helpful Map	National Forest Map: Arapaho. (See Appendix A.)
Terrain	Steep climbs up Lookout Mountain from Golden to U.S. 40. This is a climber's bicycle route, enjoyed by many bikies as a test of strength.
Roads and Traffic	Narrow road, but not very much traffic. You may see some cars carrying hang gliders because this is also a popular hang gliding take-off point.
Special Notes	This is an alternate route out of Golden that can be used for Tour 9. Steeper climbs than you would have following the I-70 corridor, but the same altitude gain from Golden to join Tour 9 at mile 9.6.

0.0 **Leave** Golden on Washington St. from under the Welcome Arch, heading **south**.

Pass Colorado School of Mines.

0.6 **Right** (W) on 19th St. at stop sign. 4′ shoulder. **Follow** Lookout Mountain sign.

1.0 **Straight ahead** (W) at traffic light. Road becomes Jefferson County Rd. 68.

1.6   **Pass through** gate and begin steep climb. No shoulder.

2.2   Views of Golden on the right. Red roofs are Colorado School of Mines. Coors Brewery in gray buildings beyond. Note the hogback ridges to the north.

3.3   **Continue** up through switchbacks along the side of the mountain. Spectacular views all the way.

Some leveling off interspersed with steep climbs.

5.3   **Pass** forest of TV antennas.

6.2   **Pass** road on right to Buffalo Bill's Grave and Lookout Park Picnic Area.

7.0   Grocery store and deli on left.

7.3   Top of climb. Elevation 7375'.

Road levels off on Lookout Mountain Rd. and then starts down toward U.S. 40.

9.0   **Finish** at U.S. 40 at T.

Retrace to Golden.

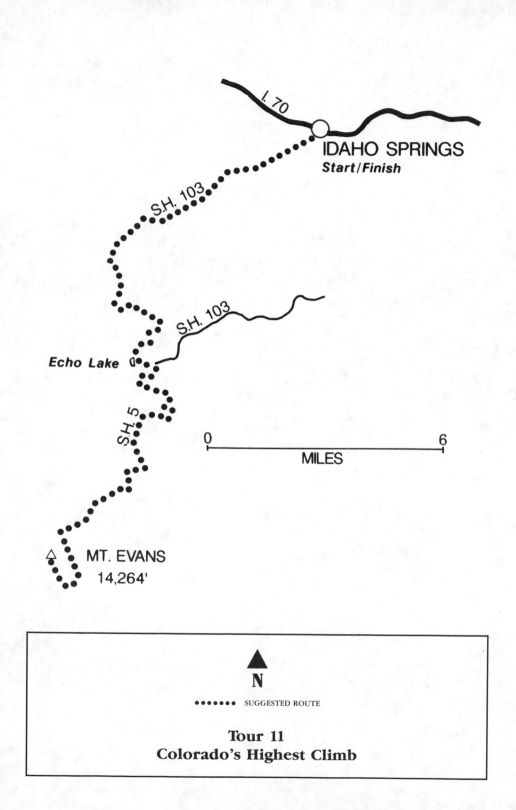

I. 70

IDAHO SPRINGS
Start/Finish

S.H. 103

S.H. 103

Echo Lake

S.H. 5

0   6

MILES

MT. EVANS
14,264'

N

••••••• SUGGESTED ROUTE

Tour 11
Colorado's Highest Climb

11

▲

Colorado's Highest Climb

Distance 57 mi round trip from Idaho Springs (7540') to the top of Mt. Evans (14,264')

Actual Climbing 6750'

Helpful Maps *Colorado Road Atlas*, page D17. National Forest Map: Arapaho. (See Appendix A.)

Terrain The road to the top of Mt. Evans is the highest paved road in North America. You climb almost 7000' in 28 mi! It's not the most enjoyable bicycle touring you can do. The main reason for making the climb is to say that you have done it. From Idaho Springs it's a very pleasant ride to Echo Lake. Beyond that the terrain is rough and steep.

Roads and Traffic Smooth road as far as Echo Lake. Then progressively rougher pavement as you climb to the summit. The higher you go the more potholes. Auto-tourist traffic may be heavy in the midsummer, but if you make the trip early in the day you will avoid most of it. Drivers are usually cautious and going slowly.

Special Notes A bicycle race, the Bob Cook Memorial, is held on this course every year in July. Record holder for the Mt. Evans Hill Climb is Alexi Grewal, Olympic Gold Medal winner, who set the record in 1984 for the climb from the National Forest Center in Idaho Springs to the top in 1 hour, 47 minutes, 51 seconds.

0.0   **Leave** Idaho Springs going **south** on Col. 103 (13th
St.), **crossing over** I-70 and immediately passing the
National Forest Information Center on the right—a
good place to buy maps and get info about camping
and hiking.

You will be cycling on a nice, smooth road winding
up through a canyon following Chicago Creek. A
relatively gentle climb.

6.8   **Curve left** and **cross bridge** over Chicago Creek
for start of steeper climbs and hairpin turns.

13.1   Road levels out at Echo Lake, elevation 10,650′,
where you will ride along the lake shore to reach the
Echo Lake Lodge and Restaurant. Good pavement
thus far.

13.7   **Right** on Col. 5, leaving Col. 103, through gate which
might be closed in bad weather.

From here on the roadbed will be rougher. The road
is narrow with no guardrails and sheer drop-offs in

*On Colorado's
highest climb, to
the top of
Mt. Evans, you
will have to dodge
potholes. This
road, closed in
the winter, is
subject to
extremes of
freezing and
thawing.*

places. Take the middle of your lane. The cars will be traveling slowly.

You will soon be above the tree line and looking down on Echo Lake.

22.9   **Pass** Summit Lake with some leveling-off places interspersed with some very steep climbing over very rough pavement.

23.1   **Continue** through another gate to steep climb over rough road.

28.4   **Reach top** 15.3 mi from Echo Lake, 28.4 mi from Idaho Springs. Elevation 14,260′ above sea level.

The views from here are spectacular to say the least. Colorado has 54 peaks that rise above 14,000′. On a clear day from here you can see many of them.

You'll see the ruins of a restaurant at the top. A fire destroyed it several years ago.

Now comes the really hard part. The 15.3 mi back to Echo Lake is not an easy descent. The roughness of the pavement and the chill factor at this altitude often make it a very uncomfortable ride. It may be snowing. If possible arrange to get a ride back down for you and your bicycle. Incidentally, the racers never ride down. The climb up is the challenge. But if you do choose to ride down, be prepared with warm clothing, and you must have a pair of warm gloves, because your hands will be out there on the brakes on the way down. Inspect your tires and brakes before you start down.

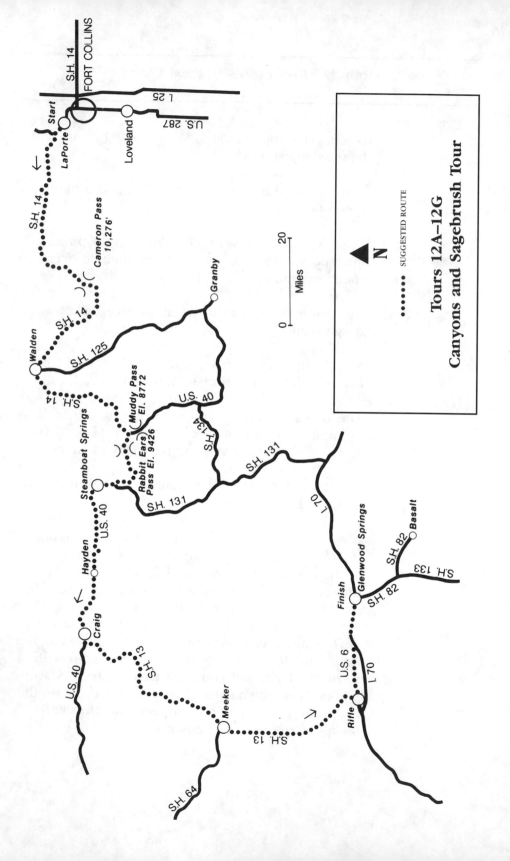

Tours 12A–12G
Canyons and Sagebrush Tour

SUGGESTED ROUTE

N

Miles
0   20

12

Canyons and Sagebrush Tour

Distance	316 mi
Suggested Time:	6 days
Total Climbing	10,700′

Starting in LaPorte (north of Fort Collins) you will ride up the beautiful Poudre Canyon and then across flat, bleak, sagebrush-covered North Park to Walden. From Walden continue southwest to cross 9426′ Rabbit Ears Pass and descend into Steamboat Springs, the popular ski-resort town. Then continue on to Craig, Meeker, Rifle, and Glenwood Springs, where a dip in the famous Hot Springs pool will make for a fitting finish of your tour.

La Porte to Walden

Distance	95 mi from La Porte (5060′) to Walden (8099′)
Actual Climbing	5300′
Helpful Maps	*Colorado Road Atlas*, pages D10, D9, D8. National Forest Maps: Roosevelt, Routt. (See Appendix A.)
Terrain	From LaPorte to Cameron Pass, elevation 10,276′, 63 mi of mostly climbing. From the top of the pass to Walden it's essentially downhill.
Roads and Traffic	Leaving the LaPorte and Fort Collins area you will usually encounter traffic, especially on weekends. After passing Red Feathers Road in Poudre Canyon there will be very little traffic to Walden and beyond.
Special Notes	From the northern edge of Fort Collins follow U.S. 287 north to La Porte and start trip from there. The Elkhorn Motel (303) 482-3579 is on U.S. 287, 1.3 mi northwest of the LaPorte traffic light. The Fort Collins Mile High KOA is 4 mi north on U.S. 287 just beyond the turn to Poudre Canyon. In the Poudre Canyon, campgrounds are plentiful, but motels are scarce—so plan ahead.

0.0   **Leave** LaPorte going **north** on U.S. 287.

4.0   **Left** (W) into Poudre Canyon on Col. 14. 4′ shoulder.

KOA Campground is located just north of entrance to Poudre Canyon on the east side of U.S. 287.

5.2   Start of climb at Open Range sign on narrow road. 1′ shoulder. Gentle upgrade along the Cache la Poudre River.

12.6   Steeper climb.

13.8   Small town of Poudre Park. Restaurant.

15.2   **Enter** Roosevelt National Forest. (For more info on National Forest campgrounds see official map of Roosevelt National Forest.)

17.1   Ansel Watrous National Forest Campground on river to the right. Elevation 5800′.

18.6   The canyon becomes narrower.

19.1   **Pass through** a short tunnel.

20.2   **Continue** out into a more open canyon.

21.8   Sharp curve and steep grades coming up.

22.2   **Cross** bridge over the river, and enter a narrow canyon. Just room for the river and the road.

24.8   Terrain flattens out to more gentle climb.

27.8   Mountain Park National Forest Campground on river on left.

29.8   Kelly Flats National Forest Campground on left.

31.9   **Cross** bridge over the river and then ride through a wide valley.

36.1   **Pass** small town of Rustic. Restaurant, grocery, gas station. Red Feathers Rd. on right.

36.2   Big Horn Cabins.

37.3   Mountain Greenery Resort. Cabins, restaurant, and campground.

37.7   Poudre River Cabins. (303) 881-2149. Best bet to call ahead for reservations if you want to stay in cabins in this area.

43.7   **Pass** State Trout Rearing Unit. Road flattens out running along more placid river. 3′ shoulder.

44.8   Big Bend National Forest Campground.

48.5   Sleeping Elephant Mountain on left, and Sleeping Elephant National Forest Campground on right.

The Canyons and Sagebrush tour follows the rushing Cache la Poudre River up through the Poudre Canyon to Cameron Pass at an elevation of 10,276′.

49.5   Spencer Heights Resort. Cabins, store, and campground.

52.3   **Cross** bridge and begin steeper climbing. 6′ shoulder starts.

Aspen Glen National Forest Campground on right.

56.4   **Pass** Laramie River Woods Landing Road.

Chambers Lake Campground on left.

60.6   Road levels off for 1.5 mi at Joe Wright Reservoir. Then starts climb up to the pass. Steady climb, but not steep.

63.5   Cameron Pass summit. Jackson County line. Elevation 10,276′.

63.6   Steep, curving downhill for 4 mi into Colorado State Forest. Careful on curves. Watch for loose gravel.

67.8   At bottom road narrows. No shoulder.

69.4   Colorado State Forest Headquarters and Campground. Now terrain is flat. You are in the North Park area riding through pine forests on both sides of the road. "Park," as in North Park, is a technical term meaning a large, relatively flat area, at a high altitude, surrounded by mountains.

73.3   Gould. Elevation here 8920′. Restaurant—no town.

75.2   North Park KOA (303) 723-4310 with camping cabins. Last place to stop before Walden.

You will now be riding through flat North Park. Medicine Bow ridge of mountains to the east. Then out of the forest into rather bleak areas of sagebrush-covered hillsides. Road is downhill and narrow, but there is little traffic.

91.6   Arapaho National Wildlife Refuge on left side of road. Sierra Madre Range of mountains beyond on the horizon.

94.8   **Finish** in Walden at T (junction of Col. 14 and Col. 125).

Walden

Population 947, elevation 8099'.

Motels, restaurants, groceries. This is the only choice for motels for many miles in any direction. We stayed at the North Park Motel (303) 723-4271. It was basic, but okay. Most of the rooms have kitchenettes. Small museum in Walden is worth a visit.

12B

Walden to Steamboat Springs

Distance 60 mi from Walden (8099′) to Steamboat Springs (6695′)

Actual Climbing 2100′

Helpful Maps *Colorado Road Atlas*, pages D8, D4, T22. National Forest Map: Routt. (See Appendix A.)

Terrain From Walden the first 37 mi are rolling or flat. After that it's a climb to the top that's 6 mi past Rabbit Ears Pass. Then a long downhill to Steamboat.

Roads and Traffic Rolling roads, no shoulder, but little traffic until you join U.S. 40 to cross Muddy Pass and Rabbit Ears Pass. Then good shoulder until the bottom of the downhill run.

Special Notes Leaving Walden you will be cycling through wide-open North Park, an arid area of sagebrush-covered hills and no trees. Be sure to start with plenty of water. No town until you reach Steamboat Springs.

0.0 **Leave** Walden heading **south** on Col. 14 and Col. 125.

1.3 **Right** (W) following Col. 14 and leaving Col. 125. Note Bikecentennial 76 sign just after turn. No shoulder, little traffic.

10.6 Terrain flattens out.

Lots of wildlife in this area—birds, small animals, and the occasional deer crossing the road.

24.3   Rolling hills again.

25.5   Steep downhill and **cross** bridge at bottom.

26.2   **Continue** into forested area with hills closer in on both sides of the road.

35.0   **Right** (W) on U.S. 40 **crossing** Muddy Pass, elevation 8772′.

Enter Routt National Forest.

36.9   Start of climb heading toward Rabbit Ears Pass. No shoulder at first, then climbing lane starts with 3′ shoulder. The last mile is steep.

38.3   Rabbit Ears Pass. Elevation 9426′ at the Continental Divide.

Continue climbing. 6′ shoulder.

40.6   Top at Routt County line. Terrain levels out and then becomes rolling.

Walton Creek National Forest Campground on left.

44.2   Another steep climb—the last climb of the day.

44.7   Meadows National Forest Campground, and at last the top! Elevation 9300′.

46.0   Steep downhill. 7% grade. 6′ shoulder.

Continue down for 7 mi. Don't let the bike get away

from you—on curves you might not be able to stay within shoulder area if you are going too fast.

48.9   Spectacular view of valley on left.

53.4   Bottom of one of Colorado's most spectacular downhill runs.

53.7   Shoulder ends. Narrow road for 4 mi. Keep alert, high-speed traffic.

56.6   **Pass** junction of Col. 131 and **continue** on U.S. 40.

57.4   Motel 8 on left, Holiday Inn on right.

57.7   **Pass** Visitor Information Center. Begin 4-lane road with 8′ shoulder into town.

59.4   **Pass** Fish Creek Park Campground on left.

Enter Steamboat Springs on Lincoln Ave. (still U.S. 40).

60.4   **Finish** in front of courthouse, corner of Lincoln Ave. and 6th St.

Steamboat Springs   Population 5098, elevation 6695′.

The town was named Steamboat Springs by early explorers who thought they heard the chugging of a steamboat around a riverbend, but instead found a spring "chugging" out of the ground. Thus, Steamboat Springs.

This is a pleasant ski resort town that is usually uncrowded in the summer. Plenty of motels, restaurants, stores, and one of the most interesting bicycle shops in Colorado. Be sure to visit the Sore Saddle Cyclery. To find it **continue west** on Lincoln Ave. to 12th St. and turn **left** (S) for 1 block to Yampa Ave. They will have information there about bike routes in and around the town if you wish to do some side trips.

Moots Bicycles are manufactered here in this odd-shaped shop. When we visited, Moots was fabricating a track tandem for the tandem racing team of Nelson Vales and Scott Berryman. World-class cyclists Alexi Grewal and Andy Hampsten ride Moots mountain bikes for fun and training when not on their regular road bikes.

A visit to The Sore Saddle Cyclery, housed in a remodeled wood-drying kiln in Steamboat Springs, will be a treat for any bikie.

Steamboat Springs to Craig

Distance	43 mi from Steamboat Springs (6695′) to Craig (6185′)
Actual Climbing	200′
Helpful Maps	*Colorado Road Atlas*, pages T22, D4, D3. National Forest Map: Routt. (See Appendix A.)
Terrain	Rolling road most of the way, following the Yampa River most of the time.
Roads and Traffic	Shoulder varies from none to 4′ to 6′. Traffic not heavy.

0.0 **Leave** Old Downtown Area of Steamboat Springs from the courthouse at Lincoln Ave. and 6th St.

Proceed west on U.S. 40. No shoulder.

3.1 Ski Town Campground on left.

5.6 Start of 6′ shoulder.

9.8 Shoulder ends. Little traffic.

11.4 Small town of Milner. Grocery store.

Rolling road following the Yampa River.

25.5   Town of Hayden. Supermarket on west edge of town, restaurant and motel.

31.9   Rest area—good picnic grounds.

40.9   Wagon Wheels Campground on left.

42.9   **Finish** in Craig at junction of Col. 13 North (corner of Victory Way and Yampa Ave.).

Craig   Population 8133, elevation 6185′.

In the peaceful Yampa River Valley, surrounded by rolling wheatfields, Craig is a typical small western town. Motels, restaurants, stores, plus two motels out of town, south on Col. 13.

12D

Craig to Meeker

Distance	49 mi from Craig (6185′) to Meeker (6249′)
Actual Climbing	900′
Helpful Maps	*Colorado Road Atlas*, pages D3, D6. (See Appendix A.)
Terrain	More rolling terrain. Hogback rock formations along the roadside. Wild, remote countryside. One climb of 2 mi to the summit of Nine Mile Gap.
Roads and Traffic	Less and less traffic as you continue on this tour route. The road winds through wide-open spaces.
Special Notes	You will be riding through remote, rather desolate areas from Craig to Meeker to Rifle. You have to be adventurous and resourceful to undertake this ride. It can be hot and dry out there. Be prepared with plenty of water and food supplies. The distances are not great, but there are very few resources to fall back on.

0.0   **Leave** Craig at corner of Victory Way and Yampa Ave. going **west** on U.S. 40 and Col. 13.

1.5   **Left** (S) on Col. 13 leaving U.S. 40. 6′ shoulder.

1.8   Holiday Inn and Super 8 Motel out here beyond

the town. No more facilities for 48 mi until you reach Meeker.

Good rolling road with 6' shoulder and little traffic.

8.6   Long downhill into wide-open space through a valley between rolling hills.

9.4   **Pass** strip mine plant and start a gradual uphill through a narrower river valley to Hamilton. No facilities there.

14.6   Start of no shoulder for 10 mi on road winding through wide-open spaces in a valley with no trees. Wild, bleak vistas on all sides.

24.6   Start of 6' shoulder through wider valley.

26.7   **Pass** Colo-Wyo Coal Co. office.

29.6   Valley narrows with rock formations near the road.

31.9   Cultivated hayfields and a farmhouse—possible emergency water source.

The trip from Steamboat Springs to Craig, Meeker, and Rifle will take you through remote and desolate sagebrush country with the occasional cultivated hayfield along the roadside.

36.9 Start of climb up to Nine Mile Gap Summit.

38.5 Top, and start down with 6' shoulder.

40.3 **Pass** Nine Mile Fishing & Hunting Office—possible water supply.

45.3 **Continue** down and pass Meeker city limit sign. But continue on for 4 mi to reach the town.

48.0 **Pass** junction of Rio Blanco County Rd. 8.

Supermarket and motel on Market St. as you enter Meeker.

49.4 **Finish** in Meeker at corner of Market St. and 6th.

Meeker Population 2356, elevation 6249'.

This is a pleasant town that feels like an oasis after the lonesome ride from Craig. The main street of town is 1 block north of Market St. Across from the courthouse on Main St. is the recently restored Meeker Hotel. It's worth a visit if just to look at the quaint lobby with its walls covered with mounted deer, elk, and bear heads. A framed copy of the *Meeker Herald*, dated Aug. 1885, displays a front-page ad for the original Meeker Hotel, claiming that it was "The only First-Class Hotel in Northwestern Colorado."

Motels, restaurants, stores. Overnight tent camping permitted in the Meeker City Park, a nice shady area 1 block south of Market St. on the riverbank. Another campground is 3 mi west of town on the route to Rifle.

12E

▲
Meeker to Rifle

Distance   42 mi from Meeker (6249′) to Rifle (5345′)

Actual   1700′
Climbing

Helpful Maps   *Colorado Road Atlas*, page D6. National Forest Map: White River. (See Appendix A.)

Terrain   Rolling road running through very unusual rocky outcroppings. As you near Rifle, the area to the east of the road is called the Grand Hogback.

Roads and   Good roads often with a good shoulder. Little
Traffic   traffic.

Special Notes   Again you must be prepared with a good supply of water and food. You will find no facilities along the road to Rifle—40 mi of open country.

0.0   **Leave** Meeker from corner of Market and 6th, going **west** on Col. 13. 8′ shoulder out of town.

Nice view to the left of a fertile valley.

2.7   **Bear left** (S) toward Rifle at Y junction with Col. 64.

Stagecoach Campground on left.

3.1   **Cross over** White River. Now no shoulder for 6.5 mi.

Many unusual outcroppings of stone and hogback ridges on both sides of the road.

9.6   Road becomes more rolling and 2′ shoulder starts.

23.0   **Pass** farmhouse, one of the few out here—possible emergency water supply.

23.4   Rio Blanco (7250′). Truck stop now closed. Nothing else here.

25.0   Shoulder ends.

25.5   Garfield County line.

25.9   Steep downhill on winding road for 7 mi.

32.9   At bottom continue through more rolling terrain.

39.3   **Pass** junction of Col. 325 and **continue south** on Col. 13. 6′ shoulder.

39.8   Rifle city limits sign.

41.4   **Left** (S) following Central Business District sign at interchange.

41.9   **Enter** Rifle going **south** on Railroad Ave. Garfield County Fairgrounds on right.

42.4   **Finish** in Rifle at 5th and Railroad Ave.

Rifle   Population 3215, elevation 5345′.

Restaurants and stores on Railroad Ave. (Col. 13). At U.S. 6 intersection on south edge of town you can

153

get tourist information at the Chamber of Commerce located in a refurbished railroad car. Motels and restaurants are at the I-70 interchange. To get to them **continue straight** ahead, **south** along Railroad Ave. for 0.5 mi, **cross** U.S. 6 and **pass under** I-70.

12F

Rifle to Glenwood Springs

Distance 27 mi from Rifle (5345′) to Glenwood Springs (5746′)

Actual Climbing 500′

Helpful Maps *Colorado Road Atlas*, pages D6, D7, T14. National Forest Map: White River. (See Appendix A.)

Terrain Relatively flat ride following the Colorado River.

Roads and Traffic You will be on U.S. 6, which is essentially a frontage road for I-70 until you join I-70 and ride on the shoulder for 5 mi before entering Glenwood Springs. (See page 30 for safe Interstate riding suggestions.)

0.0 **Leave** Rifle at corner of 5th and Railroad Ave., going **south**.

0.3 **Left** (E) at traffic light onto U.S. 6 East, which parallels I-70 and the Colorado River. 2′ or more shoulder most of the way.

6.9 **Pass through** town of Silt. Grocery, cafe, restaurant, and motel.

14.6 **Pass through** town of New Castle. Restaurant and stores.

15.5 **Pass** I-70 entrance and **continue east** on U.S. 6.

19.2   **Right** to enter I-70 at Exit #109. Do not follow Canyon Creek sign on dead-end road.

19.4   **Pass over** I-70 and **join** it to ride on the shoulder going **east**.

24.5   **Take** Exit #114 (West Glenwood) and **pass under** I-70.

24.8   **Right** (E) on frontage road at traffic light. 2' shoulder. Motels and restaurants along this strip to the east. Ami's Acres Campground (303) 945-5340 is 1 mi **west** of this Exit #114 on the frontage road.

26.8   Frontage road becomes 6th St.

26.9   **Finish** in Glenwood Springs at 6th St. and Grand Ave.

Glenwood Springs   Population 4637, elevation 5746'.

The famous Hot Springs pool and the big resort hotels are just ahead in the middle of the downtown area. There are plenty of motels, restaurants, stores,

A fitting end to this arid-country ride would be a dip in the famous Hot Springs pool in Glenwood Springs.

and a bike shop. Two campgrounds: Ami's Acres (which you passed west of town) and Rock Garden Campground (303) 945-6737 2.5 mi **east** on the new bikepath along I-70 (see below).

To continue south from Glenwood Springs see Tour 16.

12G

Glenwood Canyon

About the Area Glenwood Canyon, cut through the cliffs by the Colorado River, runs east from Glenwood Springs. It has long been a bottleneck, with a heavily traveled 2-lane road which was dangerous for automobiles and almost impossible for bicycles. Now a new elevated and cantilevered 4-lane highway is being built through the canyon, and a bicycle route is being built alongside and below the highway. The bikepath runs along the bank of the Colorado River, quietly remote from the traffic roaring by above it.

At printing neither the highway nor the bike route had been completed, but we cycled for about 5 mi on the new bikepath through the canyon, and it's an interesting out-and-back local ride.

Cantilevered I-70 sweeps through Glenwood Canyon. The new bikepath is free from highway traffic and noise.

158

0.0   **Leave** downtown Glenwood Springs at corner of 6th and Grand Ave.

Cycle east on 6th St. past the Hot Springs Lodge, ignoring the Dead End sign.

0.5   **Pass** the Vapor Caves on road running **east** along the edge of I-70.

1.0   Start of bikepath.

1.2   **Cross** bike bridge over I-70 and ride along the Colorado River.

1.9   **Cycle around** car barrier.

2.5   Rock Garden Campground at top of gentle climb. This is a good tent camping spot.

2.6   Gravel road. Dismount for deep gravel at start of descent, then ride down through S curves to bottom— again at river's edge.

2.8   **Enter** paved bikepath.

5.3   Turnaround point. This is where a construction barrier ended our trip on the day we rode it.

Eventually the bikepath will continue all the way through Glenwood Canyon. The best way to find out about the current situation is to inquire at the Alpine Bike Shop, 109 6th St. in Glenwood Springs (303) 945-6434.

It was a very enjoyable ride along the river with practically no noise from passing traffic. Rafters waved to us as they passed us on the river, and an occasional train labored uphill on the far side of the river.

159

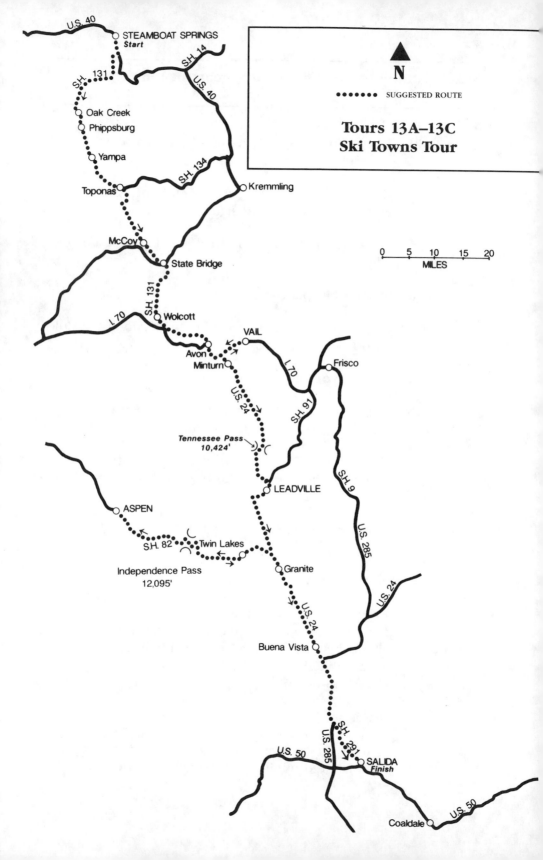

U.S. 40

STEAMBOAT SPRINGS
Start

S.H. 14

U.S. 40

S.H. 131

Oak Creek

Phippsburg

Yampa

S.H. 134

Toponas

Kremmling

N

•••••• SUGGESTED ROUTE

**Tours 13A–13C
Ski Towns Tour**

0   5   10   15   20
MILES

McCoy

State Bridge

S.H. 131

I. 70

Wolcott

VAIL

Avon

Minturn

Frisco

U.S. 24

S.H. 91

I. 70

Tennessee Pass
10,424'

LEADVILLE

S.H. 9

ASPEN

S.H. 82

Twin Lakes

U.S. 285

Independence Pass
12,095'

Granite

U.S. 24

U.S. 24

Buena Vista

S.H. 291

U.S. 285

U.S. 50

SALIDA
Finish

U.S. 50

Coaldale

13

Ski Towns Tour

Distance	284 mi
Suggested Time	3 days
Total Climbing	16,200'

This tour connects Colorado's three most famous ski resorts. The tour starts in Steamboat Springs. From there you head south, visit Vail, and then climb 12,095' over Independence Pass on the way to Aspen. From Aspen you retrace over Independence Pass and continue south to finish in Salida, where you can join connecting route Tour 24.

Steamboat Springs to Vail

Distance	95 mi from Steamboat Springs (6695′) to Vail (8150′)
Actual Climbing	4700′
Helpful Maps	*Colorado Road Atlas*, pages T22, D4, D7, D16. National Forest Maps: Routt, White River. (See Appendix A.)
Terrain	Rolling countryside. Steep descent to Colorado River at State Bridge followed by 5 mi of steep climb.
Roads and Traffic	Some narrow roads, but not much traffic until you join the I-70 corridor into Vail. (See page 30 for safe Interstate riding suggestions.)

Steamboat Springs   Population 5098, elevation 6695′.

This is a more down-to-earth, more homespun ski town than the other two on the tour. It has a pleasant small-town feeling, but there are still plenty of motels, restaurants, stores, an in-town campground, and a really marvelous bike shop. See Canyons and Sagebrush Tour 12B for more information about the Sore Saddle Cyclery.

0.0 **Leave** downtown Steamboat Springs (corner of Lincoln Ave. and 6th St.) going **south** and **east** on

U.S. 40. 4-lane road with shoulder. Nice views of ski slopes and lodges ahead.

1.2   **Pass** Fish Creek Park Campground.

2.6   End of shoulder.

4.0   **Right** (S) on Col. 131 toward Wolcott. Narrow road, no shoulder, but not much traffic.

You will be riding through a broad valley on a flat road with hayfields sweeping off on both sides.

11.2   Rolling road, getting steeper in spots. No shoulder, but little traffic on this pleasant country road winding through rolling hills.

21.2   Small town of Oak Creek. Elevation 7414'. Motel, restaurants, stores.

24.8   Small town of Phippsburg. Not much here in the way of facilities.

25.0   Road flattens out after Phippsburg, running through a broad valley with more hayfields.

28.0   Interesting hogback rock formations along here.

30.7   Small town of Yampa. Elevation 7892'. **Bear right** on Main St. to go through town. General store, restaurant, and an unpaved street back to highway.

31.6   **Right** (S) to rejoin Col. 131.

Flat or gently rolling road through aird, sagebrush-covered low hills.

40.2 Toponas (8280′). Nothing here except small grocery store.

40.8 **Pass** junction of Col. 134.

43.0 **Cross** bridge and start climb of 2 mi.

45.0 Long down. 2′ shoulder.

52.6 Eagle County line.

53.8 **Cross** Rock Creek at bottom of long down and start up onto rolling road again.

Colorado River on right.

57.5 Small town of Bond. Gas station and store.

57.8 **Cross** R.R. tracks.

59.7 Steep down to Colorado River crossing.

60.5 **Cross** bridge over Colorado River at State Bridge (6740′). No facilities here.

Steep climb up from river on rough road. No shoulder.

65.6 Top, and start down on smoother road, steep in spots, winding through a canyon to the Eagle River.

71.3 **Cross** cattle guard.

74.3 **Cross** 3 sets of R.R. tracks and narrow bridge over the Eagle River at Wolcott (6960′).

74.4 **Left** (E) on U.S. 6 toward Minturn.

75.1   **Join** I-70 East toward Denver at Exit #157 and ride on the shoulder. Use caution passing interchanges between here and the West Vail exit.

92.2   **Right** at Exit #173—West Vail.

Left and **pass under** I-70.

92.3   **Right** (E) on North Frontage Road of I-70, passing shopping center on left.

95.0   **Right** (S), **passing under** I-70 at Exit #176.

95.1   **Finish** on South Frontage Road at heart of Vail.

Vail   Population 2261, elevation 8150′.

This is perhaps the most famous ski resort in Colorado. Vail is a new town, only 25 years old, planned and built from the ground up as a community with one purpose—recreation. Skiing on the wonderful slopes here was its first sport, but later additions of golf, tennis, and other recreations continued the tradition. What with the Alpine style architecture and the "beautiful people," some visitors have likened it to a movie set.

There are plenty of motels, restaurants, and stores, and a campground beyond town to the east. To find a small, European-style hotel, easy to get to by bicycle, turn **left** (E) on the **south** side frontage road at Exit #176 and continue for 0.5 mi. Turn **right** at big stop sign and make sweeping turn going down through an S curve. **Left** at bottom for 2 blocks. **Right** at next 1-way street going to the right.

The Tivoli Lodge. (303) 476-5615. It's just 1 block east of the heart of the Village.

To find the Gore Creek Campground you must continue **east** for 6.4 mi on the South Frontage Road. **Pass** the golf course, and **pass under** I-70 3 times.

Ignore Dead End sign and **follow** campground signs to Gore Creek White River National Forest Campground.

The Vail Pass Bicycle Path continues on from this point to Breckenridge. It passes through beautiful mountain scenery, but it is not always adequate for the traffic on it. It is too narrow for the speeding downhill cyclist meeting up with the climbing cyclist, who may be walking up the very steep sections—sometimes more than 7% grades. We recommend that you avoid it on midsummer weekends when it is especially crowded. But early and late in the summer you may find it uncrowded. To ride over Vail Pass see Tour 14.

Summer visitors to Vail are often treated to a criterium bicycle race through the picturesque village streets.

Vail through Leadville to Aspen

Distance	98 mi from Vail (8150′) to Aspen (7908′)
Actual Climbing	7620′
Helpful Maps	*Colorado Road Atlas*, pages D16, T18, D23, D22, T2. National Forest Map: White River. (See Appendix A.)
Terrain	Plenty of climbing on this ride. First, over 10,404′ Tennessee Pass to Leadville with an elevation of 10,152′. Then down to the Arkansas River level before climbing up over 12,095′ Independence Pass.
Roads and Traffic	Out of Vail on I-70 you ride west on the shoulder for 5 mi. Then turn south on U.S. 24, which is narrow in spots but doesn't have a lot of traffic. The road over Independence Pass is good, but very narrow in places. As a result trucks are directed not to use this pass, and you will encounter little truck traffic up here. Trucks are advised to approach Aspen from the west side on Col. 82.
Special Notes	There are plenty of campgrounds along this route between Vail and Aspen, so that if you are camping you could break your trip up into shorter rides each day. Motels, however, are scarce, except in Leadville.
0.0	**Leave** Vail turning **left** (W) on frontage road on **north** side of I-70 at #176 interchange.

Pass shopping center on right.

2.8   **Left** at entrance ramp #173 onto I-70 (W) and ride on shoulder.

5.0   **Take** Exit #171 toward Minturn.

5.1   **Right** (S) on U.S. 24. Narrow road, no shoulder.

7.2   Small town of Minturn, elevation 7817′. Restaurants and supermarket.

10.5   Start of climb to Battle Mountain.

14.1   Top of Battle Mountain, elevation 9250′.

Steep, curving downhill.

15.6   **Cross** bridge over Eagle River at bottom.

Road flattens out, still curving and narrow. Low traffic count.

16.4   **Enter** White River National Forest.

17.3   Hornsilver National Forest Campground.

18.4   **Start climb** up away from the river. Road levels off again.

22.4   **Pass** Camp Hale Memorial. Ski troops were trained here in WW II. This is the 10th Mountain Division Memorial Highway.

23.2   **Begin climb** to Tennessee Pass. Not a steep climb.

28.5   Tennessee Pass Summit at the Continental Divide. Elevation 10,424′.

The down side of the pass is not steep either. Almost flat road right away running through a wide valley.

37.3   **Bear right** at Y to Leadville, staying on U.S. 24 through town.

Leadville

Population 3879, elevation 10,152', making this the highest incorporated city in the United States.

The silver mines of Leadville made it famous, but gold, zinc, lead, tungsten, tin, and molybdenum have also created a sometimes thriving mining community here, dating from 1860. The fortunes of Leadville have risen and fallen according to the demands for these products.

Motels, restaurants, stores, and the Sugar Loafin' Campground 3.5 mi out of town. Phone them (719) 486-1031 and ask for directions.

38.6   **Leave** Leadville from in front of City Hall on Harrison Ave. (U.S. 24) riding **south** out of town.

Continue on U.S. 24, downhill on narrow road. More traffic after Leadville.

46.8   **Cross** Arkansas River, and continue down through the valley of the (at this point) very small and quiet river.

54.0   **Right** (W) on Col. 82. No shoulder.

55.0   **Enter** San Isabel National Forest.

55.1   Rolling hills, and start of 8' shoulder.

56.9 Twin Lakes Reservoir on left, mountains of the Continental Divide beyond.

Lake View National Forest Campground.

60.4 Twin Lakes Post Office and store, elevation 9210'.

Trivia Question: What is the highest peak in Colorado? Answer: Mt. Elbert (14,433'), just 5 mi to the northwest.

End of shoulder. Narrow road running through a narrow valley.

63.2 Parry Peak National Forest Campground.

Gradual climb continues through pines and aspen groves. 2' shoulder.

72.2 Valley widens out into more arid-looking country.

73.6 Serious climbing starts with switchbacks up out of the valley. Road narrows with drop-off on left and rock cliffs on right.

75.0 More open, wider valley. Many lovely wildflowers all along this road.

76.0 Big switchback and steep climb, with drop-off on right and views of the valley you climbed from.

You will be above tree line, riding through rock-strewn fields where there are likely to be a few patches of snow even in midsummer.

78.2 Independence Pass on the Continental Divide at 12,095'.

78.3   Steep downhill on curving, narrow road.

81.3   Back into pine forest and wildflower country.

84.2   Lost Man National Forest Campground.

The road follows the Roaring Fork River downstream through greener, narrow valley. Tight curves on

The climb over Independence Pass, elevation 12,095', takes you through beautiful wildflower fields, pine and aspen groves, and above timberline.

narrow road. Pine trees and aspen again closing in on both sides.

88.4 Road really narrows through rocky cliffs. Lane only about 8′ wide, but it's so narrow that motor traffic moves slowly.

Weller National Forest Campground.

Lots of aspen in wider valley. Road widens with some shoulder off and on.

94.2 Difficult National Forest Campground. If you want to camp near Aspen this is a good choice.

Flat road into town with 3′ shoulder on left—broken shoulder on right. More traffic as you near town.

97.4 **Pass** Aspen city limits and **cross over** Roaring Fork River, following Col. 82 onto Main St. in Aspen.

98.0 **Finish** on Main St. in front of the famous Hotel Jerome (330 E. Main).

Aspen Population 3678, elevation 7908′.

Romantic Aspen in its beautiful mountain setting has carefully preserved its history. Silver mining was responsible for its 1880 beginnings. The world's largest silver nugget, weighing almost a ton, was produced in the Smuggler Mine here, and at one time Aspen was the largest city in Colorado west of the Continental Divide. The architecture of those days has been preserved and restored to its former glory. The Hotel Jerome is splendid, and the downtown streets are lined with store fronts that maintain the atmosphere of the silver bonanza days. Residential neighborhoods also abound with restored cottages and Victorian landmarks. All this nestled beneath Aspen Mountain and the famous ski slopes. Many motels, restaurants, stores, and 12 (!) bike shops. Aspen is small enough to easily get around by bicycle, and there are lots of bike riders here.

For an easy-to-reach motel, favored by bikies, turn **left** (S) on Monarch St. for 3 blocks to the edge of Wagner Park, where you will find the Limelite Lodge, at 228 East Cooper St. (303) 925-3025. There are many other equally desirable lodgings in Aspen. It would be wise to call ahead for a reservation before making the climb over Independence Pass.

Silver mining was responsible for the settlement of Aspen in the 1880s. It still has the look of those early days in its many preserved and restored buildings. Ski slopes, green in summer, loom above the town.

13C

Aspen through Buena Vista to Salida

Distance	91 mi from Aspen (7908′) to Salida (7036′)
Actual Climbing	4400′
Helpful Maps	*Colorado Road Atlas*, pages T2, D22, D23, T18. National Forest Maps: White River, San Isabel. (See Appendix A.)
Terrain	A serious climb over Independence Pass, then a rolling road south on U.S. 24 to join U.S. 50 at Salida.
Roads and Traffic	See Independence Pass information in Tour 13B. U.S. 24 South following the Arkansas River has a good shoulder almost all the way.
Special Notes	Retrace over Independence Pass and continue south. We recommend that you do not cycle on Col. 82 out of Aspen to the northwest toward Basalt. All the trucks that did not come over Independence Pass and much other traffic from the north will be on this narrow, busy road.

0.0   **Leave** Aspen from the front of the Hotel Jerome, 330 E. Main St. (Col. 82) heading **east** and **retrace** over Independence Pass. (See Tour 13B.)

37.0   Twin Lakes Post Office and store.

43.4 **Right** (S) on U.S. 24 downhill, following the Arkansas River. No shoulder for 2.6 mi.

45.0 Chaffee County line.

46.0 **Pass** small town of Granite. 6′ shoulder begins.

Rolling road, but mostly downhill through a broad valley, with the Sawatch Range of mountains in view to the west.

Signs along the highway identify "fourteener" mountain peaks of the Collegiate Range.

56.0 Mt. Harvard (14,420′).

60.4 Mt. Yale (14,196′).

63.2 Town of Buena Vista. Population 2075, elevation 7954′. Motels, a B&B, restaurants, and stores.

64.2 **Continue south** through town on U.S. 24.

65.6 Mt. Princeton (14,197′).

66.4 **Leave** U.S. 24 and go straight ahead (**south**) to join U.S. 285. 8′ shoulder.

71.8 **Pass** small town of Nathrop. Brown's Campground on east side of road.

75.4 View of Mt. Antero (14,269′).

81.0 **Left** (E) on Col. 291 toward Salida (leaving U.S. 285). 8′ shoulder.

82.6 No shoulder for 4.6 mi.

87.2   Start of 8' shoulder.

88.0   **Cross** Arkansas River.

89.6   **Enter** Salida on Col. 291, which becomes 1st St. Motels, restaurants, and stores along this stretch.

90.6   **Bear right** (S) on Oak St., still following Col. 291.

91.2   **Finish** at corner of Oak St. and Rainbow Blvd. (U.S. 50).

Right (W) on Rainbow Blvd. (U.S. 50) for Salida's motel and restaurant row. **Left** (SE) on U.S. 50 for 4-Seasons Campground, which is 1.6 mi east of town.

See Tour 24 for east-west U.S. 50 connecting route information, or Tour 28 for continuing south.

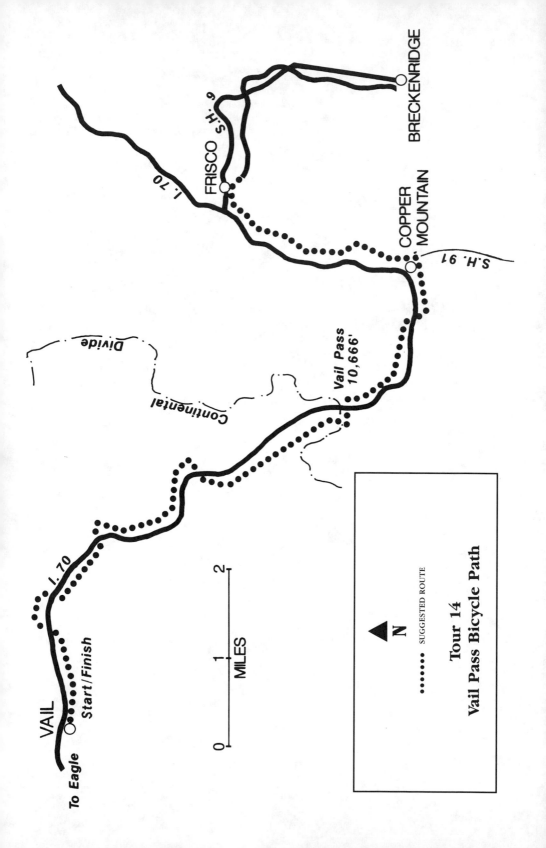

To Eagle

VAIL

Start/Finish

I. 70

Continental Divide

Vail Pass
10,666'

I. 70

FRISCO S.H. 9

BRECKENRIDGE

COPPER
MOUNTAIN

S.H. 91

MILES

0   1   2

N

·········· SUGGESTED ROUTE

Tour 14
Vail Pass Bicycle Path

14

Vail Pass Bicycle Path

Distance 47 mi round trip, riding from Vail (8150′) to Frisco (9097′)

Actual Climbing A total of 4085′ when you climb both sides of 10,666′ Vail Pass

Helpful Maps *Colorado Road Atlas*, page D16. For a map of this trip refer to the map of the Vail Pass Bicycle Path included with the *Bicycling Colorado* maps from the Colorado Department of Highways. (See Appendix A.)

Special Notes This is a ride through beautiful mountain scenery, removed from auto traffic. However, on midsummer weekends the path is sometimes so crowded with riders (often inexperienced), hikers, and skiers practicing on rollerskates that it can be dangerous. We suggest that you make this tour in early or late summer, when you will not be so likely to encounter a crowd.

0.0 **Leave** Vail from I-70 exit #176, cycling **east** on the South Frontage Road.

0.5 **Pass** big 2-way stop sign.

Pass golf course on right.

Continue on frontage road, **passing under** I-70 3 times.

Ignore Dead End sign and **continue southeast**.

6.4   **Pass** Gore Creek Campground.

12.4   **Pass through** rest area parking lot at top of Vail Pass. Elevation 10,666'.

This is a good turn-around point if you wish to return to Vail. You will have completed a 25 mi trip out and back.

12.5   **Continue** on bicycle path and **pass through** bicycle path tunnel.

Pass Copper Mountain Ski Resort.

17.5   **Cross** Col. 91.

Left (N) through parking area, and continue on bikepath.

23.5   **Right** (E) on Business Rt. 70 in Frisco. Motels, restaurants, stores, bike shop.

For return to Vail, reverse these directions.

The Vail Pass Bicycle Path follows the I-70 corridor from Vail to Breckenridge.

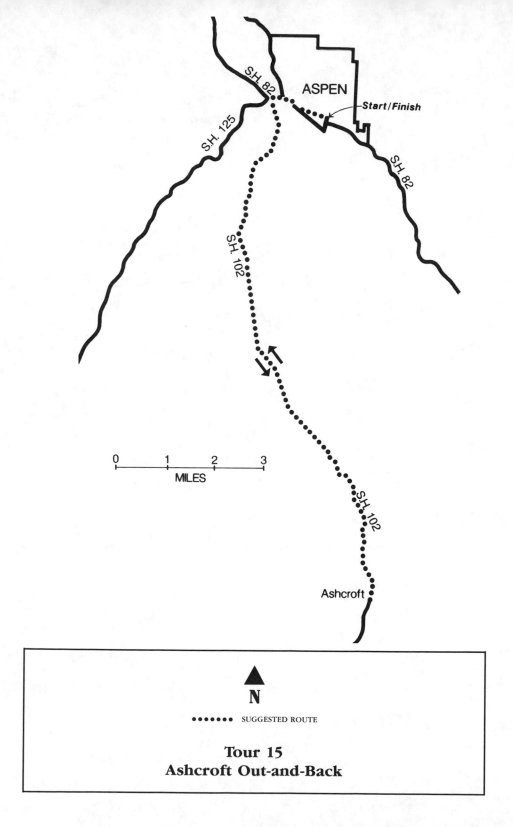

S.H. 82

S.H. 125

ASPEN

Start/Finish

S.H. 82

S.H. 102

0   1   2   3
MILES

S.H. 102

Ashcroft

▲
N

••••••• SUGGESTED ROUTE

**Tour 15
Ashcroft Out-and-Back**

15

Ashcroft Out-and-Back

Distance	26 mi round trip from Aspen (7908′) to Ashcroft (8900′)
Actual Climbing	1200′
Helpful Maps	*Colorado Road Atlas*, pages T2, D22. National Forest Map: White River. (See Appendix A.)
Terrain	Pleasant climb, steep in spots, on Castle Creek Road to the ghost town of Ashcroft. Scenic valley, with glimpses of peaks to the south.
Roads and Traffic	Narrow road, but you will encounter more bikes than cars.
Special Notes	This is a trouble-free ride through mountain greenery. The biggest hazard you may encounter will be from inexperienced riders on rented mountain bicycles. Several shops in Aspen offer to provide people with motorized transportation to the top of a climb, put them on rented mountain bicycles, and let them cruise back down to Aspen. Castle Creek Road from Ashcroft is one of their routes. Needless to say there are going to be some squirrelly riders in this situation. Luckily the Ashcroft road is wide enough that it should not be a major problem.

0.0 **Leave** Aspen going **west** on Col. 82, from the front of the Hotel Jerome at 330 E. Main St.

0.7   **Right** for 2 blocks and then **left**, still following Col. 82.

1.1   **Cross** bridge over Roaring Fork River. 4' shoulder.

1.9   **Left** on Castle Creek Rd. at traffic light.

Immediately left (S) again on road to Ashcroft (County Rd. 102).

Gradual uphill on country road following Castle Creek. No shoulder. Very little traffic.

7.7   Steeper climb. You will be riding high above the river through mountain greenery.

8.2   Back down to the river and through more open valley.

13.0   Ashcroft townsite. Wooden walkway leads you to restored ghost town off to the left.

26.0   **Retrace** down mountain to Aspen.

This scenic road leads from Aspen up to the ghost town of Ashcroft.

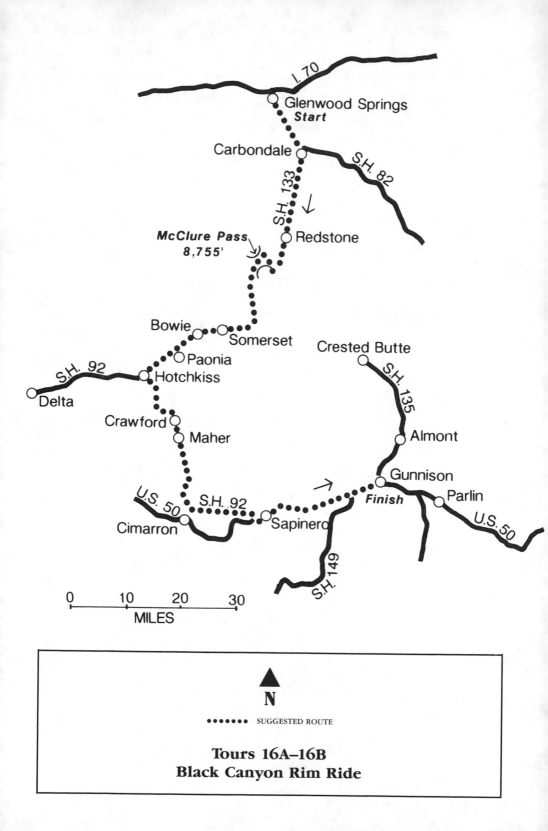

Glenwood Springs
Start

I. 70

Carbondale

S.H. 82

S.H. 133

Redstone

McClure Pass
8,755'

Bowie
Somerset
Crested Butte

Paonia

S.H. 135

S.H. 92
Hotchkiss

Delta

Crawford

Maher
Almont

Gunnison

U.S. 50
S.H. 92
Parlin

Finish

Cimarron
Sapinero
U.S. 50

S.H. 149

0   10   20   30
MILES

▲
N

●●●●●●● SUGGESTED ROUTE

Tours 16A–16B
Black Canyon Rim Ride

16

▲

Black Canyon Rim Ride

Distance	163 mi
Suggested Time	2 days
Total Climbing	8500′

This tour takes you from Glenwood Springs south to the small town of Hotchkiss. On the second day of the tour you will ride along the north rim of the Black Canyon of the Gunnison, through areas of spectacular scenery, and then to the junction of U.S. 50, and east to the town of Gunnison.

A map at this scenic overlook on the rim of the Black Canyon of the Gunnison shows the recreational area below.

187

Glenwood Springs to Hotchkiss

Distance	82 mi from Glenwood Springs (5746') to Hotchkiss (5351')
Actual Climbing	3300'
Helpful Maps	*Colorado Road Atlas*, pages T14, D7, D22, D21. National Forest Maps: White River, Gunnison Basin. (See Appendix A.)
Terrain	Rolling roads. A climb of 3.5 mi up to McClure Pass and then a descent of 8.5 mi on the other side.
Roads and Traffic	Good roads with shoulder most of the time until you pass Somerset after about 50 mi. Here the road narrows and you have to negotiate 3 sets of R.R. tracks running across the road at very sharp angles. Best to walk over these, especially if the road is wet. Traffic will be low volume on Col. 133 after you leave busy Col. 82.
	Note: From this point Col. 82, heading toward Aspen, is narrow and loaded with trucks, RVs, buses, etc. At this writing this highway is not for cycling. Possibly all this will change in a few years, after the roadway is widened. Until then, stay off this road to Aspen.
Special Notes	On Col. 133 you will be riding through some very scenic country. McClure Pass is one of Colorado's most pleasant climbs—for beauty and lack of car traffic.

0.0 **Leave** Glenwood Springs at corner of 6th St. and Grand Ave. **Cross** bridge and head **south** out of town on Col. 82.

1.5 **Bear left** at traffic light leaving Grand Ave. and continue on Col. 82. 4-lane road with 6' shoulder.

12.1 **Right** (S) on Col. 133 leaving Col. 82.

13.1 **Left** (E) to Carbondale business district.

13.7 Carbondale (6181') is a small town with interesting restaurants and stores.

13.8 **Right** (S) on S. 2nd St.

14.5 **Right** (W) at T at stop sign on 100 Rd. for 1 block.

14.6 **Left** (S) at next stop sign back to Col. 133.

You will be riding through a flat, broad river valley. 4' shoulder. This is enjoyable riding. Good tight scenery along twisting road that gives you differing and enchanting vistas. View of 12,952' Mt. Sopris to the east.

16.6 Pitkin County line. Gentle climb gradually getting steeper.

24.6 **Enter** White River National Forest.

28.6 **Left** (E) on County Rd. 15, the road to the small village of Redstone, elevation 7180'.

Redstone National Forest Campground on left.

Continue south on this back road for 1.7 mi to the

center of Redstone. Motels, stores, and restaurants, including the historic and renovated Redstone Inn (303) 963-2526. The town and the inn were originally built by a coal baron to house his coke oven workers. You'll see remains of the coke ovens as you rejoin Col. 133.

30.6   **Right** in front of Redstone Inn and **cross over** bridge back to Col. 133.

30.7   **Left** (S) on Col. 133. 2′ shoulder. The road follows the Crystal River going upstream gradually through redrock cliffs on the sides of the canyon.

35.5   Gunnison County line.

36.2   Start of steep climb up to McClure Pass, riding through aspen groves with the road getting steeper as you progress.

39.4   McClure Pass summit. Elevation 8755′.

Enter Gunnison National Forest and start steep 8.5 mi

Approaching McClure Pass on Col. 133. This is one of Colorado's most pleasant climbs—for beauty and lack of car traffic.

downhill through curves. Use caution. 3' shoulder. 20 mph speed limit sign. Bike riders should obey!

41.2   **Pass** McClure National Forest Campground.

47.9   Bottom of the long 8.5 mi downhill. From here gentle descent until you cross bridge.

53.9   **Pass** Paonia Reservoir.

56.7   **Pass** dam, and start steeper downhill.

57.3   Gunnison County Road #12 on left. Crystal Meadows Ranch Campground, restaurant, and store 1 mi down this road. It's paved here, but the rest of the road to Crested Butte is unpaved.

   Continue south on Col. 133. Road narrows on long downhill of 2.4 mi. No shoulder.

59.7   Start of 8' shoulder.

62.2   **Pass** Arco Coal Mine and Bear Coal Co.

63.3   Small town of Somerset, an old coal mining town. Small store here.

63.4   Road narrows. No shoulder through this section. Road follows canal on right. Long downhill to Paonia.

   Warning. There are three sets of R.R. tracks in the next mile that are slanted across the road at such an angle that it's almost impossible to ride over them at the 90-degree angle required for safety. Best to stop and walk each time—especially if it is raining. Some of our bikie friends, even though experienced bike handlers, have taken bad spills here on these tracks.

68.0   **Pass** small town of Bowie. Fruit market.

72.5   **Left** (SE) on Col. 187 into Paonia. Population 1424, elevation 5674'. Restaurants and stores here, and one very small motel.

73.3   **Right** (W) out of Paonia on 3rd St. to **rejoin** Col. 133.

73.5   **Left** (SW) on Col. 133. Roller-coaster road to Hotchkiss.

74.2   **Pass** Redwood Arms Motel and restaurant.

81.7   **Finish** in Hotchkiss at junction of Col. 133 and Col. 92.

Hotchkiss   Population 849, elevation 5351'.

Comfort T Lodge (303) 872-2200 is at the east edge of town. Tent camping is allowed at the Fairgrounds in Hotchkiss. Restaurants and stores.

16B

▲

Hotchkiss to Gunnison

Distance 81 mi from Hotchkiss (5351′) to Gunnison (7703′)

Actual 5200′
Climbing

Helpful Maps *Colorado Road Atlas*, pages D21, D22. National
Forest Map: Gunnison Basin. (See Appendix A.)

Terrain Serious climbing in the area overlooking the Black
Canyon of the Gunnison. But the spectacular views
make it worthwhile.

Roads and Tour starts on backcountry road through wide-open
Traffic spaces. Then more mountainous riding across the
Black Mesa. There can be some auto-tourist traffic,
but not high speed. They are enjoying the spectacular
views also.

Special Notes Be prepared with plenty of water and picnic supplies.
There are no facilities after you pass through Craw-
ford until you reach U.S. 50 at mile 54.

0.0 **Leave** Hotchkiss heading south on Col. 92.

This is a curving road with short climbs and no
shoulder. Very little traffic, but for your own safety,
take the center of your lane when you come to the
climbs, which sometimes have drop-offs and guardrails near the edge of the road.

193

Road becomes more rolling through wide-open sagebrush-covered hills.

11.1 Small town of Crawford. Motel and country store.

Continue on Col. 92 out of town down a steep, curving hill.

11.6 At bottom wider road. 3' shoulder.

12.6 **Pass** Crawford Reservoir.

14.1 Montrose County line. Shoulder broken and non-existent in some places.

16.0 Maher. Nothing there.

Start of long downhill.

25.2 At bottom **enter** Gunnison National Forest and start climb. Views of Black Canyon on the right. 2' shoulder.

28.6 Crystal Scenic Overlook. View down into the Black Canyon.

Rolling road takes you on ups and downs, averaging a mile climb followed by a mile down.

31.0 High point with vista on right of valley of the Gunnison River below.

35.0 Another bottom, and immediately start up.

35.4 Hermits Rest Scenic Overlook. Elevation 9125'. Below is the silent gorge of the Black Canyon, and in the distance the rugged San Juan Mountain Range with its

14,000' peaks. The highest in view is 14,309' Uncompahgre Peak. At this high point we found the clearest, purest air in all of our Colorado touring.

You ride through a series of climbs and descents for more than 10 mi through this area, with overwhelmingly spectacular views on your right as you pedal along the north rim of the Black Canyon of the Gunnison.

39.2   Finally start down through aspen groves with more rolling ups and downs.

45.6   **Cross** Curecanti Creek and **continue** on long, gently descending road.

47.5   **Enter** Curecanti National Recreation Area.

48.1   Pioneer Point Scenic Overlook.

52.6   **Pass** Soap Creek Road and start down.

53.5   **Cross** Blue Mesa Dam.

53.9   **Pass** Lake Fork Campground.

54.2   **Right** (E) at junction of U.S. 50 at T toward Gunnison.

55.2   **Cross** bridge over Blue Mesa Reservoir.

56.2   Sapinero, elevation 7600'. Store and restaurant.

Road winds along the edge of the reservoir. 6' shoulder.

59.4   **Cross** bridge to **north** side of reservoir.

Pass junction of Col. 149.

Short stretch of no shoulder.

76.6 Mesa Campground and store.

78.1 Begin 8' shoulder. Several motels along here on the way into town.

79.2 **Pass** road to KOA, which is 1 mi to the south.

80.8 **Finish** in Gunnison at corner of Tomichi Ave. (U.S. 50) and Main St. (Col. 135).

Gunnison Population 5785, elevation 7703'.

Motels, restaurants, stores, and bike shop. For more Gunnison information see Tour 25.

See Tour 24 for connecting route east to Pueblo; Tour 25A west to Montrose.

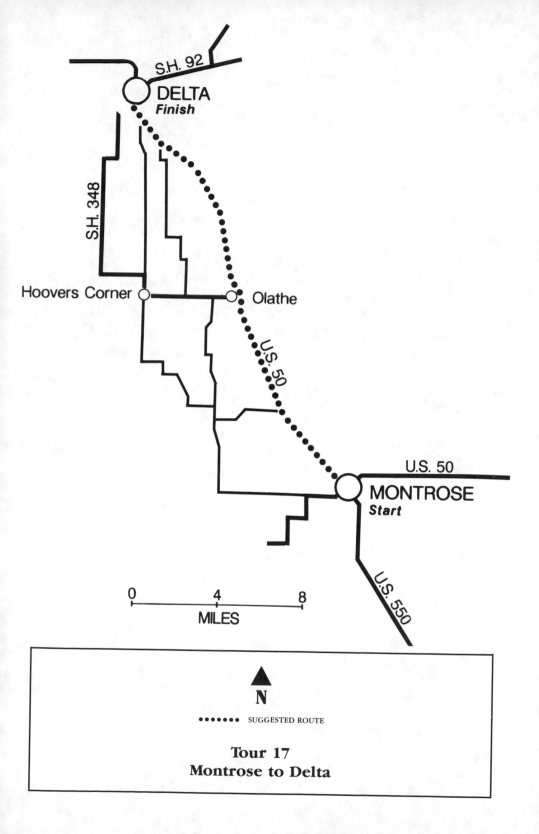

S.H. 92

DELTA
Finish

S.H. 348

Hoovers Corner

Olathe

U.S. 50

U.S. 50

MONTROSE
Start

U.S. 550

0   4   8
MILES

N

•••••••• SUGGESTED ROUTE

Tour 17
Montrose to Delta

▲

17

Montrose to Delta

Connecting route

Distance	22 mi from Montrose (5794') to Delta (4961')
Altitude Loss	833'
Helpful Map	*Colorado Road Atlas*, page D21. (See Appendix A.)
Terrain	Flat. Road parallel with the Uncompahgre River, which flows downstream to Delta.
Roads and Traffic	Wide shoulder most of the way. 6 mi stretch of no shoulder.

This short connecting route takes you from Montrose to the beginning of Tour 18, Grand Mesa Circle, in Delta.

Montrose

Population 8722, elevation 5794'.

Motels and restaurants on U.S. 50 on the east side of town. 2 in-town campgrounds, also on the east side of town: Mountain View, 1 block to the north of U.S. 50, and KOA, 2 blocks to the south. Bike shops and restaurants in the downtown area.

0.0 **Leave** Montrose on U.S. 50 going **northwest** out of town.

10.6   **Pass** intersection of Col. 348. Beginning of 2-lane highway with no shoulder.

15.4   Delta County line.

16.5   Start of 4-lane divided highway. 10′ shoulder into Delta.

21.9   **Finish** in Delta at junction of U.S. 50 (Main St.) and Col. 92.

Delta   Population 3931, elevation 4961′.

Prosperous-looking Delta owes its stability to the western-slope fruit growing industry. Western-slope peaches are rated as some of the best in the world. A unique outdoor mural at the corner of Main and 5th glorifies the local agricultural enterprises with giant blowups of fruit box labels.

Motels, restaurants, groceries, and a bike shop. Delta/Grand Mesa KOA campground is 1 mi east of town on Col. 92.

The small town of Delta owes its prosperity to the western-slope fruit growing industry and pays tribute to it with this unique outdoor mural. These are giant blowups of the actual end labels on the fruit boxes.

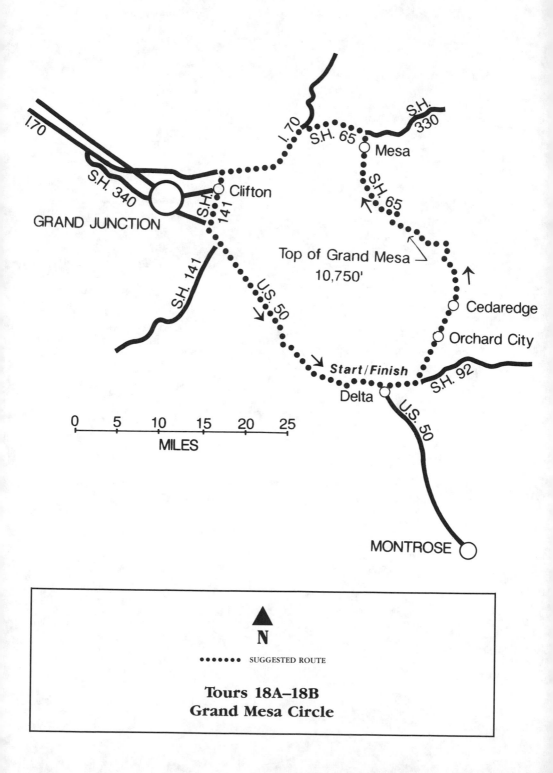

I.70

S.H. 340

GRAND JUNCTION

S.H. 141

Clifton

I.70

S.H. 65

Mesa

S.H. 330

S.H. 65

Top of Grand Mesa
10,750'

Cedaredge

Orchard City

S.H. 141

U.S. 50

Start/Finish

S.H. 92

Delta

U.S. 50

MONTROSE

| 0 | 5 | 10 | 15 | 20 | 25 |
MILES

▲
N

••••••• SUGGESTED ROUTE

Tours 18A–18B
Grand Mesa Circle

▲

18

Grand Mesa Circle

Distance	118 mi
Suggested Time:	2 days
Total Climbing	6400'

It's an exciting ride to the top of the Grand Mesa—the world's highest flattop mountain—and an equally exciting steep descent down to the Colorado River, where you join I-70 into Grand Junction. (See page 30 for safe Interstate riding suggestions.) The ride back to Delta on U.S. 50 takes you through some desert-like, remote western country.

Two cyclists head for the beginning of the climb to the top of the Grand Mesa in western Colorado.

18A

▲

Delta to Clifton/Grand Junction

Distance   79 mi from Delta (4961′) to Clifton/Grand Junction (4586′)

Actual Climbing   6000′

Helpful Maps   *Colorado Road Atlas*, pages D21, D20. National Forest Map: Grand Mesa. (See Appendix A.)

Terrain   The first 14 mi are an easy upgrade. From there you will have some serious climbing over the Grand Mesa. From the top it's downhill for 40 mi, all the way to Clifton and Grand Junction.

Roads and Traffic   You will have a variety of roads on the Grand Mesa, some newly paved and widened, and not a lot of traffic. The hazard of several cattle guards to cross on the top of the mesa may be your biggest concern.

Special Notes   You should plan to make an early morning start from Delta to ride over the Grand Mesa, to avoid afternoon thunderstorms and to reach the outskirts of Grand Junction in good time.

Delta   Population 3931, elevation 4961′.

Motels, restaurants, groceries, and bike shop. Delta/Grand Mesa KOA Campground 1 mi east of edge of town on Col. 92. (See Tour 17 for more Delta information.)

0.0 **Leave** Delta at junction of U.S. 50 (Main St.) and Col. 92.

Proceed east on Col. 92. Flat terrain with mesas and mountains on the horizon. 10′ shoulder.

1.3 **Pass** KOA Campground.

3.9 **Left** (N) on Col. 65. No shoulder.

6.0 Orchard City, elevation 5800′. You have started on gentle climb toward Grand Mesa. Areas of sand-colored mesas and hills on the left.

10.4 Start of 6′ shoulder. Passing through some of the peach-growing orchard country of the western slope of the Rockies.

14.3 Cedaredge. Population 1184, elevation 6100′. Motel, restaurants, and stores.

15.0 At traffic light start of real climb. 3′ shoulder.

17.0 Top and slight downhill.

18.1 Aspen Trails Campground on left.

20.7 Steeper climbs and S curves.

21.9 View back down into the valley on the right.

22.9 Then view down into the valley on the left.

Lots of curving around as you climb to the top of the mesa through scrub oak and aspen groves.

25.2 Cattle guards and steeper climbing in the next 2 mi.

Be careful crossing these cattle guards. Cross at a good clip, or walk over them, especially if it is raining and the rails are wet.

27.3 **Enter** Grand Mesa National Forest.

29.7 Dip down and back up through pine forests.

31.5 Ward Lake area.

31.7 Carp Lake Campground on right.

End of wide shoulder. Shoulder narrows and then ends.

32.0 Grand Mesa Lodge. Store and cafe.

34.7 At top of the mesa, cross Mesa County line. Elevation 10,750′—more than 2 mi high!

Road narrows and may be rough as you start down on rolling road from the top of the mesa.

37.2 Steep down with views of mesas ahead.

38.6 **Cross** 2 cattle guards in next mile and a half. Bumpy road.

40.6 Spruce Grove Campground and more steep downhill.

41.1 Mesa Lakes Resort with food and lodging.

42.3 Long down with view of Battlement Mesa, 15 mi to the north.

44.8 Start of 3′ shoulder, and another cattle guard to cross.

47.1   **Pass** Powderhorn Ski Area. Good smooth road with 3′ shoulder and more gentle downhill.

54.8   Small town of Mesa, elevation 5650′. Wagon Wheel Motel, (303) 268-5224, the only one for quite a few miles. Restaurant and general store.

55.3   Steep downhill.

56.4   Bridge at bottom and junction of Col. 330.

   Continue straight ahead on Col 65. 3′ shoulder.

61.0   **Start through** narrow canyon with sheer cliffs towering above the road on both sides, following the curving Plateau River, until it joins the Colorado River at the end of the canyon.

65.0   **Pass over** I-70 at Exit #49.

   Immediate left (W) on entrance ramp to I-70 West toward Grand Junction, and ride on shoulder.

70.0   **Cross** Colorado River. Use extreme caution on this narrow bridge.

   You will be passing through unusual scenery. Towering barren bluffs on the north side of the road, and lush green orchards and vegetable farms on the south side.

72.2   **Pass** Palisade Exit #42.

77.4   **Leave** I-70 at Exit #37 and cross over I-70 on Business Loop 70 to Clifton, elevation 4712′, at the eastern edge of Grand Junction.

Tour 18   Grand Mesa Circle

As you approach Grand Junction you will see just to the north of I-70 towering barren bluffs so arid that scarcely anything grows.

But just to the south of I-70 irrigation works its magic, and orchards, vine-yards, and vegetable farms flourish.

You will pass the KOA Campground on the north-west side of Business Loop 70.

78.5   **Finish** in Clifton at corner of Business Loop 70 and "F" Road at traffic light.

Best bet for overnight in the area is in Clifton, a suburb of Grand Junction.

Just beyond traffic light on Business Loop 70, on the northwest side of the road, is the Clifton Inn (303) 434-3400. The people here are very friendly to bikies, who often stop here.

Grand Junction   Population 27,956, elevation 4586'.

Grand Junction is situated in the valley of the Colo-rado and Gunnison rivers. There is some wild and wonderful scenery around here. The Colorado National Monument, to the west, contains sheer-walled canyons, redrock spires, and unearthly-looking rock formations. Bicycle races, including one stage of the Coors Classic, have been run on the Monument grounds, and because of the unusual scenery the course has been named the "Tour of the Moon." You too can tour the moon on Rim Rock Drive from the West Entrance at Fruita to the East Entrance at Grand Junction. See Tour 19.

It is our suggestion that you stay at either the camp-ground or the motel for 2 nights, leaving your gear there until the next day, and make Tour 19 to the Colorado National Monument—Tour of the Moon— from Clifton before returning to Delta.

Clifton to Delta

Distance	39 mi from Clifton (4710′) to Delta (4961′)
Actual Climbing	400′
Helpful Maps	*Colorado Road Atlas*, pages D20, D21. (See Appendix A.)
Terrain	Flat to rolling roads through some very desolate landscape.
Roads and Traffic	This is the easy way to leave the Grand Junction area. When you join U.S. 50 going south there will be a good bit of traffic. You will have a 10′ shoulder at the beginning of this ride, but 11.8 mi of no shoulder as you approach Delta.

0.0 **Leave** Clifton Inn/KOA area of Clifton on Business Loop 70 going **west**.

0.2 **Left** (S) at traffic light on Col. 141 (32nd Rd). 10′ shoulder.

Cross bridge over R.R. tracks.

2.2 **Cross** river and climb up over a ridge with short bit of narrower shoulder.

3.2 Start of 10′ shoulder.

5.8   **Left** (SE) on U.S. 50 at T, toward Delta on rolling road through desert-like area. 10′ shoulder.

Grand Mesa in view to the east.

Traffic can be heavy on this road. No problem while you have the 10′ shoulder, but at mile 24.6 you will begin the 11.8 mi of no shoulder. Use caution and your rearview mirror.

You will be riding through bleak, brown stretches of nothing but sand and sagebrush. There's nothing out there. It's okay if you like wide-open, western terrain. Be prepared, fill your water bottles.

20.8   Delta County line.

24.6   Start of no shoulder into Delta. **Caution**. The Colorado State Highway *Bicycling Colorado* map rates this a red road—"least desirable for cycling." But most of the heavy traffic is at commuting time.

36.4   Start of 10′ shoulder.

RV Campground just before river.

38.6   **Cross** Gunnison River.

39.2   **Finish** tour in Delta on U.S. 50 (Main St.) at junction of Col. 92.

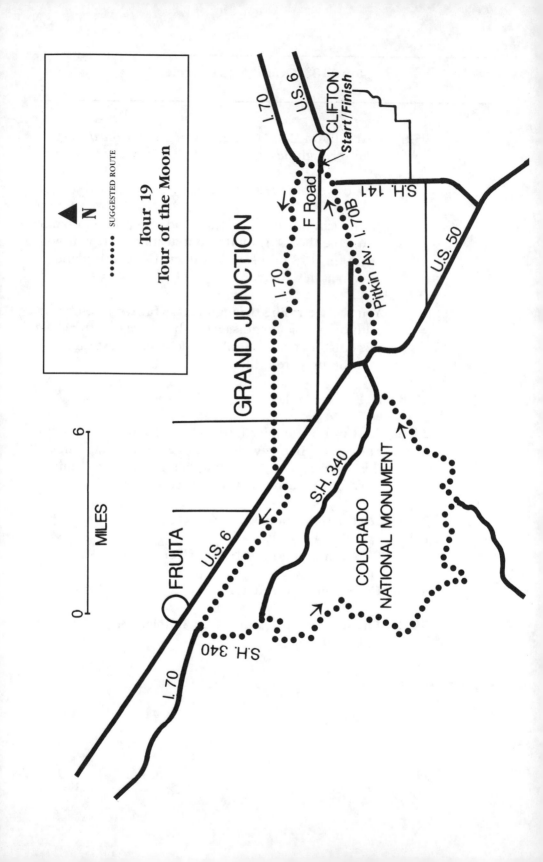

N

SUGGESTED ROUTE

Tour 19
Tour of the Moon

MILES

0   6

CLIFTON
Start/Finish

I. 70

U.S. 6

F Road

I. 70

S.H. 141

Pitkin Av.   I. 70B

U.S. 50

GRAND JUNCTION

S.H. 340

FRUITA

U.S. 6

S.H. 340

I. 70

COLORADO
NATIONAL MONUMENT

19

Tour of the Moon

Distance 56 mi round trip from Clifton

Actual Climbing 2600′

Helpful Maps *Colorado Road Atlas*, pages D20, T15. (See Appendix A.)

Terrain There are steep climbs and descents at the entrance and exit to the National Monument, and some more gentle climbs as you ride along Rim Rock Dr.

Roads and Traffic The best way to get to the Colorado National Monument by bicycle is to follow I-70 to Fruita and enter at the West Gate. (See page 30 for safe Interstate riding suggestions.)

The roads in the Monument are 2-lane with no shoulder. Traffic usually moves slowly. But take a lane when necessary. The administrators of the Monument welcome bicyclists, but hope that riders will respect other traffic, and if cars pile up behind them, will pull off to the side of the road and let the cars pass.

Special Notes The Colorado National Monument, located on a mesa west of Grand Junction, is well worth a visit. It has been a favorite ride for bicyclists, both tourists and racers, for many years. It's called the Tour of the Moon because of the spectacular moonscape-looking rock formations that cover the area. The name probably originated after one of the stages of the Coors Classic International Bicycle Race was run on the Monument grounds.

0.0   **Leave** Clifton from the corner of Business Loop 70 and "F" Road.

Proceed north on Business Loop 70.

0.6   **Enter** I-70 West at Exit #37 and ride on the shoulder. You will bypass downtown Grand Junction and its rather heavy traffic by riding on the Interstate to Exit #19 at Fruita.

6.6   **Pass** the Airport Exit #31.

Cliffs of the Colorado National Monument are in view to the south.

18.6   **Leave** I-70 at Exit #19.

Left (S) and **pass over** I-70 onto Col. 340.

The Coors International Bicycle Classic always holds one stage of the race in the Colorado National Monument grounds. It's called the Tour of the Moon because of the spectacular moonscape-looking rock formations that cover the area.

19.0   **Pass** rest area and Welcome Center on left. 4'
shoulder.

20.0   **Cross** Colorado River. End of shoulder.

21.4   **Right**, following Colorado National Monument sign
to West Entrance. The fee is $1.50 for bicyclists. Ask
for the free Bike Route map at the gatehouse.

22.0   Start of climb, through otherworldly redrock
formations.

23.8   **Pass through** 2 short tunnels.

The history of the formation of the canyon is
detailed on markers at the overlooks.

26.0   Road levels off at Visitors Center. Information about
the National Monument is available here. There is a
campground down the road to the left just before the
Visitors Center. Fee for camping is $3.00, which
you need to have in exact change if you should wish
to stop there for the night.

Continue along flat and rolling road, with many
spectacular views of rock formations, the vast plains
below, and more mesas on the distant horizon.

32.2   **Left** at "16 mi. to Grand Junction" sign.

34.4   Road levels off, passing deep canyons with sheer
redrock sides.

41.0   Start of steep downhill and sharp curves.

42.0   Another tunnel to pass through.

44.4   **Leave** Colorado National Monument at the East Gate.

Continue down on Monument Rd.

48.0 **Right** on Col. 340 at traffic light toward Grand Junction. 4' shoulder.

48.3 **Cross** bridge over Colorado River and R.R. tracks.

48.7 **Right** (S) on Business Loop 70 (1st St.), and curve **left** onto Pitkin Ave.

Proceed east on Pitkin Ave. (Business Loop 70). You will be riding in city traffic, but this is a wide 1-way street. 10' shoulder.

53.1 U.S. 6 joins Business Loop 70.

55.5 **Pass** junction of Col. 141. Highway swings **north**.

55.9 **Finish** in Clifton at corner of Business Loop 70 and "F" Road.

Clifton Inn is on the northwest side of Business Loop 70.

56.2 KOA Campground is just beyond next traffic light, also on northwest side of road.

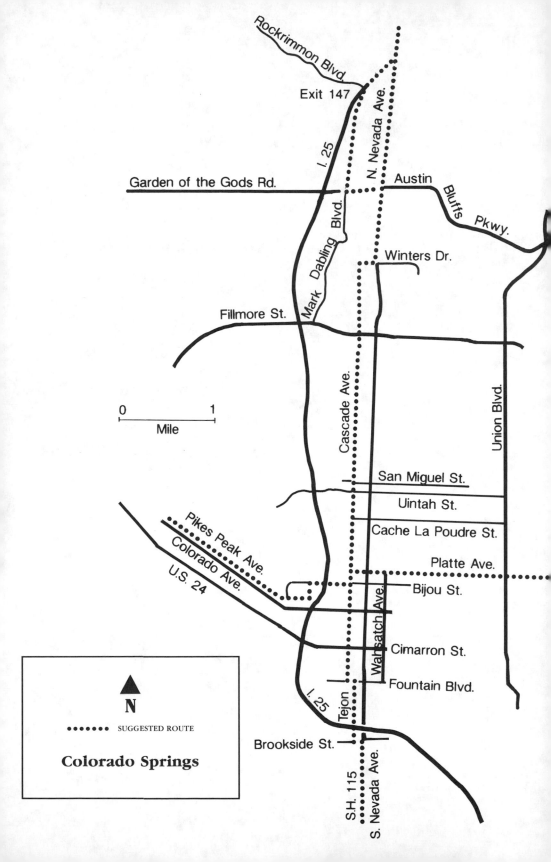

Rockrimmon Blvd.

Exit 147

I. 25

N. Nevada Ave.

Garden of the Gods Rd.

Austin

Bluffs Pkwy.

Mark Dabling Blvd.

Winters Dr.

Fillmore St.

Cascade Ave.

Union Blvd.

San Miguel St.

Uintah St.

Cache La Poudre St.

Pikes Peak Ave.

Colorado Ave.

U.S. 24

Platte Ave.

Bijou St.

Wahsatch Ave.

Cimarron St.

Fountain Blvd.

I. 25

Tejon

N

•••••• SUGGESTED ROUTE

Colorado Springs

Brookside St.

S.H. 115

S. Nevada Ave.

0   1
Mile

Colorado Springs
Population 214,821, elevation 6012'

▲

In 1806 Captain Zebulon Pike, the first official explorer of this western territory, put his own name on Pikes Peak, the mountain that looms over the town. When gold was discovered in 1859, "Pikes Peak or bust" was a rallying cry for goldseekers coming west.

Sixty-five years after Captain Pike's expedition, while surveying for the railroad routes, General William J. Palmer became enchanted with the area and established the town of Colorado Springs.

Adventurous travelers from the East and from Europe flocked to Colorado Springs in the late 1800s. So many Englishmen came that at one time it was called Little London. And as was the custom, it had its sanitariums for those seeking a cure for tuberculosis in the pure mountain air.

Bike Routes

Colorado Springs is a bustling metropolis, the second largest city in Colorado, but wide streets and an excellent Bicycle Access Map make it an easy-cycling town. The map is available from Colorado Springs Planning Dept. (See Appendix A.)

There are also bicycle club rides out of Colorado Springs every weekend. Any of the bike shops can furnish a schedule. If you have the time and the desire to see some bicycle track racing, the bike shops can also give you a schedule of the races being run weekly on the velodrome at the U.S. Olympic Training Center here.

To reach Colorado Springs by bicycle from either the north or the south, you can follow the Colorado Department of Highways Bicycle Maps. (See Appendix A.) The maps direct you along the I-25 corridor and give suggested routes for getting into or through the city. For suggestions about safe Interstate bicycle riding see page 30.

Accommodations

There are many motels, restaurants, and bike shops here. Two motels somewhat centrally located, and easy to get to by bicycle, are on N. Nevada Ave. not far from the Colorado College campus: J's Motor Hotel (719) 633-5513 and the Imperial 400 Inn (719) 636-3385. From Cascade Ave. go **east** on Cache la Poudre St. for 2 blocks to Nevada Ave. Turn **right** (S) and you will see the motels in the next 2 blocks.

Pikes Peak, most famous of the gold-rush days mountains, towers over the city of Colorado Springs.

One campground in town easily reached by bicycle is Campers Village, 1209 S. Nevada Ave. (719) 632-9737. From Cache la Poudre St. ride **south** on Cascade Ave. for 2.5 mi. **Left** (E) on Las Vegas St. for 3 blocks. **Right** (S) on Weber St. to Campers Village.

Another choice for campers is the Garden of the Gods Campground (719) 475-9450 at the edge of Manitou Springs. **Follow** the route on Tour 21 to Manitou Springs as far as Columbus Ave., at mile 4.2. Straight ahead is the campground, with good tent sites as well as AYH 4-bunk cabins. There are also many motels and other campgrounds in Manitou Springs.

Mansions Mini-Tour

In Colorado Springs's Old North End Historical District there is a fabulous collection of mansions from the 1880s. Some of the best are along Cascade Ave. north of the Colorado College campus and on Wood Ave. 1 block to the west. A leisurely bicycle ride through this area would be of interest to history and architecture buffs.

To see these mansions start at the corner of Cascade Ave. and San Miguel St.; cycle **west** on San Miguel for 1 block. **Right** (N) on Wood Ave. **Left** (W) on Fontanero St. **Left** (S) on Alamo Ave. **Right** (W) on Columbia St. **Right** (N) on Culebra Ave. **Right** (E) on Fontanero St. **Right** (S) on Cascade Ave. and back to San Miguel St.

Just to the south of this area is Colorado College, founded in 1874. Most of our tours around Colorado Springs start from the north or south edge of this campus on Cascade Ave.

For more Colorado Springs-and-vicinity route information see Tours 20, 21, 22, and 23.

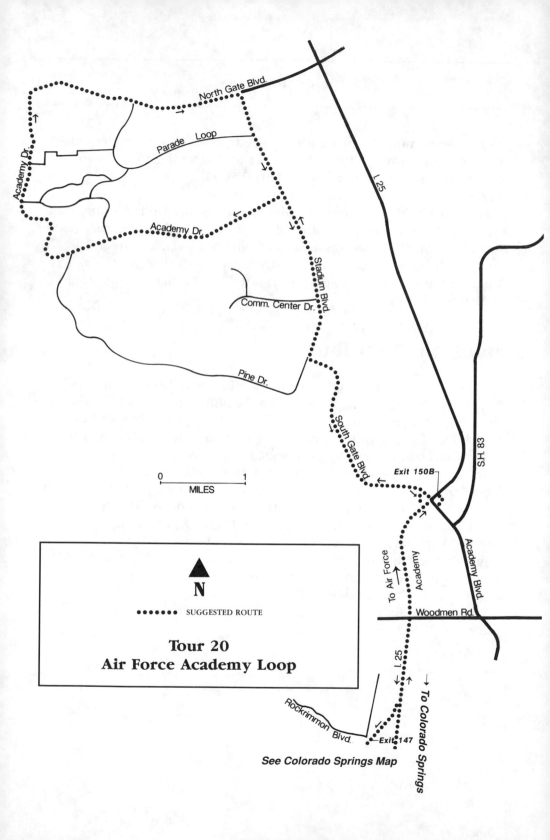

North Gate Blvd.

Academy Dr.

Parade Loop

Academy Dr.

I 25

Stadium Blvd.

Comm. Center Dr.

Pine Dr.

South Gate Blvd.

S.H. 83

Exit 150B

To Air Force

Academy

Academy Blvd.

Woodmen Rd.

I 25

0   1
MILES

N

•••••• SUGGESTED ROUTE

**Tour 20
Air Force Academy Loop**

Rockrimmon Blvd.

Exit 147

To Colorado Springs

See Colorado Springs Map

20

Air Force Academy Loop

Distance	36 mi round trip from Colorado Springs (6012′)
Actual Climbing	1800′
Helpful Maps	*Colorado Road Atlas*, pages T6, D25, D46. Colorado Springs Area Bike Map. (See Appendix A.)
Terrain	Some steep climbs on the grounds of the Academy.
Roads and Traffic	You will have to ride for 2 mi on the shoulder of I-25 from Colorado Springs to the entrance of the Air Force Academy. (See page 30 for safe Interstate riding suggestions.) On the Academy grounds you may encounter some tourist traffic, but it usually moves slowly.

0.0   **Start** tour in Colorado Springs at the **north** edge of the Colorado College campus, corner of San Miguel St. and Cascade Ave.

Cycle **north** on Cascade Ave., passing through old Colorado Springs area of fine, beautifully preserved mansions dating from the 1870s when General William Jackson Palmer established the posh resort town that became Colorado Springs.

2.2   **Right** (E) on Winters Dr. at stop light for 1 block.

2.4   **Left** (N) on Nevada. 4-lane divided highway.

223

4.7   **Merge** with I-25 and ride on shoulder for 2 mi to Exit #150B for the **south** entrance of the Air Force Academy. Use caution on narrow bridge and at interchanges.

6.7   **Exit right** at #150B (south entrance of the Air Force Academy) and **cross over** I-25 heading **west**.

7.0   **Enter** Air Force Academy on South Gate Blvd. Ask for map at gatehouse.

9.3   **Right** (N) on Stadium Blvd.

11.5 **Left** (W) on Academy Dr., following Visitors Center signs.

You are now on the course used in the road race for the World Cycling Championship here in 1986. The racers thought that the course was too easy—hills not steep enough or long enough. Make your own judgement!

15.5 Visitors Center. Air Force exhibits here plus snack shop, rest rooms, gift shop. The famous Cadet Chapel is a short walk away. Altitude here is 7280′.

Continue on Academy Dr., and up to two scenic overlooks.

22.2 **Right** (S) onto Stadium Blvd. (just before the B-25 bomber).

25.7 **Left** (E) on South Gate Blvd.

27.8 **Leave** Air Force Academy.

28.2 **Right** (S) onto shoulder of I-25. Use caution on narrow bridge and at interchanges.

31.3   **Right** (W) leaving I-25 at Exit #147 (Rockrimmon Rd.) just before No Bicycles sign.

Left (S) immediately on Mark Dabling Blvd.

32.5   **Left** (E) on Garden of the Gods Rd.

32.9   **Right** (S) on Nevada Ave.

33.7   **Right** (W) on Winters Dr. for 1 block.

33.9   **Left** (S) on Cascade Ave.

36.1   **Finish** in Colorado Springs at corner of Cascade Ave. and San Miguel St. at **north** edge of Colorado College campus.

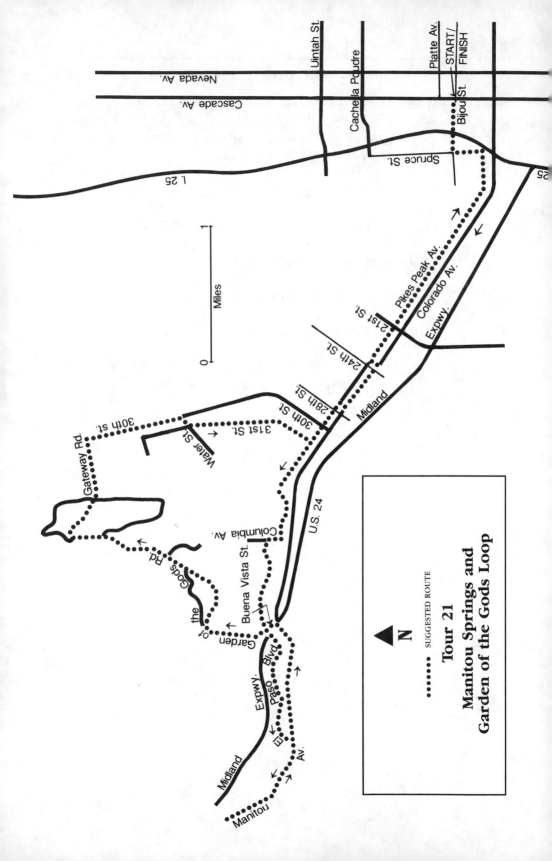

Tour 21
Manitou Springs and
Garden of the Gods Loop

• • • • • • SUGGESTED ROUTE

N

21

Manitou Springs and Garden of the Gods Loop

Distance	15 mi round trip from Colorado Springs (6012') to Manitou Springs (6412')
Actual Climbing	1000'
Helpful Maps	*Colorado Road Atlas*, pages T6, T7. Colorado Springs Area Bike Map. (See Appendix A.)
Terrain	Easy riding except for the rolling hills in the Garden of the Gods Park, which will involve some climbing.

0.0 **Start** tour at the corner of Cascade Ave. and Bijou St. in downtown Colorado Springs.

Cross bridge going **west** on Bijou St. and **continue** 1 block to Spruce St.

0.4 **Left** (S) on Spruce for 2 blocks. Follow Bike Route signs.

0.7 **Right** (W) on Pikes Peak Ave.

2.5 **Left** (S) on 24th St. for 1 block to Colorado Ave.

Right (W) on Colorado Ave. into Old Colorado City.

Between 24th St. and 27th St. you will find restored Old Colorado City, quaint shops, and restaurants (and a very good bike shop). It's well worth a visit. Lock up your bike and walk through this interesting and historical old town site established in 1859, 12 years before Colorado Springs. It was a booming frontier town—the first El Paso County settlement—set up to monopolize the wagon trade headed up Ute Pass to the gold mine camps.

2.7   **Right** (N) on 28th St. for 1 block.

Left (W) on Pikes Peak Ave. for 1.2 mi to T at Columbia Ave.

Straight ahead is the side gate of the Garden of the Gods Campground, 3704 W. Colorado Ave. (719) 476-9450. It has good tent sites and AYH 4-bunk cabins. A good choice for camping, especially if you plan to spend some time in the area.

4.2   **Right** (N) on Columbia Ave. at T for 1 block.

4.3   **Left** (W) on El Paso Blvd. and stay on El Paso for 1 mi until it curves down and ends at Manitou Ave.

Spectacular red-rock formations gave the park its name—The Garden of the Gods.

5.3   **Right** (W) on Manitou Ave. which leads you into the center of Manitou Springs.

6.0   Manitou Springs. Population 4475, elevation 6412′.

Manitou Springs, at the foot of the Ute Pass, was an area popular with early explorers and settlers, trappers and goldseekers; and before that with the Ute Indians. Then in the early 1870s it became a fashionable spa renowned for the therapeutic values of the waters of its bubbling springs.

Restored Victorian houses, studios of artists and craftsmen with the ambiance of the early days, contrast with the more carnival-like atmosphere of the Manitou Ave. shops. There are many motels, restaurants, and campgrounds in Manitou Springs.

To continue to the Garden of the Gods Park, **retrace east** on Manitou Ave. 1 mi to Buena Vista St., following Garden of the Gods sign.

7.0   **Left** (N) on Buena Vista St., curving **right** under U.S. 24 overpass, and then immediately **left** (N). Keep following Garden of the Gods signs to Garden of the Gods Rd., and enter the park on an upgrade.

7.2   **Keep right** at sign past Balanced Rock.

Continue on curving roads through spectacular red-rock formations. There are plenty of picnic places in the park. Rolling roads will give you some strenuous climbs to Gateway Rd. and the south exit at 30th St.

10.6   **Right** (S) on 30th St.

11.3   **Right** (W) on Water St. and downhill for 1 block.

229

11.4   **Left** (S) on 31st St. for 1 mi.

12.3   **Left** (E) on Pikes Peak Ave. following Bike Route sign.

14.7   **Left** (N) on Spruce St. for 2 blocks.

14.8   **Right** (E) on Bijou St. and **pass over** bridge.

15.0   **Finish** in Colorado Springs at corner of Bijou St. and Cascade Ave.

COLORADO SPRINGS
Start/Finish
See Colorado Springs Map

U.S. 24

I. 25

S.H. 9

S.H. 115

U.S. 85/87

CANON
CITY

U.S. 50

Texas Creek

S.H. 115

Penrose

Florence

U.S. 50

S.H. 67

PUEBLO

Wetmore

S.H. 96

S.H. 69

S.H. 96

Westcliffe

Silver Cliff

S.H. 165

0   15
Miles

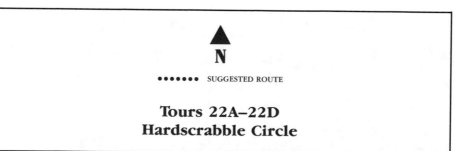

N

•••••• SUGGESTED ROUTE

**Tours 22A–22D
Hardscrabble Circle**

22

Hardscrabble Circle

Distance	185 mi
Suggested Time	4 days
Total Climbing	8000′

This tour, starting in Colorado Springs, includes the Hardscrabble Century (a 100 mi ride that starts and ends in Florence). The popular Hardscrabble Century Ride is sponsored every year in mid-September by the Colorado Springs Strada Bicycling Club.

Participation in this ride has grown steadily since 1970, when a Colorado Springs cyclist, Steve Hall, scouted the route and rode it with a few friends. Now on National Century Day hundreds of cyclists turn out for the Hardscrabble Century Ride.

Our Hardscrabble Circle is planned as a 4-day tour starting and ending in Colorado Springs, with an average riding day of 45 mi.

Terrain Some climbs and descents on Col. 115 from Colorado Springs. On the Hardscrabble Century route out of Florence the first half is strenuous climbing, the second half is easier downhill riding.

Roads and Traffic Good shoulder on Col. 115. Very little traffic on the country roads between Florence and Texas Creek, where you join U.S. 50, which has an adequate shoulder. The only narrow, no-shoulder road is on Col. 115 from Cañon City back to Florence.

Colorado Springs to Florence

Distance	42 mi from Colorado Springs (6012′) to Florence (5187′)
Actual Climbing	1500′
Helpful Maps	*Colorado Road Atlas*, pages T6, D25, D24. (See Appendix A.)
Terrain	Several long hills of a mile or more in length.
Roads and Traffic	Good wide shoulder all the way after the first few miles getting out of Colorado Springs.

0.0   **Leave** Colorado Springs from the corner of Cache la Poudre St. and Cascade Ave. at the **south** edge of Colorado College campus, cycling **south** on Cascade Ave.

2.0   **Left** (E) on Fountain Blvd. for 1 block.

       Right (S) on Tejon St. and **pass under** I-25.

2.5   **Left** (E) on Brookside for 1 block.

2.6   **Right** (S) on Nevada Ave. (Col. 115). Use caution riding in city traffic to the edge of Colorado Springs.

3.5   **Continue south** on Col. 115. Long up- and down-grades of a mile or more. 10′ shoulder. Trouble-free riding, with good views of snowcapped mountain peaks.

35.5 **Pass** small town of Penrose. Motel, restaurant.

35.8 **Cross** U.S. 50.

Col. 115 becomes a quiet country road with 2′ shoulder for 6 mi into Florence.

41.8 **Finish** in downtown Florence at junction of Col. 115 and Col. 67 North.

Florence Population 2987, elevation 5187′.

This is a small edge-of-the-mountains town. The discovery of the second oil well in the United States occurred near Florence in 1898, and coal mining was important to the development and prosperity of the town at the turn of the century.

In Florence there is one small, basic motel, The Riviera (719) 784-6570. There is also a B&B, the Florence Hotel (719) 784-3681, and there are restaurants and stores. Camping is allowed in Florence City Park, 2 blocks north of the main street on State Rt. 67 north. However, best bet for a campground would be to detour 3 mi east on U.S. 50 where Col. 115 crosses it before going into Florence. Floyd's RV Park, cafe, and store (719) 372-3385.

22B

▲
Florence to Westcliffe

Distance	39 mi from Florence (5187′) to Westcliffe (7888′)
Actual Climbing	4500′
Helpful Maps	*Colorado Road Atlas*, page D30. National Forest Map: San Isabel. (See Appendix A.)
Terrain	This is the day you will do most of the climbing, through the Wet Mountain Range, to altitudes of more than 9000′ on the way to Westcliffe.
Roads and Traffic	Low traffic count on backcountry roads.

0.0 **Leave** downtown Florence going **east** on Col. 115 to Col. 67 **south**.

0.8 **Right** (S) on Col. 67. No shoulder on flat road running through cactus-dotted landscape.

10.1 Note Hardscrabble history on Point-of-Interest sign. No doubt that the name Hardscrabble came from the difficulties the early settlers had in making a living in this rugged territory.

12.2 Small town of Wetmore, elevation 5990′. Gas station and convenience store.

Riders on one of Colorado's most famous century rides, the Hardscrabble Century, making an early morning start from Florence.

A welcome banana break is furnished by the Colorado Springs Strada Bicycling Club, sponsor of the Hardscrabble Century.

12.6 **Right** (S) at stop sign to join Col. 96. 2′ to 4′ shoulder on this road passing through wooded, rolling country.

15.4 **Enter** San Isabel National Forest and begin steeper climbing up through the Wet Mountain Range.

18.2 Terrain getting more mountainous as you proceed. It is essentially climbing, but with alternating ups and downs.

20.2 Steep climb. 8% grade just before McKenzie Junction.

22.0 **Pass** Col. 165 on the left at McKenzie Junction.

Continue west on Col. 96, which levels off somewhat running through meadowland, but climbs to over 9000′ before starting down.

28.6 High point with views of the Sangre de Cristo Mountains ahead.

29.6 Nice downhill—finally!

37.8 **Continue** on spectacular downs into small town of Silver Cliff.

Silver Cliff. Population 280, elevation 7982′. This was one of Colorado's silver-boomtowns, reaching its zenith in 1880. Small motel, restaurant, Kleins Campground.

38.2 **Continue west** to the picturesque main street of Westcliffe—end of Col. 96 at junction of Col. 69.

39.2 **Finish** in Westcliffe at junction of Col. 69.

Westcliffe   Population 324, elevation 7888′.

This is a compact little town—the big town of the Wet Mountain Valley. Westcliffe was established when the Denver and Rio Grande narrow gauge railway extended its tracks from Cañon City to 1 mile west of Silver Cliff in 1881. The Sangre de Cristo Mountains sweep up from the western edge of the valley.

After crossing the high point near McKenzie Junction cyclists can look forward to this splendid downhill run toward Silver Cliff and Westcliffe.

An ocean once covered this valley. It's easy to imagine the shoreline where the Sangre de Cristo range rises from the valley floor.

In Westcliffe there are motels, restaurants, and stores. We found that the best bet for lodging was the Westcliffe Inn, south on Col. 69 at the edge of town (719) 783-9277. It would be wise to call ahead for a reservation.

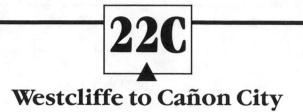

22C

Westcliffe to Cañon City

Distance   52 mi from Westcliffe (7888') to Cañon City (5332')

Actual   500'
Climbing

Helpful Maps   *Colorado Road Atlas*, pages D30, D24, T4. (See Appendix A.)

Terrain   Essentially descending, toward and along the Arkansas River.

Roads and   Low-traffic country roads until you join U.S. 50 at
Traffic   Texas Creek. 2' to 4' shoulder on U.S. 50.

  0.0   **Leave** Westcliffe going **north** on Col. 69. No shoulder to 1' shoulder on this quiet road through the Wet Mountain Valley with the towering Sangre de Cristo Mountain Range on your left.

         Gentle downgrade through ranch country, the terrain becoming more dry and barren as you progress.

13.4   Small settlement of Hillside with small store and gas station. Interesting views down the valley.

         Then start long 12 mi descent to Texas Creek through progressively steeper canyons as you approach the Arkansas River.

24.8   **Right** (E) on U.S. 50. Texas Creek Trading Post at intersection. Small store and post office dating from 1885.

Continue (E) on U.S. 50, following the Arkansas River downstream. 2' to 4' shoulder. Watch for rafts and kayaks on the whitewater of the rushing Arkansas River.

39.9   **Pass** small settlement of Parkdale.

Cross bridge over Arkansas River at the point where it enters the Royal Gorge.

41.6   Steep climb up to the Royal Gorge area. 8' shoulder.

43.0   KOA Campground on Royal Gorge Rd. 0.5 mi south, and various other campgrounds and motels in the area.

You can add a visit to the Royal Gorge Park by riding **south** on Royal Gorge Road for 4.3 mi with a very long, very steep climb on the way. Entrance fee to the park is $6.00, which allows you to ride or walk over the world's highest suspension bridge between two 150' high steel towers over the 1055' deep canyon.

Back on U.S. 50, the road flattens out and then makes a descent to the city limits of Cañon City. 6' shoulder.

49.6   **Pass** Rustic Lamphouse Campground 1 mi west of town. 4-lane, no-shoulder road into city.

50.2   **Pass** Colorado State Penitentiary.

51.3   **Left** (N) 1 block, following Business U.S. 50 to Main St.

243

51.6   **Finish** in Cañon City at corner of Main St. and 5th St.

Cañon City   Population 13,037, elevation 5332'.

Interesting turn-of-the-century buildings on Main St. Note fancy cornices and ornate tops preserved on many of them. At the corner of Main and 5th note the large sign showing the cattle brands of the area ranches. Most motels and restaurants are on U.S. 50 on the east side of town, and the RV Station Campground is at the eastern edge of the city.

Cañon City is on the route from Pueblo to Gunnison. Note the interesting roof lines on turn-of-the-century buildings on the main street.

Cañon City to Colorado Springs

Distance 52 mi from Cañon City (5332′) to Colorado Springs (6012′)

Actual Climbing 1500′

Helpful Maps *Colorado Road Atlas*, pages T4, D24, D25, T6. (See Appendix A.)

Terrain Flat road from Cañon City to Florence. Then a series of 1 mi ups and downs back to Colorado Springs.

Roads and Traffic Col. 115 is narrow and often busy between Cañon City and Florence. Best not to do it at commuting time.

0.0 **Leave** Cañon City from corner of Main St. and 5th St. going **east** on Main St.

0.4 **Right** (S) on 9th St. (Col. 115). 3′ shoulder out of town, then no shoulder on road to Florence.

8.0 Florence. Restaurants and stores.

   Continue east out of Florence on Col. 115. 2′ shoulder.

14.0 **Cross** U.S. 50 and **continue northeast** on Col. 115.

14.3 **Pass** small town of Penrose. Motel and restaurant.

Long ups and downs of a mile or more with trouble-free riding on the 10' shoulder.

46.0   **Use caution** at interchanges, which occur more frequently as you near Colorado Springs.

Col. 115 becomes Nevada Ave. at south edge of Colorado Springs.

47.3   **Left** (W) on Brookside St. for 1 block.

Right (N) on Tejon St. and **pass under** I-25.

Left (W) on Fountain Blvd. for 1 block to Cascade Ave.

49.7   **Right** (N) on Cascade Ave.

51.8   **Finish** tour in Colorado Springs at **south** edge of the Colorado College campus, corner of Cascade Ave. and Cache la Poudre St.

See page 219 for Colorado Springs information.

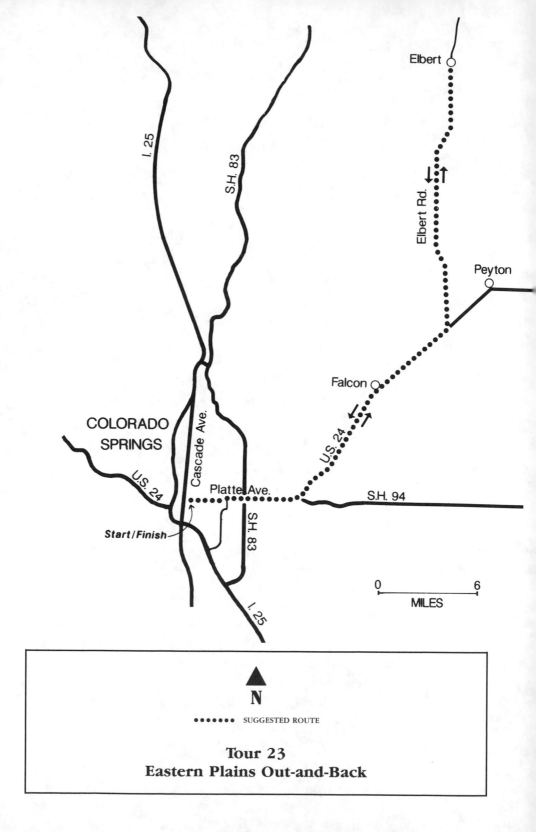

I. 25

S.H. 83

Elbert

Elbert Rd.

Peyton

Falcon

COLORADO
SPRINGS

Cascade Ave.

U.S. 24

Platte Ave.

S.H. 94

U.S. 24

S.H. 83

Start/Finish

I. 25

0   6
MILES

N

•••••••• SUGGESTED ROUTE

Tour 23
Eastern Plains Out-and-Back

23

Eastern Plains Out-and-Back

Distance   79 mi round trip from Colorado Springs (6012′)

Actual Climbing   1200′

Helpful Maps   *Colorado Road Atlas*, pages T6, T7, D25. Colorado Springs Area Bike Map. (See Appendix A.)

Terrain   Rolling grasslands. Easy riding unless you encounter a headwind. No major climbs.

Roads and Traffic   You will encounter some city traffic getting out of Colorado Springs. Then you will have an 8′ shoulder to the Elbert turnoff. The road to Elbert is rough in places, but it has a low traffic count.

Special Notes   This ride to Falcon (6830′) and Elbert (6720′), is a favorite early season ride for the local club cyclists. You ride far to the east of the mountains into remote-feeling countryside. Just a taste of the vast spaces of eastern Colorado, stretching toward Kansas. It would be a good idea to take a picnic lunch. No restaurants on this route.

The local bicycle clubs often shorten this tour to a "drive-to" starting in Falcon. This allows you to ride through the best parts of the rolling grasslands and avoid the city traffic at the edge of Colorado Springs. You can park in the Falcon Middle School parking lot and do the ride from Falcon to Elbert and retrace. Distance: 45 mi.

0.0   **Start** from downtown Colorado Springs at the corner of Cascade Ave. and Platte Ave.

Cycle east on Platte Ave. (which becomes U.S. 24) passing equestrian statue of General Palmer, founder of Colorado Springs.

3.5   **Use caution** at interchange at Academy Blvd.

Continue out of town following U.S. 24. 8′ shoulder.

6.3   **Bear left** (NE) at junction with Col. 94 staying on U.S. 24. 10′ shoulder.

You will be cycling through rolling grasslands and may see deer or elk ranging across the hills.

15.0   **Pass** Falcon Food Store.

15.5   Small town of Falcon (6830′). Convenience store. Antique Santa Fe train on the R.R. track in town when we passed through.

Continue (NE) on U.S. 24.

21.1   **Left** (N) on Elbert Rd. still through grasslands.

31.5   Elbert County line. Pine forests replace grasslands. From here on the road might not be in very good condition, but you can pick your way around potholes.

38.0   Small town of Elbert (6720′). It's not much more than a ghost town, but 0.3 mi north of town there is a gas station and general store. You'll probably be glad you brought a picnic lunch.

Return by retracing to Falcon and Colorado Springs.

70.5 To avoid traffic into town on U.S. 24, at junction of Col. 94 **take** Exit #3 (N) onto Peterson Rd., which curves to the **west** and becomes Galley Rd.

71.9 **Cross** Powers Blvd.

73.5 **Right** (NW) on San Miguel St., which curves around to the **west**.

74.4 **Cross** Academy Blvd.

74.9 **Jog left** on Chelton Rd. and back to San Miguel St., going **west**.

75.9 **Left** (S) on Alexander Rd. for 4 blocks.

76.3 **Right** (W) on Cache la Poudre St.

78.7 **Left** (S) on Cascade Ave.

79.3 **Finish** at corner of Platte Ave. and Cascade Ave.

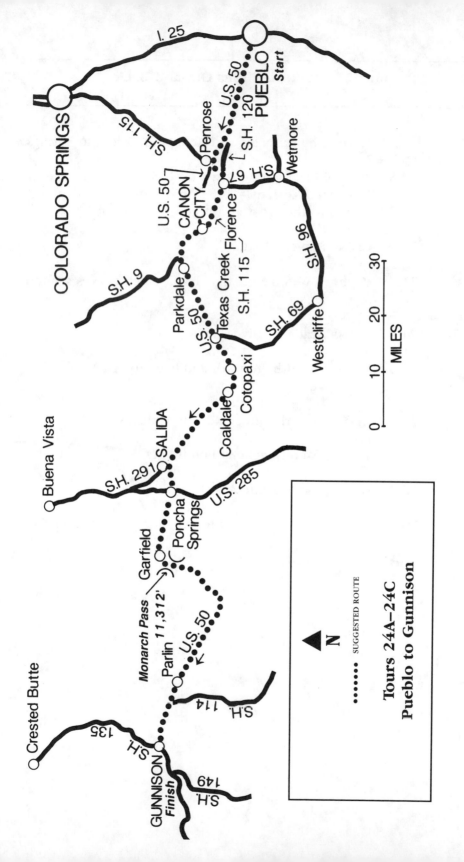

Tours 24A–24C
Pueblo to Gunnison

•••••• SUGGESTED ROUTE

N

MILES

0   10   20   30

24

Pueblo to Gunnison

Connecting route

Distance 166 mi from Pueblo (4695′) to Gunnison (7703′)

Suggested Time 3 days

Total Climbing 7900′

Terrain Long rolling ups and downs out of Pueblo on U.S. 50. After Cañon City you will ride along the Arkansas River—going upstream. There is one long climb over Monarch Pass, elevation 11,312′. Then you ride through a wide green valley following Tomichi Creek—going downstream to Gunnison.

Roads and Traffic Once you are away from Pueblo city traffic, U.S. 50 is usually not heavily traveled. Good shoulder on the route, except for these three areas: the back road from Florence to Cañon City is flat, but has a 6.5 mi stretch of no shoulder. After Texas Creek U.S. 50 has minimal shoulder for 32 mi—be alert on this stretch. The road over Monarch Pass has no shoulder, but there is a passing lane for traffic on the steep parts, thus widening the road for cyclists also.

Pueblo to Cañon City

Distance   42 mi from Pueblo (4695′) to Cañon City (5332′)

Actual Climbing   1000′

Helpful Maps   *Colorado Road Atlas*, pages T21, D31, D24, T4. (See Appendix A.)

Pueblo   Population 101,686, elevation 4695′.

Motels, restaurants, stores, and bike shops. See page 335 for more Pueblo information.

0.0   **Leave** midtown Pueblo from the corner of 4th St. and Greenwood St., following 1-way Greenwood St. **north** to 25th St.

Left (W) on 25th St. for 1 block to Elizabeth St.

Right (N) on Elizabeth St. to U.S. 50.

2.8   **Left** (W) on U.S. 50 and out of town. **Use caution** as you pass the shopping center areas at the edge of town, and be alert for turning cars.

U.S. 50 runs through arid plains, a rolling road with long ups and downs. 10′ shoulder.

9.8   Best Western Inn at Pueblo West (719) 547-2111. A good solution to an overnight stay in this area—easy to get to by bicycle. To reach the motel, **left** (S) on McCulloch Blvd. for 0.5 mi to the motel.

25.0   Floyd's RV Park (719) 372-3385. Cafe and store.

28.0   **Right** at cloverleaf exit for Col. 115.

   Left (S) on Col. 115, crossing over U.S. 50. Nice change to quiet country road, 2′ shoulder.

34.0   Florence. Population 2987, elevation 5187′. For more information about Florence see Hardscrabble Tour 22A.

   Continue west out of Florence on Col. 115 toward Cañon City. Flat road, no shoulder for 6.5 mi. Then 3′ shoulder into town.

42.0   **Finish** in Cañon City at junction of Col. 115 and U.S. 50.

Cañon City   Population 13,037, elevation 5332′.

Most motels and restaurants are on U.S. 50, toward the east end of town. RV Station campground at east edge of town. The downtown area is 1 block to the north of U.S. 50. Main St. is interesting with turn-of-the-century and earlier buildings along both sides of the street. At corner of Main and 5th St. note the large sign showing the cattle brands of the area ranches.

Cañon City to Salida

Distance	59 mi from Cañon City (5332′) to Salida (7036′)
Actual Climbing	2200′
Helpful Maps	*Colorado Road Atlas*, pages T4, D24, D23, T18. National Forest Map: San Isabel. (See Appendix A.)

0.0   **Leave** Cañon City going **west** on U.S. 50 with a climb out of town, passing Colorado State Penitentiary. 6′ shoulder.

2.0   **Pass** Rustic Lamphouse Campground.

Road flattens out at Royal Gorge area.

8.6   KOA campground 0.5 mi south on Royal Gorge Rd. There are several other campgrounds in the area.

To visit Royal Gorge turn **left** (S) on Royal Gorge Rd. for 4.3 mi to entrance gate. Very long, very steep climb involved in getting to the park. Entrance fee is $6.00, which allows you to ride or walk over the Royal Gorge Bridge and includes one other ride on aerial tram or incline railway.

Continue west from Royal Gorge area on U.S. 50.

9.8   Steep downhill. 8′ shoulder.

11.6   At bottom **cross** the Arkansas River at the point where it enters the Royal Gorge.

The Arkansas is a famous white-water river. You'll
see kayaks and river rafters all along this stretch.
The road runs along the river, a continual climb
upstream. If you're lucky you'll pick up a tail wind.
Plenty of picnic spots and campgrounds but not
many motels along this next stretch.

22.7   Texas Creek. Small store and a post office dating
from 1885.

Road has minimal shoulder for next 32 mi—watch in
your rearview mirror for RVs and trucks.

33.5   Loma Linda Motel and KOA Campground.

35.0   Small town of Cotopaxi with grocery store.

39.0   Small town of Coaldale. Lazy J Motel, Cafe, and
Campground.

Spectacular views of the Sangre de Cristo Mountains
ahead.

55.0   Beginning of 8′ shoulder.

57.2   Four Seasons Campground. Good tent sites on the
river.

59.0   **Finish** in Salida at junction of U.S. 50 (Rainbow
Blvd.) and Oak St.

Salida   Population 4870, elevation 7036′.

Plenty of motels and restaurants on 2 mi stretch of
U.S. 50 as you enter town. Other stores and a bike
shop in the real town center, which is to the north of
this highway. It's worth cycling in to see the old
town in contrast to the tourist-oriented area where
the motels are located.

24C

Salida to Gunnison

Distance	65 mi from Salida (7036′) to Gunnison (7703′)
Actual Climbing	4700′
Helpful Maps	*Colorado Road Atlas*, pages T18, D23, D22. National Forest Maps: San Isabel, Gunnison. (See Appendix A.)

0.0 **Leave** Salida on U.S. 50 West. 4-lane highway with 3′ shoulder.

4.0 **Pass** small town of Poncha Springs, **continuing west** on U.S. 50.

9.9 Poncha Springs/Salida KOA Campground.

12.7 Start of climb up to Monarch Pass. No shoulder, but passing lane for traffic on the steep parts.

16.8 Monarch Motel and restaurant.

20.6 **Pass** Monarch Ski Area.

22.4 Monarch Pass crest on the Continental Divide. Elevation 11,312′. Gain of 4276′ from Salida.

Steep descent. 6% grade. No shoulder, but continuous climbing lane for oncoming traffic helps widen the road for you too. Sharp curves. Don't let your speed get away from you.

32.8 **Pass** small town of Sargents. Cafe and grocery.

Gradual downhill. No shoulder for 2 mi.

34.5 Start of 4' shoulder.

40.8 **Pass** Monarch Valley Ranch Campground.

44.8 Gunnison County line. 10' shoulder starts.

Level road running through wide green valley following Tomichi Creek.

53.1 **Pass** small town of Parlin. Small store and gas station.

63.3 Tomachi Village Motel and Restaurant.

65.1 **Finish** in Gunnison at corner of U.S. 50 (Tomichi Ave.) and Col. 135.

Gunnison   Population 5785, elevation 7703'.

Motels, restaurants, stores, and a good bike shop. KOA Campground 1.6 mi west, on road running south from U.S. 50. Follow signs. For more information about Gunnison see Tour 25A.

The route follows U.S. 50 through the broad valley of Tomichi Creek as it nears Gunnison.

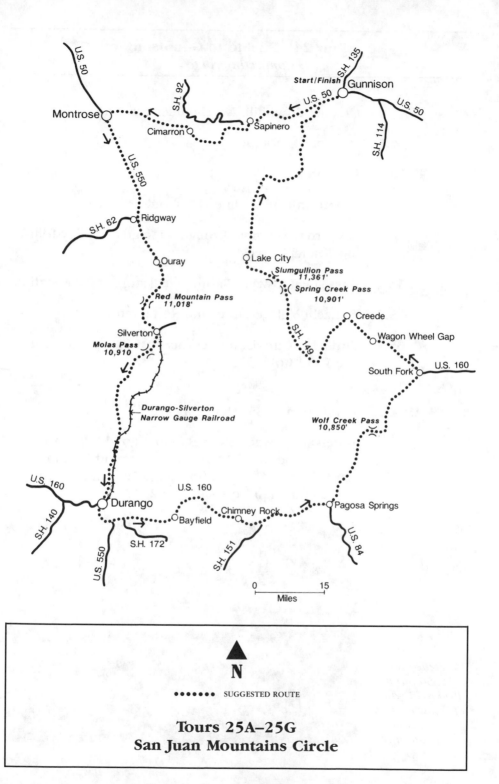

U.S. 50

S.H. 135

S.H. 92

Start/Finish
Gunnison

U.S. 50

U.S. 50

Montrose

Cimarron

Sapinero

S.H. 114

U.S. 550

S.H. 62   Ridgway

Lake City

Ouray

Slumgullion Pass
11,361'

Red Mountain Pass
11,018'

Spring Creek Pass
10,901'

Creede

Silverton

Wagon Wheel Gap

Molas Pass
10,910'

S.H. 149

South Fork   U.S. 160

Durango-Silverton
Narrow Gauge Railroad

Wolf Creek Pass
10,850'

U.S. 160

U.S. 160

Chimney Rock

Pagosa Springs

S.H. 140

Durango

Bayfield

S.H. 172

S.H. 151

U.S. 84

U.S. 550

0   15
Miles

N

••••••• SUGGESTED ROUTE

Tours 25A–25G
San Juan Mountains Circle

25

San Juan Mountains Circle

Distance	413 mi
Suggested Time	7 days
Total Climbing	23,900′

Gunnison, 196 miles southwest of Denver, is the starting point for this tour, which takes you through some of the most beautiful and rugged mountain areas in Colorado. This is one of the most popular tours conducted by The Colorado Heart Cycle Association (see Appendix B), a nonprofit cycling group which has been conducting tours since 1978. It is a difficult tour and you should be in excellent cycling condition to ride it. You should also be sure to have adequately low gears on your bicycle.

Gunnison to Montrose

Distance	66 mi from Gunnison (7703′) to Montrose (5794′)
Actual Climbing	2800′ in 3 climbs
Helpful Maps	*Colorado Road Atlas*, pages D22, D21. National Forest Maps: Gunnison Basin, Uncompahgre. (See Appendix A.)
Terrain	Serious climbing and steep downhills, except for 25 mi out of Gunnison.
Roads and Traffic	Good shoulders over much of the route, but some riding on narrow, no-shoulder roads. Moderate traffic on U.S. 50.

Gunnison Population 5785, elevation 7703′.

Settled in 1874 in the fertile Gunnison River valley, the town was named for Captain John Gunnison, who had surveyed a railroad route through the area as early as 1853. Cattle ranching is important in the valleys of the Gunnison River and Tomichi Creek. You will be riding through cattle country as you approach Gunnison from the east, and as you continue west you will enter the Curecanti National Recreation Area, created by the construction of 3 dams on the Gunnison River.

An interesting side trip to make from Gunnison is the 56 mi round trip to Crested Butte for lunch. See Tour 26.

In Gunnison there are plenty of motels, restaurants, stores, and a good bike shop. There is a KOA Campground to the southwest 1.6 mi out of town off of U.S. 50. The Tomichi Village Motel (303) 641-1131 just east of Gunnison is the traditional starting point for the Heart Cycle Group. If you are driving to the start of this tour you can arrange to leave your car parked at the motel until your return.

0.0   **Leave** Gunnison from the corner of U.S. 50 (Tomichi Ave.) and Col. 135 (Main St.) going **west**. 10′ shoulder.

1.6   KOA Campground on road to the left—1 mi south.

You will be cycling on a flat road joining and following the Gunnison River. 4′ shoulder along this stretch except for about 2 mi with no shoulder.

Pass through rocky canyon. You will be in the Curecanti National Recreation Area.

9.6   **Follow** along **north** edge of Blue Mesa Reservoir.

11.5   Stevens Creek Campground.

Some climbing through mesa country alongside the Blue Mesa Reservoir. Bleak-looking landscape.

21.6   **Cross** bridge over Blue Mesa Reservoir. Now good 6′ shoulder through big open spaces.

24.9   Small settlement of Sapinero. Elevation 7600′. Small store.

27.2 **Pass** Blue Mesa Dam and start first real climb of the day.

Lake Fort Campground (0.3 mi north on Col. 92).

28.9 Top of climb. Cafe and store.

Start of no shoulder on narrow rolling road.

32.7 Steep downhill with hairpin turn and more sharp curves through narrow canyon.

34.8 Bottom. Start 2.2 mi climb up out of canyon and into open fields. Highest point at 8704′.

37.1 Long, steep downhill into green meadowland area. No shoulder, but climbing lane for oncoming traffic helps widen the road for you too.

41.3 Cimarron Valley RV Park.

41.9 Montrose County line.

43.3 Pleasant Valley Ranch Campground and store.

43.5 Start of 6′ shoulder. Still going down.

45.9 Small town of Cimarron. Elevation 6900′. Small motel, cafe, store.

46.3 End of descent. End of shoulder. Beginning of another climb.

47.7 Start of 3′ shoulder.

51.3 Cerro Summit. Elevation 7909′.

51.4 Steep downhill.

55.5 At bottom into arid sagebrush country. 10′ shoulder starts.

58.1 **Pass** junction of Col. 347, road to Black Canyon of the Gunnison Monument.

60.6 RV Camperland.

64.3 Montrose city limits at end of long downhill.

66.0 **Finish** in Montrose on Main St. (U.S. 50) at corner of Townsend Ave. (U.S. 550).

Montrose   Population 8722, elevation 5794′.

In Montrose there are plenty of motels and restaurants on U.S. 50 as you enter town. Two in-town campgrounds: Mountain View (1 block to the north of U.S. 50) and KOA (2 blocks to the south). Bike shops and restaurants in the downtown area and more motels south on U.S. 550. On U.S. 550 as you leave town going south, you will see the Russell Stover Candy Factory, which has a factory store for all you chocolate freaks!

Montrose to Ouray

Distance	37 mi from Montrose (5794') to Ouray (7706')
Actual Climbing	2100'
Helpful Maps	*Colorado Road Atlas*, pages D21, D27. National Forest Map: Uncompahgre. (See Appendix A.)
Terrain	Mostly a gentle, continuous climb.
Roads and Traffic	An equal amount of shoulder and no-shoulder riding through this popular area. In July and August there will be quite a bit of traffic on these roads. Best plan: get an early start before the traffic builds up.
Special Notes	This is quite an easy riding day. But it's good to arrive early in Ouray and have time to explore the town. You should also plan to get a very early start on the next day because you will have a lot of climbing to do.

0.0 **Leave** Montrose from corner of Main St. and Townsend Ave. (U.S. 50 and U.S. 550).

Proceed south on U.S. 550 out of town on wide 4-lane highway with 10' shoulder.

3.4 Ute Indian Museum just off highway to the right is worth a visit.

4.8   Beginning of 15 mi of no shoulder. You will be riding through a broad, flat valley with mountains in the distance.

12.7   Small town of Colona. Small cafe.

16.1   Road gets a bit wider with gradual climb into more forested, narrower canyon.

18.4   Scenery becomes more interesting and now you will have a 4' to 2' shoulder for 7 mi.

25.4   End of shoulder on downhill into small town of Ridgway. Motel, cafe, store.

27.0   Junction of Col. 62.

   Stay on U.S. 550, straight ahead to Ouray. Steady, but not steep climbing.

29.2   Webers Campground.

31.6   Sunshine Valley Ranch Campground.

32.7   KOA Campground is west on Col. 23.

   Continue climb through some of the most beautiful scenery in Colorado, following the Uncompahgre River upstream.

33.9   **Enter** Uncompahgre National Forest.

35.6   Picnic area in Ouray City Park at north edge of town.

37.2   **Finish** in Ouray on Main St. at corner of 7th Ave.

Ouray   Population 684, elevation 7706'.

This is the town that is called the "Switzerland of America," perhaps because of the sharply rising Alpine-like peaks that jut up from the very edge of town. Dating from 1891, Ouray is a fascinating old mining town, its main street now walked by tourists rather than miners.

Riding into Ouray, a fascinating old mining town dating from 1891. With its spectacular mountain backdrop it's easy to see why Ouray is called the "Switzerland of America."

Motels, restaurants, and stores. An in-town campground, the 4J + 1 + 1 (303) 325-4418, is 2 blocks west of Main St. A good motel we have stayed in is the Best Western Twin Peaks Motel (303) 325-4427, 1 block west of Main St. on the road to Box Canyon Falls. During July and August it would be wise to phone ahead for a reservation, because this little mountain town is filled to capacity on many nights during the tourist season.

25C

Ouray to Durango

Distance	74 mi from Ouray (7706′) to Durango (6512′)
Actual Climbing	5900′
Helpful Maps	*Colorado Road Atlas*, pages D27, D33, T5. National Forest Maps: Uncompahgre, San Juan. (See Appendix A.)
Terrain	Mountainous! Three major climbs to passes at 11,000′, 10,900′, and 10,600′. And as many descents. Be sure to carry warm clothing—for the altitude and for the chill factor on the long, fast downhills.
Roads and Traffic	There is a shoulder on the road a good bit of the way. Many switchbacks and curves and sometimes a sheer drop-off down the mountain side—take the middle of your lane when necessary and make the motor traffic wait until it's safe for them to pass. Or stop and get off the road until the line of cars passes.
Special Notes	You should make a very early start on this day. There will be less traffic early in the day, and less chance of rain or wind or lightning in the high country in the morning.

0.0 **Leave** Ouray on Main St. (U.S. 550) going **south**.

Start climb immediately, with switchbacks leading you up out of town. Not much shoulder at the beginning of this road, which is called the "Million Dollar Highway" because it was so expensive to build, as are all mountain highways.

2.8   **Ride through** short tunnel.

4.7   **Ride through** snowshed tunnel.

6.2   Road flattens out. A small respite through open valley for 2 mi.

Climb again to 10,000′ elevation mark.

13.7   Red Mountain Pass. Elevation 11,018′. A gain of 3300′ in the first 13.5 mi.

Steep descent with sharp curves. 3′ shoulder.

16.3   Road flattens out through wider valley and then descends through a narrow canyon.

23.7   **Left** (E) on Col. 110 into Silverton. Elevation 9318′. Restaurants, stores, hotels. Good place for a coffee

The Million Dollar Highway that runs from Ouray toward Durango has many switchbacks and steep climbs.

stop. Silver Lakes Campground 0.5 mi beyond town on Col. 110. There are passenger trains to Durango on the Silverton & Durango Narrow Gauge Railroad from here every day during the summer season. If you're really hurting from the climbing you might consider taking the train to Durango. They take bikes.

24.9   Back on U.S. 550, start second climb up to Molas Pass.

31.6   Top of Molas Pass. Elevation 10,910'.

31.8   Steep descent on south side. It will be cold on these descents. Put on your warm-ups before starting down.

36.0   Bottom at Lime Creek, and start up for the last climb, to Coal Bank Summit.

39.0   Coal Bank Pass. Elevation 10,640'. Snow was in the air as we crossed the summit in June!

Steep downhill for 6 mi.

45.0   **Pass** Purgatory Ski Area.

Cyclists on the Heart Cycle Tour of the San Juans meeting up with their sag wagon at the top of Molas Pass, elevation 10,910'.

49.7   Gas station and store. Start of 8′ shoulder.

57.1   Steep downhill—7% grade.

58.8   **Cross** Durango & Silverton R.R. tracks.

59.9   KOA Campground.

63.2   Small town of Hermosa. Gas station and market.

        Continue on flat road into Durango through a wide green valley. Durango & Silverton R.R. tracks on east side of road.

        Pass United Campground (303) 247-3853 on County Rd. 203 to the east (near 37th St.).

71.9   **Pass** motel and restaurant area.

        You will be entering Durango on Main Ave. (U.S. 550).

74.4   **Finish** in Durango just **north** of the restored Old Town on Main Ave. at the junction of Camino del Rio.

Durango
Population 11,649, elevation 6512′.

Nestled at the base of the San Juan Mountains, Durango is the bustling hub city of southwest Colorado. Many of the original buildings, constructed during Durango's pioneer days in the late 1800s, are still standing, carefully restored. The jewel of the old downtown is the Strater Hotel. Go into the lobby and you'll get the feel of the old days.

Two thousand years ago the region was home to the cliff-dwelling Anasazi Indians. You can visit the

273

remains of these cliff dwellings in nearby Mesa Verde National Park. but it doesn't make a very good bike ride. The roads in the park are narrow and crowded with buses and RVs. And there is a long, dangerous tunnel to ride through. The best way to see Mesa Verde is to declare an off-the-bike day and take a commercial bus tour from Durango to the park. (For more info see page 305.)

In Durango there are plenty of motels, restaurants, stores, and bike shops. A motel often used by bikies is the Comfort Inn (303) 259-5373 on Main Ave. near 29th St. It would certainly be wise to have an advance reservation in this popular tourist town.

See page 305 for more information about Durango.

25D

Durango to Pagosa Springs

Distance   60 mi from Durango (6512') to Pagosa Springs (7079')

Actual Climbing   3100' in 4 climbs

Helpful Maps   *Colorado Road Atlas*, pages T5, D33, D34. National Forest Map: San Juan. (See Appendix A.)

Terrain   Rolling roads through semi-arid country, with several long, not very steep climbs.

Roads and Traffic   Good shoulder most of the time. Not too much traffic.

0.0   **Leave** Durango at junction of Main Ave. (U.S. 550) and Camino del Rio.

      Proceed south on Camino del Rio to U.S. 160.

0.8   **Stay** on the right and join U.S. 160 East, curving left toward Pagosa Springs. 8' shoulder. Use caution at interchanges.

2.2   **Continue** straight ahead at traffic light.

      Durango Mall on left.

4.3   **Leave** U.S. 550 and head **east** on U.S. 160. 3' shoulder.

7.1   KOA Campground.

Rolling road through semi-arid countryside. 10′ shoulder.

17.6   **Bear left**, staying on U.S. 160 to bypass Bayfield.

19.0   Cafe and gas station.

19.4   Deli and convenience store.

27.9   Archuleta County line. Shoulder narrows.

Climb of 1 mi.

30.7   Begin long descent.

37.7   **Cross** Piedra River at bottom.

41.4   Chimney Rock, restaurant and campground.

43.7   **Pass** junction of Col. 151 and **continue** through wider, greener valley. 4′ shoulder.

52.7   Another climb of 1 mi with rugged San Juan Mountains in view.

56.1   Gas station and store.

57.8   **Pass** Super 8 Motel.

57.9   Long descent into Pagosa Springs.

60.3   **Finish** in downtown Pagosa Springs on U.S. 160.

Pagosa Springs   Population 1331, elevation 7079′.

Motels, restaurants, stores. KOA Campground 2 mi east of town on U.S. 160.

25E

▲

Pagosa Springs to Creede

Distance	66 mi from Pagosa Springs (7079′) to Creede (8852′)
Actual Climbing	4500′
Helpful Maps	*Colorado Road Atlas*, pages D34, D28, D29. National Forest Maps: San Juan, Rio Grande. (See Appendix A.)
Terrain	The one big climb of the day is over Wolf Creek Pass on the Continental Divide at an elevation of 10,850′.
Roads and Traffic	Some riding on no-shoulder roads. In general, not a lot of traffic.

0.0 **Leave** Pagosa Springs going **northeast** on U.S. 160.

Bear left (N) toward Del Norte. 8′ shoulder.

2.3 KOA Campground.

You will be riding through a lush, forested valley on a slight upgrade toward the San Juan Mountains and Wolf Creek Pass. An ideal cycling road.

Elk Meadows Campground.

14.3 Start climb to the pass. Climbing lane with 2′ shoulder.

23.8 Wolf Creek Pass on the Continental Divide. Elevation 10,850′. A gain of 3771′ from Pagosa Springs.

23.9 Start descent. 6% grade. 8′ shoulder.

25.0 **Pass** Wolf Creek Ski Area.

Snowshed (approximately 50 yds.). Watch for ice on the road.

26.0 Road narrows. 2-lane, no shoulder with drop-off. Take the middle of your lane; don't risk cycling close to the drop-off.

Road work going on in this area in the summer of 1988. May soon be upgraded to wider highway.

34.3 Motel and store at bottom. Continue on through narrow canyon running alongside the south fork of the Rio Grande.

35.7 Park Creek National Forest Campground.

36.4 Rio Grande County line.

38.0 Fun Valley Campground, motel, and grocery store.

43.4 **Left** (NW) on Col. 149 at the town of South Fork, elevation 8180′, winding through Rio Grande Valley going upstream. No shoulder. Start 700′ climb to Creede.

52.9 Palisade National Forest Campground.

55.2 Blue Creek Lodge and Restaurant.

Pass big scree fields coming down toward highway and river.

56.6   Small town of Wagon Wheel Gap, elevation 8390'. Restaurant, lodge, and store. Good snack stop.

You will be riding along the Rio Grande River through a wider valley. 3' shoulder.

60.3   **Warning**. Three sets of R.R. tracks in the next 2.5 mi crossing the highway. Make sure you cross them at a 90-degree angle. If traffic is heavy or if it is raining, it's smart to get off the bike and walk over the tracks.

65.5   **Finish** in downtown Creede.

Creede   Population 610, elevation 8852'.

This small town doesn't have a history of law and order. Bat Masterson was once the town marshal, and most of the early-day residents were gunslingers, fugitives from justice, saloon keepers, or miners in search of silver ore. In 1892 $100,000 worth of ore was being shipped out of Creede every month. Silver mining still goes on in the area—when the price of silver is high enough. However, much of the time the mines are closed. The small downtown district is well worth a stroll. The road up the canyon leads to Creede's Historic Mining District.

The Wason Ranch and Cabins, (719) 658-2413, in Creede is favored by bikies. There is also a motel, the Snowshoe, (719) 658-2315. Restaurants and stores.

Creede to Lake City

Distance	51 mi from Creede (8852′) to Lake City (8671′)
Actual Climbing	3200′ in 2 climbs
Helpful Maps	*Colorado Road Atlas*, page D28. National Forest Map: Gunnison Basin. (See Appendix A.)
Terrain	Flat roads at beginning of day. Then two passes—Spring Creek, elevation 10,901′ and Slumgullion, elevation 11,361′.
Roads and Traffic	Low traffic count on these country roads.
Special Notes	Of interest on this ride is the view from a roadside rest area of the Rio Grande Pyramid. This is the location of the headwaters of the Rio Grande River as it starts the 1850 mi journey to the Gulf of Mexico.

0.0   **Leave** downtown Creede on Col. 149 riding out through a wide valley on a flat road going **southwest**. No shoulder.

Enter Rio Grande National Forest.

6.3   Marshall Park National Forest Campground on road to the left.

Continue on mostly level road through wide valley of the Rio Grande River with spectacular views of snowcapped mountains. 3′ shoulder. Riding through grasslands—cattle country.

20.0   **Start** first climb of the day.

Hinsdale County line.

After leaving Creede the San Juan Mountains tour continues through the wide valley of the Rio Grande River with a view of the Rio Grande Pyramid—headwaters of the river where it starts its 1850 mi journey to the Gulf of Mexico.

23.7   South Clear Creek National Forest Campground.

Steep climb up to roadside rest area with view of Rio Grande Pyramid—headwaters of the Rio Grande River.

26.0   Long downhill and then a series of ups and downs. Essentially up with a few long downs thrown in. Watch for beaver dams in streams alongside the road.

32.8   Into open range. Use caution on the cattle guards. Cross them at a good speed going straight across the rails.

33.4   Spring Creek Pass, on the Continental Divide at 10,901′.

Steep downhill. 2′ shoulder, but bumpy roadbed.

35.7   At bottom **cross** several creeks. No shoulder here.

Start up again. Steep and bumpy road. Evergreen forests closing in on both sides of the road. 2′ shoulder.

40.7   Slumgullion Pass. Elevation 11,361′.

Start down on steep 7% grade with aspen groves and evergreens on each side. Watch for loose gravel in turns.

45.4   Sharp curve at Lake San Cristobal overlook and more steep downhill.

48.2   Wood Lake Campground.

More gentle downhill for 2 mi into Lake City. No shoulder.

51.0   **Finish** in downtown Lake City.

Lake City   Population 206, elevation 8671′.

Lake City was one of the earliest settlements in western Colorado. It served as a railroad shipping center for the gold and silver mines that were in the surrounding San Juan Mountains.

Motels and cabins, restaurants and stores. River Fork Campground is 1 block to the east of town.

Lake City to Gunnison

Distance	59 mi from Lake City (8671') to Gunnison (7703')
Actual Climbing	2300'
Helpful Maps	*Colorado Road Atlas*, pages D28, D22. National Forest Map: Gunnison Basin. (See Appendix A.)
Terrain	The road follows the river downstream for the beginning of the ride. Then two climbs of about 1000', some roller-coaster, and finally a flat ride into Gunnison.
Roads and Traffic	Low traffic count on country roads. 4' shoulder on U.S. 50 going into Gunnison.

0.0   **Leave** Lake City on Col. 149 going **north**. Narrow road with no shoulder through a valley that follows the Lake Fork of the Gunnison River.

5.2   Narrow canyon. Just room for the road and the river.

10.7   **Climb up** and out into open, wider valley with the river in a rocky canyon below on the right. 4' shoulder. There is a series of short climbs where you leave the river, but in general it's a downhill ride following the river downstream. Shoulder width varies.

24.3   **Pass** road to Blue Mesa and start climb.

29.0   Some steep descents.

31.8   **Cross** bridge at bottom and start up through an arid, bleak area on a roller-coaster road.

46.4   Reach Blue Mesa Reservoir and ride alongside.

49.1   **Cross** bridge over end of Reservoir.

49.2   **Right** (E) on U.S. 50. 4′ shoulder on level road through the Gunnison River valley.

51.4   Beaver Creek Campground.

Short stretch of no shoulder.

54.8   Mesa Campground and store.

56.3   Begin 8′ shoulder.

57.4   **Pass** road to KOA Campground, which is 1 mi to the south.

59.0   **Finish** tour in Gunnison on U.S. 50 (Tomichi Ave.) at corner of Main St. (Col. 135).

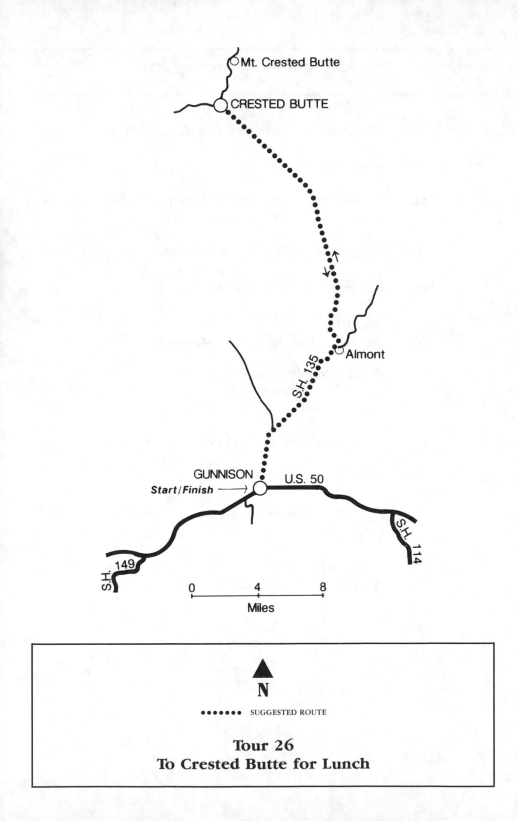

Mt. Crested Butte

CRESTED BUTTE

Almont

S.H. 135

GUNNISON
Start/Finish ➞   U.S. 50

S.H. 114

S.H. 149

0   4   8

Miles

N

•••••• SUGGESTED ROUTE

Tour 26
To Crested Butte for Lunch

26

To Crested Butte for Lunch

Distance	56 mi round trip from Gunnison (7703′) to Crested Butte (8885′)
Actual Climbing	1200′
Helpful Maps	*Colorado Road Atlas*, page D22. National Forest Map: Gunnison Basin. (See Appendix A.)
	This is a good 1-day trip with a special lunch stop in Crested Butte. Many good restaurants.
Terrain	Uphill going. Nice long descent for your return to Gunnison.
Roads and Traffic	Mostly no-shoulder riding. Not a lot of traffic.

0.0 **Leave** Gunnison from corner of U.S. 50 (Tomichi Ave.) and Col. 135 (Main St.).

Ride north on Col. 135. 6′ shoulder out of town.

2.5 **Pass** Blue Horizon Campground.

3.1 **Cross** river. Begin no-shoulder road through wide Gunnison River valley.

10.5 Almont, elevation 8010′. Taylor River and East River converge here.

Cross bridge and **continue north** on Col. 135.

10.9 **Begin** a bit steeper climbing through open valley with green mountainsides sweeping up and more rugged mountain peaks visible in the distance. Views of the Maroon Bells and Snowmass Mountain to the north.

Continue north through the broad Slate River valley.

28.0 **Finish** in downtown Crested Butte. You will have a wide choice of restaurants for your lunch stop.

Crested Butte Population 959, elevation 8885'.

Snowcapped peaks look down on this historic town with its old miners' houses, store fronts, hotels, and saloons that look as if they dated from 1880—when the town was incorporated at the peak of the gold and silver boom in this area. In the same year the Denver and Rio Grande Narrow Gauge Railroad was built along what is now Col. 135 from Gunnison,

A spring rainstorm has just passed through the mountain town of Crested Butte. The town was founded in 1880 at the peak of the gold and silver boom.

and Crested Butte served as a supply center for out-lying mining camps such as Aspen.

Because of its mountain trails and back roads, the Crested Butte area has become a Mecca for mountain bicycle enthusiasts. Every year mountain bikers gather here for Fat Tire Bike Week, the oldest continuing mountain bike festival held in the United States.

Retrace on Col. 135 to Gunnison. Nice downhill practically all the way back.

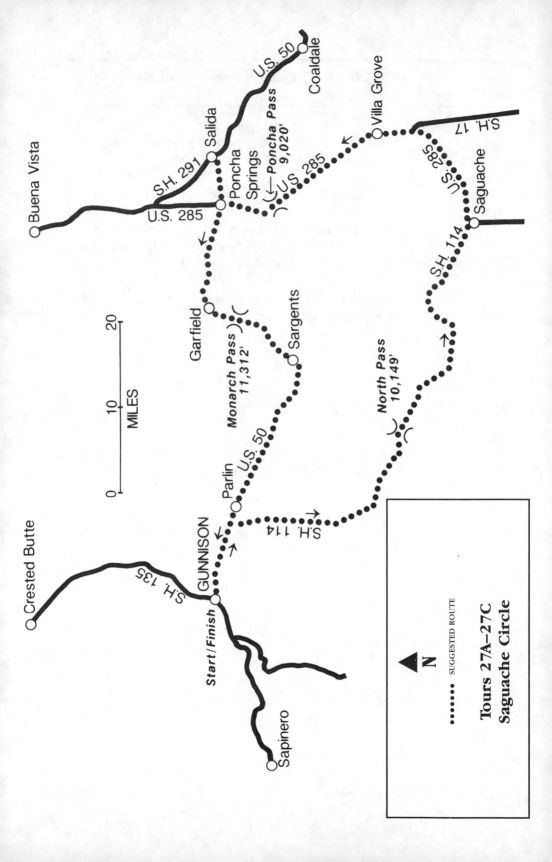

Tours 27A–27C
Saguache Circle

Saguache Circle

Distance	183 mi
Suggested Time	3 days
Total Climbing	8100'

Start this tour in Gunnison, population 5785, elevation 7703'. There are plenty of motels, restaurants, stores, and a good bike shop here. For more information about Gunnison, see Tour 25A. KOA Campground is on a road to the south of U.S. 50, 1.6 mi west of Gunnison. Follow the signs.

On the first day of the tour you will ride through some delightful country that is relatively free of "tourism," or traffic of any kind. 8 mi east of Gunnison turn south on a little-traveled road, crossing North Pass to the town of Saguache. Then you cycle east and north crossing Poncha Pass to Salida. On the third day you cross Monarch Pass and return to Gunnison.

Gunnison to Saguache

Distance	72 mi from Gunnison (7703′) to Saguache (7697′)
Actual Climbing	2500′
Helpful Maps	*Colorado Road Atlas*, pages D22, D28, D29. National Forest Maps: Gunnison Basin, Rio Grande. (See Appendix A.)
Terrain	Delightfully curving and rolling road through a remote valley, with one major climb over North Pass.
Roads and Traffic	Very little traffic. This winding road is good for cycling, but not so desirable for driving, thus not many cars or trucks.

The Saguache Circle tour, heading east out of Gunnison, follows sinuous Tomichi Creek.

0.0 **Leave** Gunnison from corner of U.S. 50 (Tomichi Ave.) and Col. 135 (Main St.) going **east**.

The road is gently rolling through a wide valley following Tomichi Creek. 10′ shoulder.

8.3 **Right** (S) on Col. 114. There is a store and gas station on U.S. 50 just beyond this turn. Last chance to replenish food or water. No facilities on Col. 114 for the next 64 mi to Saguache.

Almost level, gradually climbing road through another valley. No shoulder. Rough road.

16.7 Better roadbed through open range country. Watch out for cattle on the highway.

The valley narrows down periodically, then opens up into flat meadows. The road continues to curve with limited views ahead, so that you have that subtle anticipation and surprise as to what's beyond the next turn.

On the backcountry road over North Pass this logging truck was the only traffic we saw for miles and miles. This is a delightfully remote area—a pleasure for cyclists.

21.9   Slightly steeper road, with pine forests closing in on each side of the road.

23.4   Picnic area (with outhouse).

26.5   The terrain levels off and opens up into another valley of meadowland. 3′ shoulder.

32.7   **Enter** Gunnison National Forest.

38.2   Start of real climb. Last 0.5 mi gets steeper.

40.4   Top of North Pass, elevation 10,149′, on the Continental Divide.

Start steep down. 6% grade. 2′ shoulder.

45.9   Bottom. And then flat or rolling road, and a couple more steep downhills to the valley on the east side of the pass.

50.3   **Continue** on an almost level road following the Saguache Creek valley through more meadowland and cattle country.

51.7   End of shoulder.

66.3   Straight road through broad valley with arid mountains rising on both sides.

71.5   **Join** U.S. 285, straight ahead, at **west** edge of Saguache.

71.7   Supermarket on left.

71.9   Small, basic motel on left, Hillside Motel.

Right (S) on 4th St. following big arrow sign for the Historic Saguache Hotel.

72.1   **Finish** in Saguache at corner of U.S. 285 and 4th St.

Saguache   Population 656, elevation 7697'.

This is a small, not very prosperous town, whose main claim to fame these days is the Historic Saguache Hotel. You should call the hotel for reservations (719) 655-2347 because the only other choice for accommodations for miles around is the small, basic Hillside Motel on U.S. 285 in Saguache.

If you are adaptable and ready to appreciate western backcountry, you will enjoy a stay in this area. It's remote and rough, and definitely not touristy.

27B

Saguache to Salida

Distance 46 mi from Saguache (7697') to Salida (7036')

Actual 1300'
Climbing

Helpful Maps *Colorado Road Atlas*, pages D29, D23, T18. National Forest Maps: Rio Grande, San Isabel. (See Appendix A.)

Terrain The one climb of the day is over 9010' Poncha Pass.

Roads and Low traffic count on good roads with 2' to 8'
Traffic shoulders.

0.0 **Leave** Saguache on U.S. 285 going **northeast** (to Poncha Springs and Salida). 8' shoulder.

Flat road out into sagebrush-covered fields heading toward the Sangre de Cristo mountain range.

14.4 **Continue** (N) on U.S. 285 at junction of Col. 17.

19.4 Small settlement of Villa Grove (7980'), almost a ghost town. Grocery store and a laundromat. (The landromat offers hot showers. Western nostalgia would lead you to think that the cowboys come here for a shower on Saturday night.)

You will be riding through a broad, arid valley that sweeps up to the Sangre de Cristo mountain range to the east, looking much like an ocean beach, which of course it once was. 2′ shoulder.

27.0   Start of climb. 5′ shoulder.

34.0   Top. Poncha Pass, elevation 9010′. Saguache County line.

Start down. 7 mi descent. 3′ shoulder.

41.5   **Pass through** Poncha Springs (7469′).

41.6   **Right** (E) on U.S. 50. 4-lane highway with 3′ shoulder.

46.0   **Finish** in Salida on U.S. 50 (Rainbow Blvd.—motel row).

Salida   Population 4870, elevation 7036′.

Motels and restaurants along the 2 mi stretch of U.S. 50 as you enter town. More stores and restaurants to the north of U.S. 50 in the old part of town.

The motel row in Salida (which looks just like the motel row in many of the other towns on the tours) offers the traveler plenty of overnight choices. The more interesting part of the old town is a few blocks away and is worth a visit.

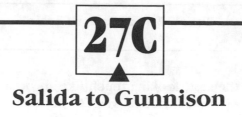

Salida to Gunnison

Distance	65 mi from Salida (7036′) to Gunnison (7703′)
Actual Climbing	4300′
Helpful Maps	*Colorado Road Atlas*, pages T18, D23, D22. National Forest Maps: San Isabel, Gunnison Basin. (See Appendix A.)
Terrain	Serious climb over Monarch Pass. Then level road following Tomichi Creek into Gunnison.
Roads and Traffic	There will be more traffic on U.S. 50 than you have encountered on the 2 previous days. There are stretches of no-shoulder on the Monarch Pass road.

0.0 **Leave** Salida going **west** on U.S. 50. 4-lane highway with 3′ shoulder.

4.0 **Pass through** Poncha Springs.

12.7 Start of climb up to Monarch Pass. No shoulder, but passing lane for traffic on the steep parts helps widen the road.

22.4 Top. Monarch Pass, elevation 11,312′. Gain of 4276′ from Salida.

Steep descent for 7 mi. 6% grade. Sharp curves. No

shoulder, but continuous climbing lane for oncoming traffic, which helps widen the road for you too.

32.8 Pass small town of Sargents. Cafe and grocery store.

34.5 Start of 4′ shoulder.

40.8 Monarch Valley Ranch Campground.

44.8 Gunnison County line. 10′ shoulder.

Level road running through wide green valley following Tomichi Creek.

53.1 Pass small town of Parlin. Small store and gas station.

65.1 Finish tour in downtown Gunnison at corner of U.S. 50 (Tomichi Ave.) and Col. 135 (Main St.).

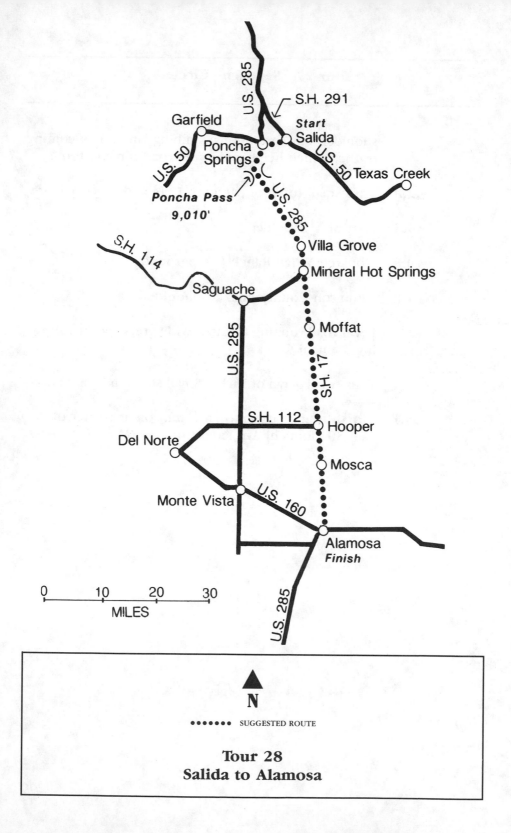

S.H. 291

U.S. 285

S.H. 291

Garfield

Start
Salida

U.S. 50

U.S. 50

Poncha
Springs

Texas Creek

U.S. 285

Poncha Pass
9,010'

S.H. 114

Villa Grove

Mineral Hot Springs

Saguache

U.S. 285

Moffat

S.H. 17

S.H. 112

Hooper

Del Norte

Mosca

Monte Vista

U.S. 160

Alamosa
Finish

U.S. 285

0   10   20   30
MILES

▲
N

•••••••• SUGGESTED ROUTE

**Tour 28
Salida to Alamosa**

28

Salida to Alamosa

Connecting route

Distance	82 mi from Salida (7036′) to Alamosa (7544′)
Actual Climbing	2000′
Helpful Maps	*Colorado Road Atlas*, pages T18, D23, D29, D35, T1. National Forest Maps: San Isabel, Rio Grande. (See Appendix A.)

Salida   Population 4870, elevation 7036′.

Plenty of motels and restaurants on 2 mi stretch of U.S. 50. Other stores and a bike shop in the town center, which is to the north of U.S. 50.

0.0   **Leave** Salida at junction of U.S. 50 and Col. 291.

Proceed west on U.S. 50. 4-lane highway with 3′ shoulder.

4.0   **Left** (S) on U.S. 285 at Poncha Springs.

4.2   Start of climb up to Poncha Pass. 3′ shoulder.

11.8   Poncha Pass. Elevation 9010′. Saguache County line.

Start down. 3′ shoulder.

16.8 Start of 5′ shoulder. The valley on the east side of the road slopes up to the Sangre de Cristo mountain range, looking like the beach of the ocean that was once here.

22.2 **Continue** through broad San Luis Valley. 2′ shoulder. Not much farming in this part of the valley—some cattle grazing.

26.2 Villa Grove (7980′). Almost a ghost town. Grocery store and laundromat. (The laundromat offers hot showers.)

30.6 **Bear left** on Col. 17, leaving U.S. 285. Watch for oncoming traffic—there are no stop signs at this intersection.

32.3 Mineral Hot Springs. Nothing there.

Col. 17 is a flat, straight road through the San Luis Valley. 2′ shoulder. There are some irrigated fields along the roadside, but mostly long stretches of arid landscape. If you study the map you'll find that this is the longest stretch of straight road in the western half of Colorado. It's not an interesting cycling road, but your best bet for going south. Less traffic than on parallel U.S. 285.

44.2 Small settlement of Moffat. Food store.

62.0 Alamosa County line. Small settlement of Hooper at the junction of Col. 112. Restaurant, gas station, grocery.

68.2 Road to the Great Sand Dunes National Monument to the left.

68.8 Tiny town of Mosca. Small motel, cafe, and grocery.

82.4 **Finish** in Alamosa. Population 6830, elevation 7544'. Motels, restaurants, bike shop, stores, Adams State College.

Join U.S. 160 (east to Walsenburg, west to Durango). See connecting route Tour 31.

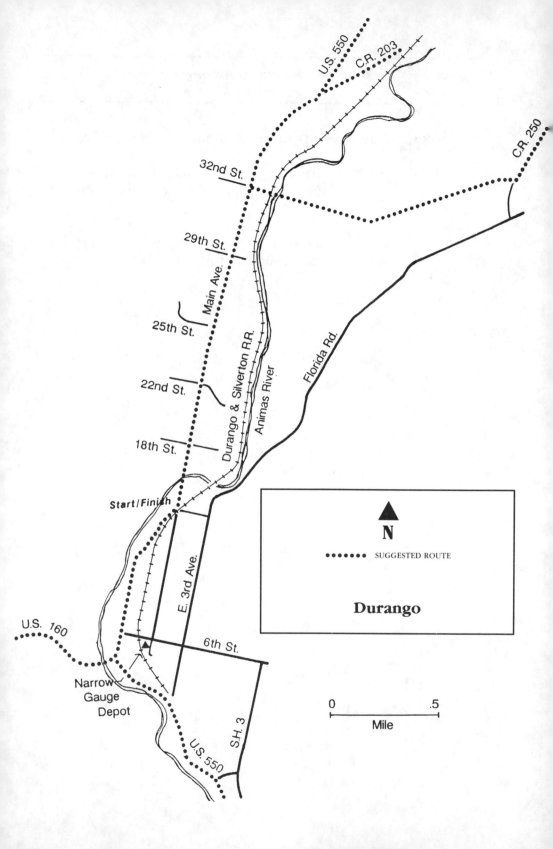

U.S. 550

C.R. 203

C.R. 250

32nd St.

29th St.

Main Ave.

25th St.

22nd St.

Durango & Silverton R.R.

Animas River

Florida Rd.

18th St.

Start/Finish

E. 3rd Ave.

N

•••••• SUGGESTED ROUTE

Durango

U.S. 160

6th St.

Narrow
Gauge
Depot

S.H. 3

U.S. 550

0   .5

Mile

Durango
Population 11,649, elevation 6512'

▲

Durango is nestled in the heart of the spectacular San Juan Mountains. It is one of the overnight stops on the week-long San Juan Mountains Circle (Tour 25), but the area is so interesting that it is worth staying here for a few extra days, allowing time for some side trips.

The Train Trip

Durango was settled in the wake of the gold and silver rush in 1880. The famous Durango & Silverton Narrow Gauge Railroad was built to transport the silver ore out of the mountains. Now it makes the 90 mi round trip to Silverton and back 4 times a day, through the magnificent Animas River Gorge, with passengers instead of silver ore. You can take your bicycle with you on a 1-way trip, and then ride back to Durango, or continue on to Ouray. Or you can reverse the trip and get on the train after cycling into Silverton from Ouray and ride on the train to Durango. Usually reservations are necessary in advance, so if you plan to do this, check with the railroad (303) 247-2733. The cost of a round-trip ticket is $32.30. If you want to go 1-way with your bicycle, the cost is $21.55, plus a small baggage charge for your bicycle.

Mesa Verde

Mesa Verde National Park, east of Durango in the high plateau country, was the home of cliff-dwelling people from about the year A.D. 550. For over 700 years this group of Indians known as the Anasazi lived and flourished here, building elaborate stone cities recessed in canyon walls on top of their mesa. Then in the late 1200s they abandoned their homes and moved away. If you have an interest in archeology you will want to visit Mesa Verde.

Unfortunately, it is not a good bicycle tour. After you enter the park you would have to ride through a rather dangerous tunnel. And you would have 21 mi of narrow, RV-clogged roads, traveling across the top of the mesa through rather uninteresting terrain, before you reach the cliff dwellings. The best way to see Mesa Verde is to leave your bicycle at your motel or campground for a day and sign up for a Mesa Verde bus tour. The cost is $27.00 for the tour, which leaves at 8:30 A.M. and returns at 5 P.M. The tour company told us that they would pick you up at your motel or campground in Durango before the tour if you call and make a reservation (303) 259-4818. It's the best way to see the remains of the marvelous and mysterious Anasazi civilization.

Accommodations

The old town area of Durango, where the Durango & Silverton Railway Station is located, is worth visiting. Several of the original hotels are restored and are catering to the tourist trade. The Strater Hotel on Main Ave. is the most famous. It's a little more expensive than the average motel, but its luxurious furnishings and atmosphere make it well worth the price.

The Durango & Silverton Narrow Gauge Railroad, originally built to transport silver ore out of the mountains, is now one of Durango's most popular tourist attractions. It passes through the beautiful Animas River Gorge.

An easy-to-reach motel, favored by bikies, is the Comfort Inn on Main Ave. near 29th St. (303) 259-5373. An excellent choice of campgrounds is the United Campground of Durango (303) 247-3853. It is 1 mi north of the edge of town just past 37th St. on County Rd. 203. (The narrow gauge train on its way to Silverton passes right through this campground.) There are many more motels, campgrounds, restaurants, bike shops, and stores.

For more Durango-and-vicinity route information see Tours 25C, 25D, 29, 30A, and 31A.

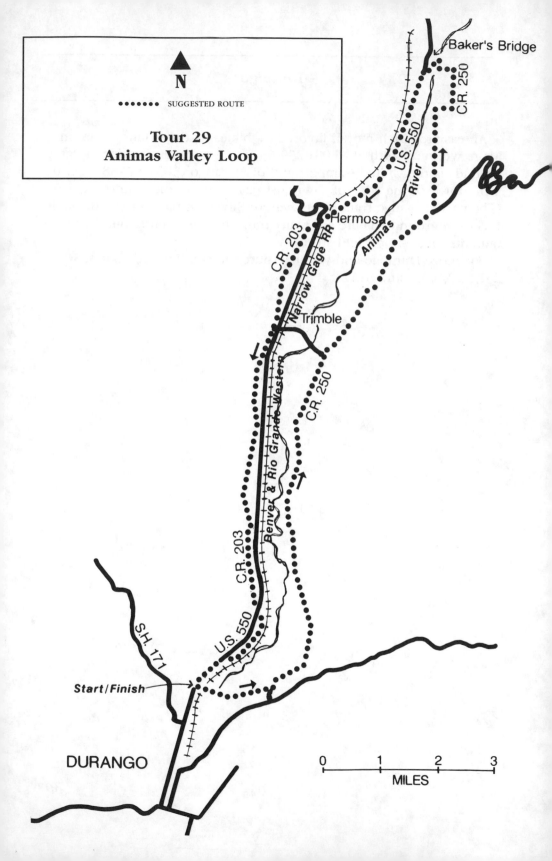

N

•••••• SUGGESTED ROUTE

Tour 29
Animas Valley Loop

Baker's Bridge

C.R. 250

U.S. 550

Animas River

Hermosa

C.R. 203

Narrow Gage RR

Trimble

C.R. 250

Denver & Rio Grande Western

C.R. 203

U.S. 550

S.H. 171

Start/Finish

DURANGO

0   1   2   3

MILES

29
Animas Valley Loop

Distance   27 mi round trip from Durango (6512')

Actual Climbing   600'

Helpful Maps   *Colorado Road Atlas*, pages T5, D33. National Forest Map: San Juan. (See Appendix A.)

Terrain   Beautiful river-valley riding, with a climb up from the river after crossing Baker's Bridge.

Roads and Traffic   Very quiet back roads along the east side of the Animas River going north. More traffic on the return to Durango on the west side of the river.

Special Notes   This is one of the favorite local rides for Durango area cyclists. It takes you through some lovely western farmland, past some of the older ranches in the area, and across the river at the famous 1-lane Baker's Bridge. Take a picnic and stop at this river crossing for lunch. Part of the movie *Butch Cassidy and the Sundance Kid* was filmed at this river location.

0.0   **Leave** Durango from Main Ave. (U.S. 550) and 32nd St. (at parking lot of North City Market store).

Proceed east on 32nd St., down over the narrow gauge railway tracks and the river.

1.3   **Left** (N) at T onto County Rd. 250.

You will be riding up the east side of the Animas River, passing some of the old La Plata County ranches. Low traffic count on this road, except perhaps at commuting times. This high road gives you a good view of the valley of the Animas River on the left.

7.6   Kimos Store. Now closed.

7.8   **Pass** junction of Col. 252, which goes to Trimbles Landing.

11.0   **Bear left** at Y (staying on pavement) on flat, straight road through pine forests to Baker's Bridge.

14.2   **Cross over** Animas River on 1-lane Baker's Bridge.

Left (S) on County Rd. 250.

14.5   **Pass** KOA Campground.

Continue through intersection, crossing cattle guard, and climbing up to U.S. 550.

14.6   At top of climb, walk over dangerous cattle guard just before U.S. 550. You have to stop before entering the highway anyhow.

Left (S) on U.S. 550. 10′ shoulder.

Cross R.R. tracks just before small town of Hermosa.

18.2   **Right** (SW) on County Rd. 203.

Cross bridge and continue past homes and ranches overlooking the river, which is now to the east.

25.0   **Cross** U.S. 550 on County Rd. 203. **Don't merge** with U.S. 550.

Immediately right (S) on **east** side of U.S. 550 on County Rd. 203.

25.2   **Pass** United Campground on left.

26.6   **Merge** with U.S. 550 (at 37th St.) and **continue south** back into Durango on Main Ave.

27.0   **Finish** at corner of Main Ave. and 32nd St.

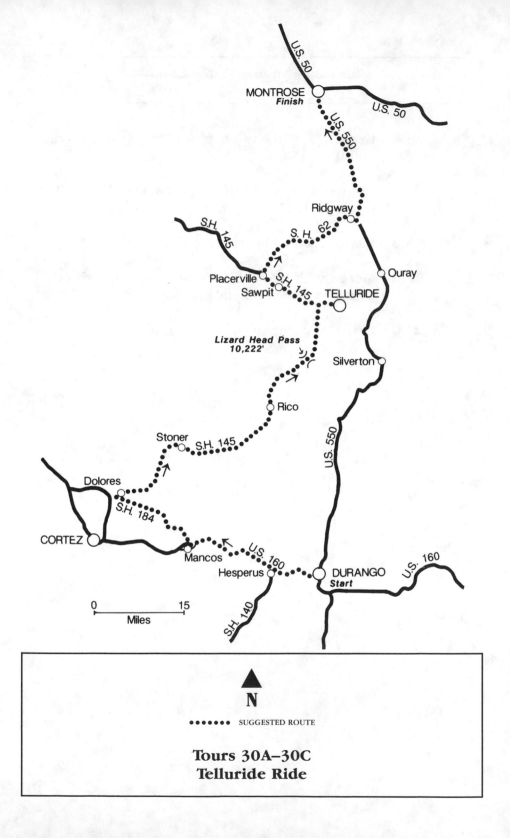

U.S. 50

MONTROSE
Finish

U.S. 50

U.S. 550

Ridgway

S.H. 145

S. H. 62

Ouray

Placerville

S.H. 145

Sawpit

TELLURIDE

Lizard Head Pass
10,222'

Silverton

Rico

Stoner

S.H. 145

Dolores

S.H. 184

U.S. 550

CORTEZ

Mancos

U.S. 160

Hesperus

DURANGO
Start

U.S. 160

S.H. 140

0   15
Miles

N

•••••• SUGGESTED ROUTE

Tours 30A–30C
Telluride Ride

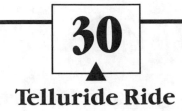

30

▲
Telluride Ride

Distance	181 mi
Suggested Time	3 days
Total Climbing	8000′

Start this tour in Durango. It follows the road on the west side of the San Juan Mountains, going north from Dolores to Telluride and then north to flatland and into Montrose.

Start of gentle climb up to Lizard Head Pass on the way to Telluride.

Durango to Dolores

Distance	48 mi from Durango (6512′) to Dolores (6939′)
Actual Climbing	2200′
Helpful Maps	*Colorado Road Atlas*, pages T5, D33, D32. National Forest Map: San Juan. (See Appendix A.)
Terrain	Some climbing out of Durango going west. Then rolling road across the Colorado Plateau.
Roads and Traffic	After leaving the Durango area, good shoulder on roads all the way to Dolores.

0.0 **Leave** Durango at junction of Main Ave. (U.S. 550) and Camino del Rio.

Proceed south on Camino del Rio to U.S. 160 West.

0.8 **Right** (W) at traffic light on U.S. 160 West. Cross over Animas River. 6-lane highway out of town.

3.8 Start climb up Hesperus Hill. 8 mi of climb. 4′ shoulder.

Hesperus. Country store.

11.6 At top the elevation is 8200′. A gain of 1688′ from Durango.

Steep down. 4′ shoulder.

22.8   Montezuma County line.

Continue on rolling road over the Colorado Plateau. The La Plata Mountains are to the north. 10′ shoulder.

28.5   Small town of Mancos on left. Motel, restaurant, and grocery at intersection of Col. 184.

28.6   **Right** (NW) on Col. 184 toward Dolores. Nice road. 4′ shoulder and not much traffic through pine forests and farmland. The heights of Mesa Verde are visible to the south.

46.6   **Right** (NE) at T onto Col. 145. 8′ shoulder.

47.0   **Cross** Dolores River.

47.8   **Finish** in Dolores on Col. 145.

Dolores   Population 802, elevation 6936′.

Motels, restaurants, grocery. Dolores River RV Park Campground 2 mi east of town.

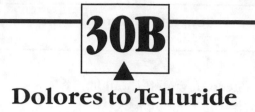

Dolores to Telluride

Distance	66 mi from Dolores (6939′) to Telluride (8745′)
Actual Climbing	4000′
Helpful Maps	*Colorado Road Atlas*, pages D32, D26, D27. National Forest Maps: San Juan, Uncompahgre. (See Appendix A.)
Terrain	Beautiful scenery on the relatively level road going north from Dolores along the Dolores River with the rugged San Juan Mountains in view to the east. Serious climbing over Lizard Head Pass before reaching Telluride.
Roads and Traffic	3′ shoulder most of the way to Lizard Head Pass on Col. 145. Usually not much traffic.

0.0 **Leave** Dolores going **east** out of town on Col. 145. No shoulder.

1.8 Dolores River RV Park.

6.0 Level road, upstream along the Dolores River. 3′ shoulder starts.

11.2 **Enter** San Juan National Forest.

14.8 Small town of Stoner. Store, Stoner Creek Campground.

Rolling and curving road with the Dolores River on the right and redrock formations on the cliffs on the left.

24.8   Priest Gulch Campground and Store.

31.2   **Cross** Dolores River.

32.4   Dolores County line.

36.6   Small settlement of Rico (8827′). Small grocery store, and not much else.

Road gets a little steeper. Rugged San Juan Mountain peaks coming into view to the east.

44.6   Start of gentle climb up to Lizard Head Pass. So far you have had a view of the rugged mountains without rugged terrain to ride through. That will change.

49.6   Lizard Head Pass. Elevation 10,222′. San Miguel County line.

Steep down on north side of pass.

54.6   After hairpin curve, steep climb for 2 mi.

56.6   Top. Alta Lake Road on right. Mountain peaks on both east and west sides now.

59.0   More steep downhills. Don't let your speed build up too much.

62.0   **Right** (E) on Col. 145 Spur to Telluride.

65.4   Telluride Visitor Information center at west edge of town.

65.6   **Finish** in Telluride on W. Colorado Ave. at corner of Aspen St.

Telluride

Population 1047, elevation 8745′.

A charming, Victorian-looking town, Telluride was incorporated in 1879 under the name Columbia. Later to ease postal service confusion between it and other Columbias, the town was renamed Telluride for a gold-bearing ore, tellurium, found in the San Juan Mountains. Gold, silver, copper, lead, and zinc were all mined here. The mountains surrounding the town contain 350 mi of tunnels leading into these mines. After 1900, mining profits dwindled and Telluride became almost a ghost town, until the sixties when skiing in winter and music festivals in the summer brought it back to life.

There are a good number of motels, restaurants, stores, a bike shop, and a campground in Telluride. The Victorian Inn (303) 728-6601 just south of W. Colorado Ave. on Aspen St. is favored by bikies. An advance reservation would be a good idea, because the town becomes crowded in summer when a festival is in progress. Telluride's campground is at the far eastern edge of town.

Telluride is a remote mountain village with many charming Victorian houses. It was named for the gold-bearing ore, tellurium, which was mined here in the 1800s.

318

30C

▲

Telluride to Montrose

Distance 67 mi from Telluride (8745′) to Montrose (5794′)

Actual Climbing 1800′

Helpful Maps *Colorado Road Atlas*, pages D27, D21. National Forest Map: Uncompahgre. (See Appendix A.)

Terrain High point is at Dallas Divide, elevation 8970′. After that it's essentially downhill.

Roads and Traffic You may encounter heavy traffic on U.S. 550 north from Ridgeway, and there are 14.4 mi of no-shoulder road along here.

0.0 **Leave** Telluride from corner of Aspen St. and W. Colorado Ave. and retrace on Col. 145 spur going **west**.

3.4 **Continue west** at intersection on Col. 145 toward Placerville.

Start down steep curving road. No shoulder.

6.8 Road levels off but continues down, running alongside San Miguel River between more redrock cliffs.

12.2 Small settlement of Sawpit. Restaurant. Start of 2′ shoulder.

15.8 Placerville (7300'). Cross Leopard Creek to junction of Col. 62.

16.4 **Right** (NE) on Col. 62 going uphill following Leopard Creek. 5' shoulder.

29.4 Ouray County line. High point at the Dallas Divide, elevation 8970'.

Steep downhill, followed by more moderate long downhill through ranching country.

40.0 Town of Ridgway. Population 369, elevation 6985'. Motel, restaurants, stores.

(If you want to return to Durango, **right** (S) to Ouray. See Tours 25B and 25C, to Ouray and Durango.)

43.6 For Montrose, **left** (N) at T on U.S. 550. No shoulder.

Continue on U.S. 550 following the Uncompahgre River downstream. Start of 6' shoulder.

49.2 No paved shoulder from here for 14.4 mi.

54.8 Small town of Colona. Small cafe.

55.0 Montrose County line.

63.6 Beginning of divided highway with 10' shoulder.

63.8 Ute Indian Museum on left.

67.0 **Finish** tour in Montrose at junction of U.S. 550 and U.S. 50.

Montrose   Population 8722, elevation 5794'.

Motels, restaurants, stores, bike shops, two in-town campgrounds. For more information about Montrose see Tour 25A.

You can make connections here to cycle east on U.S. 50. Refer to Tour 25A for Gunnison, and Tour 24 for the Pueblo to Gunnison connection route. You will have to ride these in the reverse of directions given.

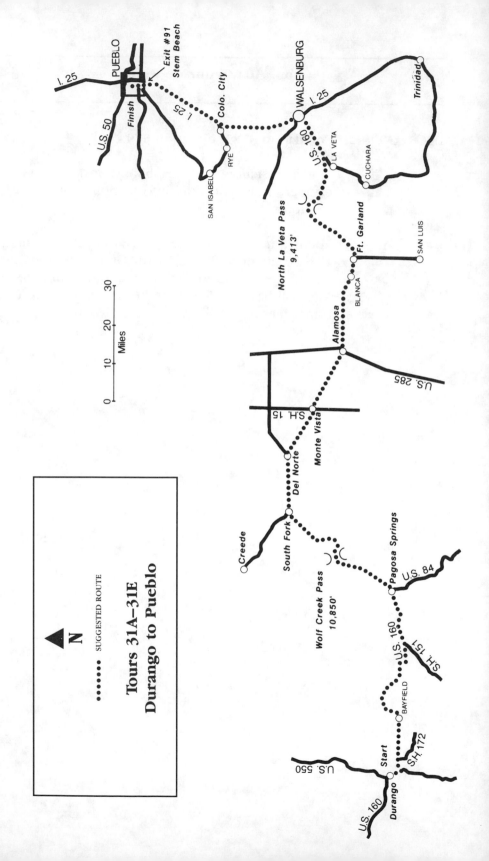

N

········· SUGGESTED ROUTE

**Tours 31A–31E
Durango to Pueblo**

31

Durango to Pueblo

Connecting route

Distance	278 mi
Suggested Time	5 days
Total Climbing	9700′
Terrain	Rolling road at the beginning of this ride. There is a climb over Wolf Creek Pass, elevation 10,850′. Then more rolling road until after Alamosa where you will be cycling through the flat San Luis Valley. Then a climb up to North La Veta Pass, elevation 9413′, and a steep down. From Walsenburg follow the more or less flat I-25 corridor north to Pueblo.
Roads and Traffic	You will be following U.S. 160 from Durango to Walsenburg—a good road with good shoulders except over Wolf Creek Pass where the road narrows and has no shoulder. Going north from Walsenburg to Pueblo you have no choice but to follow the I-25 corridor, which gives you a wide Interstate shoulder, or adjacent frontage roads. (See page 30 for safe Interstate riding suggestions.) U.S. 160 and I-25 in this area are not heavily traveled roads.

Durango to Pagosa Springs

Distance	60 mi from Durango (6512′) to Pagosa Springs (7079′)
Actual Climbing	3100′
Helpful Maps	*Colorado Road Atlas*, pages T5, D33, D34. National Forest Map: San Juan. (See Appendix A.)

Durango

Population 11,649, elevation 6512′. (See page 305 for more information about Durango.)

0.0   **Leave** Durango at junction of Main Ave. (U.S. 550) and Camino del Rio.

      Proceed south on Camino del Rio to U.S. 160.

0.8   **Stay** on the **right** and join U.S. 160 East, curving **left** toward Pagosa Springs. 8′ shoulder. Use caution at interchanges.

      Durango Mall on left.

4.3   **Leave** U.S. 550 and **continue east** on U.S. 160. 3′ shoulder.

7.1   KOA Campground.

Rolling road through semi-arid countryside. 10′ shoulder.

17.6   **Bear left**, staying on U.S. 160 to bypass Bayfield.

27.9   Archuleta County line. Shoulder narrows.

Start climb of 1 mi.

30.7   **Begin** long descent.

37.7   **Cross** Piedra River at bottom.

43.7   **Pass** junction of Col. 151 and continue through wider, greener valley. 4′ shoulder.

52.7   Another climb of 1 mi with rugged San Juan Mountains in view.

57.9   Long descent into Pagosa Springs.

60.3   **Finish** in Pagosa Springs. Population 1331, elevation 7079′. Motels, restaurants, stores. KOA Campground 2 mi east of town.

Pagosa Springs to Del Norte

Distance	59 mi from Pagosa Springs (7079′) to Del Norte (7874′)
Actual Climbing	4000′
Helpful Maps	*Colorado Road Atlas*, pages D34, D28, D29. National Forest Maps: San Juan, Rio Grande. (See Appendix A.)

0.0   **Leave** Pagosa Springs going **northeast** on U.S. 160.

        Bear left (NE) toward Del Norte. 8′ shoulder.

2.3   KOA Campground.

        You will be riding through a lush, forested valley on a slight upgrade toward Wolf Creek Pass. An ideal cycling road.

5.4   Elk Meadows Campground.

14.3   **Start climb** to the pass. Climbing lane and 2′ shoulder.

23.8   Wolf Creek Pass. Elevation 10,850′.

23.9   **Start descent**. 6% grade. 8′ shoulder.

25.0   Wolf Creek Ski Area.

        Pass through snowshed (approximately 50 yds.).

26.0   Road narrows. 2-lane, no shoulder with drop-off. Take the middle of your lane.

Road work going on in this area in the summer of 1988. May soon be upgraded to wider highway.

34.3   At bottom through narrow canyon alongside South Fork of the Rio Grande.

35.7   Park Creek National Forest Campground.

36.4   Rio Grande County line.

38.0   Fun Valley Campground, a motel and a grocery store.

43.4   **Bear right** at South Fork (8180′), staying on U.S. 160.

46.6   KOA Campground.

More scenic, greener valley. 10′ shoulder.

58.8   **Finish** in Del Norte. Population 1709, elevation 7874′. Motels, restaurants, stores.

31C

Del Norte to Alamosa

Distance	32 mi from Del Norte (7874′) to Alamosa (7544′)
Actual Climbing	none
Helpful Maps	*Colorado Road Atlas*, pages D29, D35, T1. National Forest Map: Rio Grande. (See Appendix A.)

0.0 **Leave** Del Norte on U.S. 160 going **east**.

Rolling road through rolling countryside. 10′ shoulder.

11.0 Movie Manor Motel and RV Park next to an outdoor movie.

14.2 Monte Vista. Population 3907, elevation 7663′. Motels, restaurants, store. The Monte Valley Inn, an old-style downtown hotel looks interesting.

21.0 Rio Grande County line. 6′ shoulder.

29.0 Start of 4-lane highway with 3′ shoulder.

32.0 **Finish** in Alamosa. Population 6830, elevation 7544′. Motels, restaurants, stores.

31D

▲

Alamosa to Walsenburg

Distance	77 mi from Alamosa (7544′) to Walsenburg (6185′)
Actual Climbing	2200′
Helpful Maps	*Colorado Road Atlas*, pages T1, D36, D30, D31. (See Appendix A.)

0.0 **Leave** Alamosa on U.S. 160 going **east**. 10′ shoulder.

Cross the Rio Grande River.

This road, called the Navajo Trail, runs through the flat San Luis Valley.

3.4 KOA Campground.

15.5 Costilla County line. **Continue** on U.S. 160 toward the Sangre de Cristo Mountains in the distance. 8′ shoulder.

21.2 Small town of Blanca. Restaurant and store.

Blanca Peak, 14,345′, in view to the north.

25.8 Fort Garland. Motel and restaurant. Ute Creek RV Park.

Restored frontier army post, Fort Garland, built in 1858, 0.2 mi down road out of town to the south.

Continue on U.S. 160, follow curving road through arid foothills.

39.9   Start climbing. 4′ shoulder.

47.2   North La Veta Pass, elevation 9413′. Huerfano County line at top.

Steep down. 6′ shoulder.

View of Spanish Peaks ahead.

57.2   **Right** (S) on county road to visit small town of La Veta. Narrow road, no shoulder, no traffic. Spanish Peaks to the south rising above the Cuchara Valley.

61.1   La Veta. Population 612, elevation 7013′. Motels, a B&B, restaurants and stores, campgrounds. A good overnight stopping place. (See Tour 33, Cuchara Valley Circle, for more information about this area.)

Leave La Veta on Col. 12 going **north**, back to U.S. 160. 2′ shoulder climbing up out of town.

U.S. 160, a good road with wide shoulders, sweeps across North La Veta Pass, elevation 9413′, between Alamosa and Walsenburg.

Tour 31 Durango to Pueblo
Connecting route

65.8 **Right** (E) on U.S. 160. Rolling road. 8′ shoulder.

73.2 Marlboro Inn and Restaurant.

74.0 Lathrop State Park Campground.

77.2 **Finish** in Walsenburg. Population 3945, elevation 6185′. Motels, restaurants and stores, campground.

31E

▲

Walsenburg to Pueblo

Distance 50 mi from Walsenburg (6185′) to Pueblo (4695′)

Actual Climbing 400′

Helpful Maps *Colorado Road Atlas*, pages D31, T21. (See Appendix A.)

0.0 **Leave** Walsenburg following Col. 10 **east** (E. 5th St.) to join I-25 at Exit #50.

1.0 **North** on I-25 to ride on shoulder. Refer to Colorado State Highway Bicycle Strip Map for latest information about negotiating the I-25 corridor (see Appendix A). Or follow Bike Route signs on and off the Interstate where indicated. (See page 30 for safe Interstate riding suggestions.)

42.0 **Take** Exit #91, Stem Beach, for Pueblo, and **cross over** I-25.

Right (N) on frontage road. No shoulder, no traffic.

46.2 **Straight ahead** at traffic light onto Lake Ave. 4-lane road with shoulder.

49.1 **Left** (NW) on Abriendo Ave. for 1 block.

Immediate right (NE) on Main St.

49.8   **Left** (NW) on Elizabeth St.

50.0   **Finish** in downtown Pueblo at corner of Elizabeth St. and 4th St.

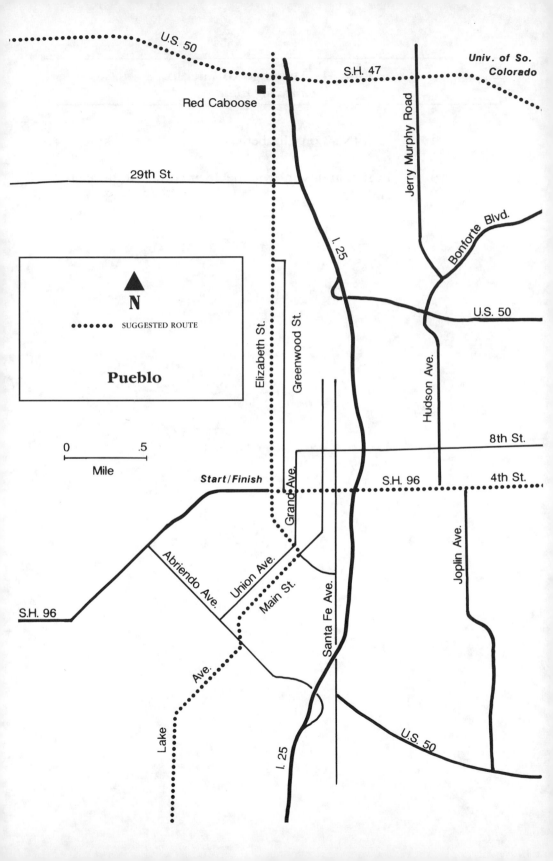

U.S. 50

S.H. 47

Univ. of So.
Colorado

Red Caboose

Jerry Murphy Road

Bonforte Blvd.

29th St.

I. 25

U.S. 50

N

SUGGESTED ROUTE

Elizabeth St.

Greenwood St.

Hudson Ave.

Pueblo

0   .5

Mile

8th St.

Start/Finish

Grand Ave.

S.H. 96

4th St.

Abriendo Ave.

Union Ave.

Main St.

Santa Fe Ave.

Joplin Ave.

S.H. 96

Lake   Ave.

I. 25

U.S. 50

Pueblo

Population 101,686, elevation 4695'

▲

As early as 1842 a fort was built here at the confluence of Fountain Creek and the Arkansas River. It was called El Pueblo because it resembled the adobe dwellings of the southwest Indians. El Pueblo was a natural crossroads for explorers, Indians, mountain men, traders, and trappers; and it served as an important trading post along the U.S. and Mexican border. It was from here that Zebulon Pike launched his expedition to the nearby mountain that was named for him. The El Pueblo Fort was abandoned in 1854 after a massacre by the Ute Indian tribe.

During the gold-rush days in the late 1800s other small communities were again established along Fountain Creek and the Arkansas River, and they were later consolidated to become the town of Pueblo. By 1890 four railroads had reached Pueblo, and it became the great iron and steel city of the new West.

Bike Routes

To reach Pueblo by bicycle from either the north or south (connecting to Colorado Springs or Trinidad) you can follow the Colorado Department of Highways Bicycle Maps (see Appendix A). The maps direct you along the I-25 corridor and give suggested routes for getting into or through the city. For suggestions about safe Interstate bicycle riding see page 30.

Pueblo is on the Bikecentennial Route that passes through Colorado on the way to Kansas and the East Coast (see Appendix A). In 1976 thousands of bicyclists, following this route, rode across the United States to celebrate the 200th birthday of the country. Since then more thousands have cycled on all or part of the route, passing through Pueblo.

Accommodations

There are plenty of motels, restaurants, stores, and bike shops here. An excellent information center is located in a little red caboose, near the corner of U.S. 50 and Elizabeth, southwest of the I-25 interchange #101. The people there can furnish you with information about historic mansions, museums, and other points of interest in the Pueblo area.

A good choice for a motel, easy to get to by bicycle, is the Best Western Inn at Pueblo West (719) 547-2111. To reach it, leave the area of the red caboose on Elizabeth St. **Left** (W) on U.S. 50 and ride 7 mi to McCulloch Blvd. **Left** (S) on McCulloch Blvd. for 0.5 mi to the motel. There is a KOA campground 7 mi north on I-25 at Exit #108. Follow the frontage road **north** from the intersection of U.S. 50 to Exit #104. Then ride on the shoulder of I-25 to Exit #108 to reach the campground.

For more Pueblo-and-vicinity route information see Tours 31, 32, and 33.

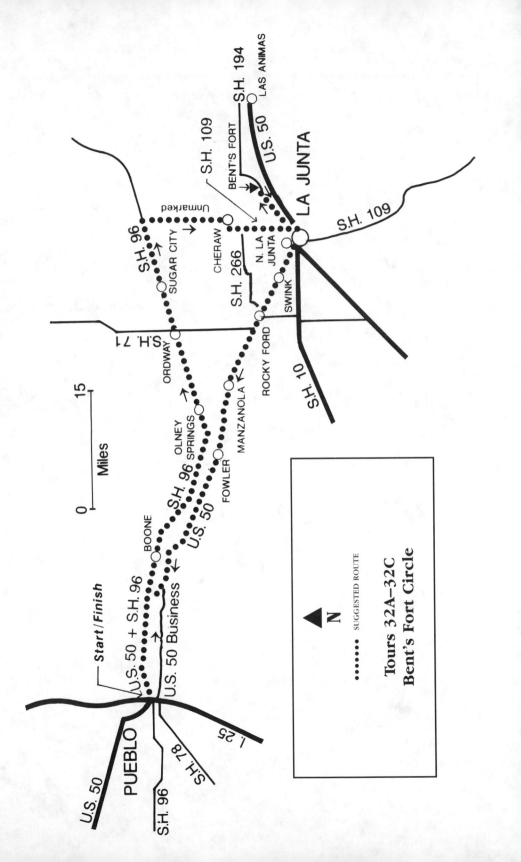

**Tours 32A–32C
Bent's Fort Circle**

N

•••••• SUGGESTED ROUTE

Miles

0   15

PUEBLO

U.S. 50

S.H. 96

S.H. 78

I 25

Start/Finish

U.S. 50 + S.H. 96

U.S. 50 Business

BOONE

S.H. 96

OLNEY SPRINGS

ORDWAY

S.H. 71

SUGAR CITY

S.H. 96

FOWLER

U.S. 50

MANZANOLA

ROCKY FORD

SWINK

S.H. 266

N. LA JUNTA

CHERAW

Unmarked

S.H. 109

BENT'S FORT

S.H. 194

LAS ANIMAS

U.S. 50

LA JUNTA

S.H. 109

S.H. 10

32

▲

Bent's Fort Circle

Distance	168 mi
Suggested Time	3 days
Total Climbing	700′

The tour starts in Pueblo and takes you out through the eastern grasslands. This is a tour to make in September. The cooler days will make riding out into the eastern plains more enjoyable, and since you will have no high mountain passes to cross you will not have to worry about early snowstorms.

The real highlight of this tour is a visit to the restored Bent's Fort east of Pueblo on the plains near the Arkansas River. It was built in 1834 and also served as a frontier trading post for the Bent-St. Vrain Company, pioneers in extending fur trading and other trading enterprises along the Santa Fe Trail. It was the frontier hub from which American trade and influence radiated south into Mexico, west to New Mexico and beyond, and north to Wyoming. You will reach Bent's Fort on the second day of this tour.

32A

Pueblo to Ordway

Distance	51 mi from Pueblo (4695′) to Ordway (4312′)
Actual Climbing	none
Helpful Maps	*Colorado Road Atlas*, pages T21, D31, D42. (See Appendix A.)
Terrain	No climbing on this trip, riding through wide-open eastern grasslands.
Roads and Traffic	There will be some city traffic as you leave Pueblo. Then you will have traffic-free roads out onto the plains.

Pueblo   Population 101,686, elevation 4695′.

Motels, restaurants, stores, bike shops. See page 335 for more information about the Pueblo area.

0.0   **Leave** Pueblo on Col. 96 from the downtown area at the corner of Elizabeth St. and 4th St.

Proceed east on Col. 96 (4th St.)

0.5   **Pass under** I-25.

U.S. 50 joins Col. 96.

3.1   **Bear right** on Col. 96 and U.S. 50, **continuing east**. 10′ shoulder. Caution at narrow underpass.

There will be heavy traffic on U.S. 50, but it has a good wide shoulder.

14.1   **Left** (N) on Col. 96, leaving U.S. 50, and then curving around to the **east**. 3′ shoulder.

Very little traffic on this road through flat, arid plains. The Arkansas River is a mile over to the south.

20.2   Small town of Boone.

22.4   **Cross** R.R. tracks slanted across road. Be sure to cross at 90-degree angle.

This is flatland riding. No trees near the road. It can be very hot out here in the middle of summer, but nice in the spring or fall.

33.3   Crowley County line.

35.4   **Pass** junction of Col. 167. 5′ shoulder.

40.0   Olney Springs. Cafe and grocery store.

Trouble-free riding, through farming area in a more fertile, wide valley. You truly feel that on a clear day you can see forever.

45.3   **Pass** junction of Col. 207.

51.0   **Left** (N) on Colorado St. and over R.R. tracks and **finish** in the small eastern plains town of Ordway. Nice change.

Ordway

Population 1135, elevation 4312′.

Restaurants and stores, and the only choice for an overnight stop. The Hotel Ordway (719) 267-3541, looks basic but okay. Call ahead to be sure they have rooms available. The Junction Campground and Store (719) 267-3262, is at the intersection of Col. 96 and Col. 71, 0.6 mi east.

Note: If for some reason you can't find a place to stay in Ordway, you should **not** continue on with the second day of this tour looking for lodging, because you will not find anything out there before arriving in La Junta. Instead, detour 12 mi **south** on Col. 71 to Rocky Ford to find a motel, or to the KOA campground 8 mi **east** of Rocky Ford. (See Rocky Ford information at end of Tour 32B.)

Ordway to Bent's Fort to Rocky Ford

Distance   56 mi from Ordway (4312') to Rocky Ford (4178')

Actual Climbing   150'

Helpful Maps   *Colorado Road Atlas*, pages D42, T17. (See Appendix A.)

Terrain   From Ordway you will cycle east through more open grassland, south to the small town of North La Junta, and then 6.5 mi east to Bent's Fort, before continuing on to Rocky Ford. Flatland riding all the way.

Roads and Traffic   Shoulders on some of the roads. The 6.5 mi road approaching Bent's Fort has no shoulder. Traffic count is low all the way.

0.0   **Leave** Ordway by retracing to Col. 96.

Left (E) on Col. 96.

0.6   **Left** (N) joining Col. 71.

The Junction Campground and Store is at this intersection.

Cross R.R. tracks.

0.8   **Right** (E) on Col. 96, leaving Col. 71. Rough road. 3' shoulder.

5.7   **Right** (S) following Col. 96 to Sugar City. No facilities.

5.8   **Left** (E) on narrow country road, still Col. 96, and out into the grasslands. Real wide-open spaces. This is all easy riding if the wind is with you.

14.5   **Right** (S) on unmarked road toward Cheraw. Narrow road, no traffic. Grasslands on both sides of the road.

21.2   **Cross** 2 bridges over dry stream beds.

25.6   Small town of Cheraw. Cafe.

25.7   **Right** (W) on Col. 109.

26.7   **Left** (S) following Col. 109 toward La Junta.

28.3   **Pass** junction of Col. 266.

31.9   Start of 8′ shoulder, and start down toward the Arkansas River.

33.9   Small town of North La Junta.

34.2   **Left** (E) on Col. 194 following Bent's Fort sign. Narrow country road through flat terrain. No shoulder. Not much traffic.

40.7   **Right** at entrance to Bent's Fort. Walk over cattle guard just after turn at entrance.

You will find a parking lot at the entrance. However, you can continue on toward the fort on your bicycle for about a quarter of a mile on a paved path. Ahead you will see the old fort isolated in the bleak countryside, looking much as it did in 1846.

An 1840s visitor to Bent's Fort, Mathew C. Field, described the fort as "an air-built castle which had dropped to earth before me in the midst of the vast desert."

As you approach it on the path from the parking lot, you still have the feeling that it appears miraculously complete and self-sufficient in remote and rather

Bent's Fort on the plains east of Pueblo is a carefully restored frontier trading post dating from 1834. It was one of the important stops on the old Santa Fe Trail.

desolate surroundings. It is one of the most impressive historic sites that we visited while gathering touring information for this book.

Entry fee is $1.00 for bicyclists. Ask for a plan of the fort as you enter.

You will be free to roam around, visit the Bent-St. Vrain Company trade room, the military quarters, the kitchen. You will probably see a cooking demonstration showing how the pioneers started a fire and baked a pie on the hearth. You may even be offered a piece of the pie. Bent's Fort closes at 4:30 P.M., so make sure you arrive early enough to enjoy it.

41.0   **Leaving** the fort, **retrace** on Col. 194 to North La Junta.

47.5   **Left** (S) on Col. 109 toward La Junta. 4' shoulder.

Cross bridge over Arkansas River and R.R. tracks.

48.5   **Right** (W) on 3rd St. into La Junta.

La Junta   Population 8338, elevation 4066'.

This was the junction—*la junta*—of the old Navajo and Santa Fe trails. Originally located at Bent's Fort, the town was moved to its present location when the railroad came through. It's now a major stop for Amtrak trains. There are several motels, restaurants, and stores here. You can make it your overnight stop if you spent too much time at Bent's Fort.

Continue west on 3rd St.

49.7   **Jog right** on a short street to join U.S. 50.

Left (W) onto U.S. 50 toward Rocky Ford. 6' shoulder.

50.6   Luxury 8 Motel just out of town.

51.9   KOA Campground. 2.2 mi west of La Junta.

Continue west on U.S. 50. 4-lane highway with 10' shoulder.

54.9   Small town of Swink.

You are now entering the famous Rocky Ford melon-growing region. If you make this trip in late August or in September, it will be at the height of the melon season, and you will pass many roadside melon stands for the next 15 mi. The Rocky Ford cantaloupes have the reputation of being the best in the world.

55.6   **Finish** in Rocky Ford on U.S. 50.

Rocky Ford   Population 4804, elevation 4178'.

This is a small town, but there is a large motel and restaurant complex on U.S. 50 as you enter town. It has two names: High Chaparral or Melon Valley Inn. (719) 254-3306. It would be a good idea to call ahead for reservations.

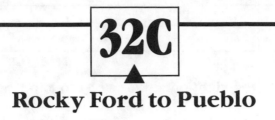

Rocky Ford to Pueblo

Distance	61 mi from Rocky Ford (4178') to Pueblo (4695')
Actual Climbing	550'
Helpful Maps	*Colorado Road Atlas*, pages D42, D31, T21. (See Appendix A.)
Terrain	Not quite so flat as the road out to Ordway. You will have some rolling road after Fowler.
Roads and Traffic	8' to 10' shoulder most of the way. City traffic to deal with as you return to Pueblo.

0.0   **Leave** Rocky Ford on U.S. 50 going **west**. 4-lane highway with 8' shoulder.

Pass more of those fruit stands. You really should stop and sample the cantaloupes.

9.2   Small town of Manzanola. Restaurant and stores.

Start of 2-lane road. 8' shoulder, except for a narrow bridge to cross in 4 mi.

18.0   Small town of Fowler. Restaurant, motel, campground. Just 1 mi west of town at Stiles Auction Barn there is an interesting cafe where we once had an excellent old-fashioned Sunday dinner. You may want to try it. No guarantees.

20.4   Pueblo County line.

Just a little bit of rolling road here, and mountains coming into view ahead.

37.3   **Bear right** on U.S. 50 to Pueblo.

Pass junction of Col. 96, and **continue straight** on U.S. 50. 4-lane with 10′ shoulder.

51.0   **Exit** from U.S. 50 (N) on Col. 47 (University Blvd.).

51.2   **Bear right** following "Bikecentennial 76" sign. 5′ shoulder.

52.8   Pueblo city limits.

University of Southern Colorado on the right.

Shopping center mall on the right.

Pass over R.R. bridge and **under** I-25.

56.0   **Left** (S) on Elizabeth St. toward downtown Pueblo. The Red Caboose information center is at the southwest corner of this intersection.

60.6   **Finish** tour in Pueblo on corner of Elizabeth St. and 4th St.

See page 335 for more Pueblo information.

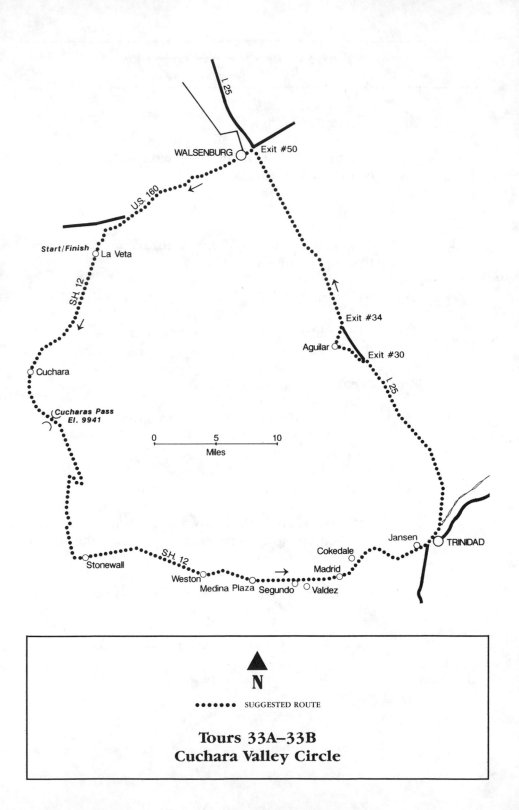

I. 25

WALSENBURG — Exit #50

U.S. 160

Start/Finish — La Veta

S.H. 12

Cuchara

Cucharas Pass
El. 9941

Exit #34

Aguilar — Exit #30

I. 25

0   5   10
Miles

Jansen — TRINIDAD

Cokedale

Stonewall

S.H. 12

Madrid

Weston

Medina Plaza   Segundo   Valdez

N

●●●●●●● SUGGESTED ROUTE

Tours 33A–33B
Cuchara Valley Circle

33

Cuchara Valley Circle

Distance	126 mi
Suggested Time	2 days
Total Climbing	5600'

September is the ideal time to ride this tour. You will have cool nights and warm days, and the aspen on the hillsides will be taking on a beautiful yellow glow. It's nice here in the summer too. The tour starts in La Veta, a delightful small town on Col. 12, at the base of the famous Spanish Peaks. It follows Colorado Highway 12 along the Pugatoire River, through some beautiful mountain scenery.

Colorado Highway 12 has been named the "Scenic Highway of Legends." Many of the legends involve tales of lost gold. According to Indian lore, the Aztecs found a rich vein of gold on the Spanish Peaks and transported quantities of it to Mexico to adorn shrines there.

The Coronado expedition came to the Spanish Peaks area in 1540 from Mexico, and the monks, left behind to convert the Indians to Christianity, extracted great quantities of gold from the Aztec mines. They departed for Mexico with pack animals loaded with the gold, but were never heard of again. Other legends persist: tales of lost gold hidden around the Spanish Peaks, and to this day never found.

The legend of the naming of the Purgatoire River dates from 1595. Spanish conquistadores from Mexico City died while searching for gold in the valley. The river was named when later explorers found the bones and armor of these first explorers beside the river. They named it "El Rio de Las Animas Perdidas en Purgatorio"—The River of Souls Lost in Purgatory—because the men had died without receiving the last rites of their church. The name was shortened to Purgatoire River, and then named by cowboys of the area, who couldn't handle the French, the Picketwire River. At one spot along Col. 12 you will pass a small store named the Picketwire.

33A
▲
La Veta to Trinidad

Distance 69 mi from La Veta (7013′) to Trinidad (6025′)

Actual Climbing 4000′

Helpful Maps *Colorado Road Atlas*, pages D31, D37, D36, T24. National Forest Map: San Isabel. (See Appendix A.)

Terrain There is one major climb to cross Cucharas Pass, elevation 9941′. Delightfully rolling road most of the rest of the time.

Roads and Traffic Quiet back road, with low traffic count. Shoulder varies from none to 4′. City traffic to deal with when you reach Trinidad.

La Veta Population 612, elevation 7013′.

There are several motels, restaurants, a grocery store, and campgrounds. The Chamber of Commerce on Main St. can give you more history of the area. The Log Haven Motel and RV Park is located at the south edge of town. One of the most desirable places to stay is the 1899 Inn, a B&B on the main street of town. It has 5 rooms to rent, serves a delicious breakfast, and it's really necessary to call ahead for a reservation. (719) 742-3576.

0.0   **Leave** La Veta going **south** on Col. 12, from in front of the 1899 Inn on Main St.

0.6   Log Haven Motel and RV Park.

Continue on Col. 12 toward Cuchara. No shoulder on curving, rolling road. Spanish Peaks to the left. The Sangre de Cristo mountain range ahead.

The Spanish Peaks dominate the Cuchara Valley and are the inspiration for many legends of lost gold hidden there by early Spanish explorers.

8.4   **Cross** Cucharas River, riding through Swiss-like green fields sweeping up toward snowcapped mountain peaks, with cattle peacefully grazing beside the road.

11.8   Small town of Cuchara. Restaurant, country store, the Cuchara Inn.

12.6   Road widens and small shoulder begins. Nice, new (1988) blacktop road for easy cycling.

12.8   **Enter** San Isabel National Forest.

13.6   Start of climb. The spectacular aspen foliage in the fall is a treat while climbing up to the pass.

18.0   Top of Cucharas Pass, elevation 9941'.

        Cross cattle guard. Use caution.

        Steep down through open areas of rolling hills. 2' shoulder.

24.2   Start of short climb up to North Lake.

24.8   Top at North Lake.

26.6   **Cross** cattle guard on downgrade.

28.2   Monument Lake on the left.

        More downhill on that nice, new blacktop road.

33.4   Small settlement of Stonewall. Mountain Inn Motel and general store.

        After Stonewall, road flattens out. Still a 2' shoulder on a quiet road.

34.6 Picketwire, small store.

37.6 **Pass** New Elk Mine.

Road joins and runs alongside Purgatoire River.

41.0 Golden Eagle Mine.

You are now entering a famous old coal mining area.

Cokedale, which you will pass farther down the road, has been listed in the National Register of Historic Places as the best example of an intact coal camp in Colorado.

Less spectacular scenery along here. No shoulder.

44.6 **Cross** slanted R.R. tracks. Caution, cross at 90-degree angle.

44.8 Small town of Weston. Country store.

46.0 **Cross** Purgatoire River.

48.4 Medina Plaza, the first of a series of small settlements without much in the way of facilities.

Pass through Segundo, Valdez, Madrid, and finally reach Trinidad, all named by the early Spanish settlers.

53.8 Start of 4′ shoulder.

58.0 Start of 2.5 mi climb up away from the river. 8′ shoulder.

59.6 Cokedale, the historic coal camp town, less than a mile in on an unpaved road to the left. Worth a visit.

A large number of small miners' houses line the unpaved streets, looking much as they did before the mine closed. This town was developed in 1907 by the Carbon Coal and Coke Company. It was considered a model mining camp. When the coke ovens shut down in 1947, the townspeople were offered a chance to buy their houses at the rate of $100 per room. The average house would consist of 4 rooms.

The Cokedale Post Office is in a building dating from the turn of the century; and the postmistress, who was born nearby, will be happy to talk to you about the history of the area.

60.6   **Return** to Col. 12 and continue climb.

61.6   Top of climb.

62.4   Long downhill to Trinidad Lake.

65.8   Town of Jansen at bottom. Start of 2' shoulder.

67.0   Trinidad city limits.

   Enter town on Robinson Ave.

   Left (N) at T on San Juan Ave. for 2 blocks.

67.8   **Right** (E) on Stonewall Ave. and curve **left**.

68.2   **Right** (SE) on University St. and **pass under** I-25.

68.4   Colorado Welcome Center on the left. Stop here for information, free coffee, and restrooms.

   Cross Purgatoire River on University St.

68.7 **Right** (SW) at traffic light onto Main St.

68.8 **Finish** in Trinidad at corner of Main St. and Country Club Dr. (also called Santa Fe Trail).

There are several motels, restaurants, and groceries near this downtown area. For a campground and/or motel that bikies find reasonably priced and easy to get to:

Proceed south on Country Club Dr.

Pass entrance to the Country Club Inn on right.

Cawthorn Motel and Campground on right 0.8 mi up Country Club Dr.

Trinidad   Population 9663, elevation 6025′.

In the early 1700s Spanish explorers and French traders crossed over Raton Pass from New Mexico to the site of Trinidad, and the Hispanic influence is

The restored territorial-style adobe Baca House is in Trinidad's Historic District.

still apparent in the names of cities, towns, and counties of the area.

In 1821 the mountain branch of the Santa Fe Trail angled southwest from Bent's Fort on the eastern plains to the site of Trinidad on the Purgatoire River and then headed south. The restored Baca House, the Bloom House, and a Pioneer Museum are located on Main St. in Trinidad's National Historic District.

Trinidad to La Veta

Distance	57 mi from Trinidad (6025′) to La Veta (7013′)
Actual Climbing	1600′
Helpful Maps	*Colorado Road Atlas*, pages T24, D37, D31. (See Appendix A.)
Terrain	Rolling terrain with no very steep climbs.
Roads and Traffic	To get from Trinidad to Walsenburg you have to ride on the I-25 shoulder. (See page 30 for safe Interstate riding suggestions.) The traffic count here on the southern section of I-25 is usually low. You can make a short detour to the old town of Aguilar for a change of pace. The roads from Walsenburg back to La Veta have good shoulders.

0.0 **Leave** Trinidad from corner of Main St. and Commercial Ave.

Proceed northwest on Commercial Ave.

Pass under I-25.

0.5 **Straight ahead** (N) at traffic light on Arizona Ave. for 9 blocks.

1.2 **Right** (E) on Goddard Ave.

1.8   **Pass under** I-25.

Left (N) and **enter** I-25 and ride on shoulder. (Don't take frontage road at this point.)

Traffic count should be low on this stretch of I-25. You will be riding through rolling, wide-open arid countryside. There's not much out there, and very few chances to replenish your water bottle, so be prepared.

For a temporary escape from Interstate riding you can take Exit #30 and detour through the small town of Aguilar, which was a center of activity during the coal mining days, but now is very quiet.

17.6   **Take** Exit #30 off of I-25.

Left (W) and **pass over** I-25 and over R.R. bridge.

Quiet little back road. No shoulder, no traffic. The Spanish Peaks are visible ahead.

20.9   **Left** (W) on Main St. in village of Aguilar. Food market, Mexican restaurant, and a variety store.

21.8   **Continue** on Business 25 to return to I-25. 3' shoulder.

23.6   **Right** over R.R. tracks.

Pass under I-25.

23.7   **Left** (N) to join I-25 at Exit #34, and ride on shoulder going **north**.

23.8   Truck stop restaurant at Exit #34.

26.8   Rest area.

28.8   Huerfano County line.

31.4   **Pass** Exit #42 to Walsenburg.

39.8   **Leave** I-25 at Exit #50 to Walsenburg.

40.0   **Left** and **pass under** I-25 on U.S. 160 West. 0.5 mi
of no shoulder.

You will be entering Walsenburg on E. 5th St.
(U.S. 160).

41.0   **Left** (S) at traffic light on Main St.

Walsenburg   Population 3945, elevation 6185′.

First settled in 1859, this town was another of the
Spanish-name towns. It had the wonderfully elegant
name of La Plaza de Los Leones. But in 1870 Fred
Walsen, a Prussian immigrant, established a trading
post at the plaza, and three years later the town was
incorporated and named after him. Motels, restaurants, stores, and a campground here.

41.1   **Right** (W) at traffic light on W. Seventh St. (following
U.S. 160).

Continue west on U.S. 160. 8′ shoulder.

44.4   Lathrop State Park entrance.

52.6   **Left** (SW) on Col. 12. 3′ shoulder. The Spanish Peaks
dominate the view to the south.

Cross R.R. tracks.

57.2   **Finish** tour in La Veta on Main St. (Col. 12).

Appendix A:

Sources for Important Maps, Directories, and Information

Pierson's Colorado Road Atlas. A spiral-bound 82-page book with 45 large-scale sectional road maps of all areas of the state, and street maps of 26 cities. Shows altitude of mountain peaks and passes. Includes a directory of all cities and towns giving population and elevation. Size: 8-1/2 × 11. Cost: $11.95. If you can't find one in your map store call Pierson Graphics Corp. (303) 623-4299 at 899 Broadway, Denver, CO 80203, or the Boulder Map Gallery (see below). You'll find that this book will answer 95% of your routing questions. We highly recommend it. When we're on tour we carry this book with us in a rear pannier.

National Forest Service Maps. Large, detailed maps of each National Forest area in Colorado, with National Forest Campgrounds indicated. Total of 11 maps. From U.S. National Forest Service, P.O. Box 25127, Denver, CO 80225. Cost: $2.00 each. Although these maps are somewhat bulky (typically 26″ × 40″), their 1/2 inch = 1 mile scale is ideal for cycling. These maps cover all the roads and highways within and without the National Forests. Explicit information is given for the hundreds of National Forest campgrounds and picnic grounds.

Boulder Map Gallery, 1708 13th St., Boulder, CO 80302, carries a large variety of maps, including National Forest Maps, USGS Topographical Maps, locally published highway maps, local bicycle maps, and the *Pierson Colorado Road Atlas*, mentioned above. Order by mail, telephone, or at the Boulder shop. (303) 444-1406. They will accept Visa or Master Card charges.

Bicycling Colorado maps prepared by the Colorado Department of Highways. An overall map of the state showing shoulder width on all state and national highways, with suitability for cycling indicated by color. Also included are four detailed strip maps showing the bicycle routes that run on and parallel to I-25, I-70, and I-76 from one end of the state to the other. Order from Colorado Department of Highways, 4201 E. Arkansas, Rm. 117, Denver, CO 80222. Cost: $2.50. Or call the Bicycle Program of the Colorado Dept. of Highways' Bike Hot Line (303) 757-9281 for more information.

Colorado Map. Our favorite all-around map of the state of Colorado is the one that's available at any Best Western motel in Colorado. It's free. No need to book a room. We like it because it's small enough to handle easily (only 18″ × 27″), and it clearly shows the National Forests and the Continental Divide.

Denver Bicycle Route Map. A detailed map of the city indicating bike paths and streets suitable for cycling—published by the Denver Bicycle Touring Club. Order from Denver Bicycle Map, 2916 S. Downing St., Englewood, CO 80110. Cost: $3.50.

City of Boulder Bicycling Map. From Bicycle Program, Transportation Division, Box 791, 1739 Broadway, Boulder, CO 80306. Cost: $2.00.

Boulder County Cycling Guide. Approved routes throughout the county. Order from Boulder County Bicycle Program, Public Works Dept., P.O. Box 471, Boulder, CO 80306. Cost: $3.00.

City of Fort Collins *Tour de Fort* Bike Map. From Bike Map, Transportation Division, 300 W. LaPorte Ave., Fort Collins, CO 80521. Free.

Colorado Springs Area Bicycle Access Map. From Planning Department, P.O. Box 791, 30 S. Nevada Ave., Colorado Springs, CO 80901. Cost: $1.00.

Colorado Campground Directory. $2.00 by first-class mail from Campground Directory, 5101 Pennsylvania Ave., Boulder, CO 80302. Or free at many Tourist Information Centers throughout the state. A rather complete listing of the commercial campgrounds. (See above for National Forest Service Campgrounds.)

AAA Tour Book for Colorado. A good directory to carry for listings of motels on the most traveled routes, as well as background information about most of the towns in the state. Campers should pick up a copy of the AAA CampBook for a listing of campgrounds. Free to AAA members at any AAA office in the U.S.

Bikecentennial Maps are available for the route through Colorado as a part of the Transamerica Bicycle Trail, which crosses the U.S. from coast to coast. One shows the route from Rawlins, Wyoming, to Pueblo, Colorado. The second shows the route from Pueblo, Colorado, to Larned, Kansas. Cost: $6.95 each. (Or $4.95 for members of Bikecentennial).

Bikecentennial is a non-profit service organization for recreational touring bicyclists. It serves its members in numerous ways: developing and mapping a nationwide network of bicycle touring routes, providing organized tours for members, a quarterly magazine, discounts on maps and books. Yearly membership: $22.00. Bikecentennial, P.O. Box 8308, Missoula, MT 59807. (406) 721-1776.

The Colorado Tourism Board, P.O. Box 38700, Denver, CO 80238, will send you a packet of Tourist Information about the state. Free.

Public Information Office of the Colorado State Highway Dept. (303) 757-9228 can often give you updated information about road conditions, improvements, and detours, but *not* information about weather or driving conditions.

The *Rocky Mountain News*, a Denver daily paper, publishes on its weather page a list of phone numbers in cities throughout Colorado that you can call to get information about weather and driving conditions. Refer to this list for information about a specific area.

Appendix B:

Colorado Bicycle Touring Organizations

Denver Bicycle Touring Club (DBTC)

This club is one of the largest and most active in the country, and has three or four rides every weekend. DBTC, P.O. Box 8973, Denver, CO 80201. For a recorded message giving the current tour schedule of DBTC call (303) 798-3713.

Colorado Mountain Club (CMC)

The CMC is a statewide organization with chapters in various Colorado cities. Hiking, climbing, backpacking, and ski touring, as well as bicycle touring. Denver clubrooms of CMC, 2530 W. Alameda Ave., Denver, CO 80219. (303) 922-8315.

The Boulder Bicycling Group of CMC

Active since 1971, the Boulder Bicycling Group of CMC has local club rides every weekend, as well as overnight tours to other parts of the state. Boulder CMC, P.O. Box 1105, Boulder, CO 80306.

Strada Bicycle Club

Sponsors the Hardscrabble Century Ride (see Tour #22) as well as other weekend rides. Strada, P.O. Box 2513, Colorado Springs, CO 80901.

Other Clubs

Several cities throughout Colorado have active bicycle touring clubs. The best way to find out about their scheduled tours is to inquire at the local bike shop.

Appendix B

The Colorado Heart Cycle Association

Founded in 1978 by a cardiologist to promote bicycling for health and physical fitness. A non-profit organization that each year conducts a series of strenuous week-long, sag-wagon, motel-oriented tours in the Colorado Rockies. Cost averages $300.00 per person. Heart Cycle, P.O. Box 10743, Denver, CO 80210. (303) 278-1359.

Ride the Rockies

Sponsored by the *Denver Post* newspaper, "Ride the Rockies" is an annual, week-long, very strenuous mass ride. Primarily a camping tour. The *Denver Post* provides camping areas and transports your tent and sleeping bag. Limited to 2000 riders. You have to sign up early to get on this tour. Registration fee $90.00. The *Denver Post*, 650 15th St., Denver, CO 80202. (303) 820-1338.

HELMETS ARE REQUIRED ON ALL THESE TOURS.

Appendix C:

Rides at a Glance

One-Day Out-and-Back

Tour		Miles	Days	Total Climb in feet	Start/Finish
10	Lookout Mountain Climb	36	1	1700	Golden
11	Colorado's Highest Climb	57	1	6750	Idaho Springs
14	Vail Pass Bicycle Path	47	1	4085	Vail
15	Ashcroft Out-and-Back	26	1	1200	Aspen
23	Eastern Plains Out-and-Back	79	1	1200	Colorado Springs
26	Crested Butte for Lunch	56	1	1200	Gunnison
12G	Glenwood Canyon	10-30	1	varies	Glenwood Springs

One-Day Loops

Tour		Miles	Days	Total Climb in feet	Start/Finish
2	Left Hand Canyon Ride	65	1	4800	Boulder
4	NCAR Loop	9	1	750	Boulder
6	Windsor Loop	33	1	300	Fort Collins
19	Tour of the Moon	56	1	2600	Clifton (Grand Junction)
20	Air Force Academy Loop	36	1	1800	Colorado Springs
21	Manitou Springs and Garden of the Gods Loop	15	1	1000	Colorado Springs
29	Animas Valley Loop	27	1	600	Durango

Appendix C

Multi-Day Circle Tours

Tour		Miles	Days	Total Climb in feet	Start/Finish
3	Cheyenne Circle	219	4	3900	Boulder
7	Trail Ridge Circle	248	5	13,208	Loveland
9	Georgetown Overnight	108	2	7800	Golden
18	Grand Mesa Circle	118	2	6400	Delta
22	Hardscrabble Circle	185	4	8000	Colorado Springs
25	San Juan Mountains Circle	413	7	23,900	Gunnison
27	Saguache Circle	183	3	8100	Gunnison
32	Bent's Fort Circle	168	3	700	Pueblo
33	Cuchara Valley Circle	126	2	5600	La Veta

Multi-Day Non-Circle Tours

Tour		Miles	Days	Total Climb in feet	Start	Finish
12	Canyons and Sagebrush Tour	316	6	10,700	LaPorte (Ft. Collins)	Glenwood Springs
13	Ski Towns Tour	284	3	16,720	Steamboat Springs	Salida
16	Black Canyon Rim Ride	163	2	8500	Glenwood Springs	Gunnison
30	Telluride Ride	181	3	8000	Durango	Montrose

Connecting Routes

Tour		Miles	Days	Total Climb in feet	Connecting with these tours
1	Denver's Stapleton Airport to Boulder	44	1	600	2,3,4,5,8,
5	Boulder to Fort Collins via Loveland	54	1	600	6,7,12, (1,2,3,4,5,8,)
8	Boulder to Golden	26	1	800	7,9,10, (2,3,4,5,8)
17	Montrose to Delta	22	1	-833	18,25,30
24	Pueblo to Gunnison	166	3	7900	13,16,22,25,26,27,28,31,32
28	Salida to Alamosa	82	1	2000	13,24,27,31
31	Durango to Pueblo	278	5	9700	24,25,28,30,32,33

Bibliography

Ballantine, Richard. *Richard's New Bicycle Book*. New York: Random House, 1987.

Bergstrom, Leslie. *Trips on Wheels: 15 Driving Tours from the Front Range*. Colorado Springs: Graphic Services, 1985.

Bridge, Raymond. *Bike Touring*. San Francisco: Sierra Club Books, 1979.

De Haan, Vici. *Bicycling the Colorado Rockies*. Boulder: Pruett Publishing, 1985.

De Haan, Vici. *Bike Rides of the Colorado Front Range*. Boulder: Pruett Publishing, 1981.

Delong, Fred. *Delong's Guide to Bicycles and Bicycling*. Radnor, PA: Chilton Books, 1978.

Ferguson, Gary. *Freewheeling: Bicycling The Open Road*. Seattle: The Mountaineers, 1984.

Forester, John. *Effective Cycling*. Cambridge, MA: MIT-Press, 1984.

Graves, Clifford L., M.D. *My Life on Two Wheels*. La Jolla, CA: Manivelle Press, 1985.

Hawkins, Karen and Gary. *Bicycle Touring in the Western United States*. New York: Random House, 1982.

Kingbay, Keith. *Inside Bicycling*. Chicago: Henry Regnery Company, 1976.

McCullagh, James C. *The Complete Bicycle Fitness Book*. New York: Warner Books, 1984.

Rakowski, John. *Adventure Cycling In Europe*. Emmaus, PA: Rodale Press, 1981.

Sloane, Eugene A. *The Complete Book of Bicycling*. New York: Simon and Schuster, 1988.

Sloane, Eugene A. *Sloane's Handy Pocket Guide to Bicycle Repair*. New York: Simon and Schuster, 1988.

Van der Plas, Rob. *The Bicycle Touring Manual*. San Francisco: Bicycle Books, 1987.

Walton, Bill and Rostaing, Bjarne. *Bill Walton's Total Book of Bicycling*. New York: Bantam Books, 1985.

Wilhelm, Tim and Glenda. *The Bicycle Touring Book*. Emmaus, PA: Rodale Press, 1980.

Index

Index